Praise for *The 30-Minute Vegan's Taste of Europe*

Named one of the Top 5 Cookbooks of 2012 by *Vegeta[...]* 10 Vegan Cookbooks of 2012 by *VegNews* magazine, [...] next, this globetrotting culinary tour deliciously m[...] World with modern vegan sensibilities."

 —Colleen Patrick-Goudreau, best-selling autho[...] and *The 30-Day Vegan Challenge*

"Any European delicacy or tradition you thought you [...] Mark has beautifully captured all the taste of Europe with fresh, fast, and healthy recipes!"

 —Lindsay S. Nixon, author of *The Happy Herbivore Cookbook, Everyday Happy Herbivore,* and *Happy Herbivore Abroad*

"These quick and tasty recipes are ideal for anyone who wants to transition to a vegan diet . . . without knowing it!"

 —Brendan Brazier, author of *Thrive Foods*

"This tasty culinary expedition provides a perfect combination of exotic and familiar dishes to enthrall any curious cook. I am eternally grateful to Mark Reinfeld for veganizing these exquisite traditional recipes so we may enjoy them while sustaining a healthful and compassionate diet."

 —Julieanna Hever, MS, RD, CPT, *Plant-Based Dietitian* and author of *The Complete Idiot's Guide to Plant-Based Nutrition*

"The once sparse space of vegan cookbooks is starting to fill up fast. *The 30-Minute Vegan's Taste of Europe* fills the vegan international cuisine void nicely."

 —CookbookMan.com

"A delightful cookbook which will appeal to not just vegans but also those who are gluten-intolerant."

 —*Tucson Citizen*

"The classic dishes of Europe used to seem 'above and beyond' either my culinary talents or the parameters of plant-based fare, but *The 30-Minute Vegan's Taste of Europe* changes all that. Mark Reinfeld has created a culinary treasure trove, even masterf[...] learned to love as a student in England. Imagine it: tea time, with [...]

 —Victoria Moran, author of *Main Street Vegan* and director[...] Main Street Vegan Academy

Praise for *The 30-Minute Vegan's Taste of the East*

"Mark and Jennifer are on the cutting edge of healthy dining. This is vegan cuisine at its finest."
 —Cher

"Whether you are vegan or not, this is a very appealing collection of recipes. I know they're going to become part of my culinary life."

— Deborah Madison, author of *Vegetarian Cooking for Everyone* and *Local Flavors*

"The vegan's answer to Rachael Ray and Mr. Food, this is recommended for anyone wishing to re-create their favorite Asian restaurant dishes without the meat."

— *Library Journal*

"A new recipe book that will inspire you to cook . . . Will be useful for those wanting to try new flavors or improve their health through diet."

— CurledUpWithAGoodBook.com

"An extraordinary compilation of vegan dishes . . . The recipes' instructions are described at length in user-friendly detail. Simple cooking charts, suggested preparation techniques, cooking tips, and more round out this excellent, easy-to-use addition to any vegan cookbook collection."

— *Midwest Book Review*

"With wonderful recipes on every page, this book takes you on a culinary journey through India, China, and Japan imparting all you need to know to re-create the flavors of the east."

— *The Vegetarian*

Praise for *The 30-Minute Vegan*

"A must-have for every kitchen, *The 30-Minute Vegan* is everything a cookbook should be— these recipes are fast, easy, and ridiculously good."

— Rory Freedman, coauthor of the *New York Times* best seller *Skinny Bitch*

"This book is filled with delicious, exciting, healthful recipes that are accessible for everyone. You'll love it whether you're a vegan, or you just want to eat like one once in a while."

— Ellie Krieger, RD, best-selling author of *So Easy: Luscious Healthy Recipes for Every Meal of the Week* and host of Food Network's *Healthy Appetite*

"One of the very best vegan cookbooks of all time. Fabulous recipes, healthy food, clear directions, and delicious results!"

— John Robbins, author of *The Food Revolution* and *Diet for a New America*

"*The 30-Minute Vegan* is a fail-safe cookbook designed to save you time and eliminate stress in the kitchen. With a well-planned collection of fast, simple, and healthy recipes, the duo is determined to keep home dining diverse and your diet in tip-top shape."

— *VegNews*

the
30-MINUTE
VEGAN
Soup's On!

Other books by Mark Reinfeld:

The 30-Minute Vegan's Taste of Europe

The 30-Minute Vegan with Jennifer Murray

The 30-Minute Vegan's Taste of the East with Jennifer Murray

The Complete Idiot's Guide to Eating Raw
with Bo Rinaldi and Jennifer Murray

Vegan Fusion World Cuisine with Bo Rinaldi

the
30-MINUTE
VEGAN

Soup's On!

MORE THAN **100**

*quick and easy recipes
for every season*

Mark Reinfeld

Da Capo
∞
LIFE
LONG

A Member of the Perseus Books Group

Designed by Trish Wilkinson
Composition by Cynthia Young

Library of Congress Cataloging-in-Publication Data
Reinfeld, Mark.
    The 30-minute vegan : soup's on! : more than 100 quick and easy recipes for every season / Mark Reinfeld.
        pages cm
    Includes bibliographical references and index.
    ISBN 978-0-7382-1673-7 (pbk.) —
ISBN 978-0-7382-1674-4 (e-book)
1. Vegan cooking.   2. Soups.   3. Quick and easy cooking.   I. Title.   II. Title: Thirty-minute vegan : soup's on!
 TX837.R4464 2013
 641.5'636—dc23
 2013021677

Published by Da Capo Press
A Member of the Perseus Books Group
www.dacapopress.com

Note: The information in this book is true and complete to the best of our knowledge. This book is intended only as an informative guide for those wishing to know more about health issues. In no way is this book intended to replace, countermand, or conflict with the advice given to you by your own physician. The ultimate decision concerning care should be made between you and your doctor. We strongly recommend you follow his or her advice. Information in this book is general and is offered with no guarantees on the part of the authors or Da Capo Press. The authors and publisher disclaim all liability in connection with the use of this book.

Da Capo Press books are available at special discounts for bulk purchases in the U.S. by corporations, institutions, and other organizations. For more information, please contact the Special Markets Department at the Perseus Books Group, 2300 Chestnut Street, Suite 200, Philadelphia, PA, 19103, or call (800) 810-4145, ext. 5000, or e-mail special.markets@perseusbooks.com.

10 9 8 7 6 5 4 3 2 1

Soup's On! is dedicated to my parents,
Martin and Roberta Reinfeld,
whose unconditional love and support
continue to inspire me.

Contents

Foreword by Dr. Neal Barnard   *xiii*

Welcome to *Soup's On!*   1
How to Use This Book   5

PART ONE

The Art of Soup Creation   **19**

Soup Terms   20
The Template Recipe   20
Soup Stock   22
Basic Vegetable Stock   25
Mushroom Stock   26
Roasted Vegetable Stock   27
Dashi   28
Basic Tamari Stock   29

PART TWO

Vegetable-Based Soups   **33**

Versatile Miso Soup with Pickled
   Ginger   34
Cleansing Burdock Soup with Ginger
   and Dandelion Greens   35
Truffled Wild Mushroom Consommé
   with Grilled Baby Asparagus   36
Mayan Tomato and Corn Soup   38

French Onion Soup   40
Broiled Zucchini Soup with Saffron   42
Thai Coconut Soup with Lemongrass   43
Ragout of Spring/Summer Vegetables   45
Fried Green Tomato Soup au Gratin   46
Szechuan Hot and Sour Vegetable Soup   47
Four Mushroom and Baby Spinach
   Soup   48
Roasted Brussels Sprouts and Red
   Cabbage Soup   49
New Orleans Corn and Bell Pepper
   Soup (Maque Choux)   50
Peasant Vegetable and Toasted
   Spice Soup   51
Indian Chutney Stew with
   Tamarind   52
Portuguese Kale and Potato Soup
   (Caldo Verde)   54
Irish Cabbage and Potato Stew   55
Jamaican Jerk Plantain Soup   56
Tropical Coconut Yam Soup   58
Ragout of Fall Vegetables   60
Ratatouille Stew with Grilled
   Broccoli Rabe   61
Roasted Root Vegetable Soup   63
Roasted Beet Borscht   64
African Peanut Soup   65

CONTENTS

PART THREE

Soups and Stews with Grains, Legumes, and Pasta 67

Fire-Roasted Tomato and Rice Soup with Spinach 69

Andean Incan Stew with Quinoa 70

Wonton Soup 72

Vietnamese Pho Real Bowl 74

Matzo Ball Soup 75

French Bouillabaisse 77

Un-Chicken Noodle Soup 79

Hot Pot with Soba Noodles, Seared Shiitake Mushrooms, and Baby Bok Choy 80

Veggie Gumbo 82

Israeli Couscous Soup with Sun-Dried Tomatoes 83

Black-Eyed Peas and Collards Stew 85

Caribbean Red Bean and Rice Soup 86

Orzo Minestrone with Broiled Fennel 88

Persian Lima Bean and Dill Soup 90

Three Sisters Soup 91

Ethiopian Stew 92

Greek Lentil Soup with Grilled Bell Pepper 94

Coconut Greens Soup with Polenta 96

Coconut Curry Veggie Soup with Tofu 97

Tibetan Noodle Soup (Thenthuk) 98

BBQ Tempeh and Roasted Corn Stew 99

Indian Mulligatawny 101

Greek Fasolada Soup with Cannellini Beans 102

Himalayan Dal with Curried Chickpeas 103

Polish Vegan Sausage and Sauerkraut Stew 105

Tofurky and Rice Soup 106

Spanish Rice and Artichoke Heart Stew 107

Italian Wedding Stew with Vegan Sausage 108

Black Bean Tomato Soup with Polenta Dumplings 109

Veggie Coq au Vin 112

Split Pea Soup 113

Brazilian Black Bean Soup with Baked Plantain 114

Adzuki Bean Soup with Enoki Mushrooms 116

North African Tagine with Broiled Tofu 117

Mushroom Barley Soup 119

Cha-Cha Chili with Tempeh 120

PART FOUR

Creamy Blended Soups 123

Creamy Fire-Roasted Tomato Soup with Dill 125

Roasted Red Pepper Soup 126

Cream of Mushroom Soup 127

Coconut Carrot Soup with Ginger and Dill 128

Corn Chowder 129

Spinach Soup with Vegan Yogurt and Toasted Sesame Seeds 130

Creamy Parsnip Soup with Smoked Cherry Tomatoes 131

Garlic Lovers' Roasted Garlic Soup 133

Mideast Chickpea Soup 135

Roasted Squash with Coconut Soup 136

Creamy Broccoli Soup with Shiitake Mushrooms 137

Bavarian Asparagus Soup with Hazelnuts 139

Creamy Grilled Vegetable Soup with Cilantro Cream 140

Grilled Eggplant Soup with Pine Nuts 142

Cheesy Cauliflower Soup 144

Holy Mole Soup with Veggies 145

Italian Pesto Soup with Gnocchi 146

Creamy White Bean Soup with Broiled Artichoke Hearts 148

Curried Pumpkin Soup 150

Green Bean Amandine Soup 151

Rosemary Potato Soup with Roasted Leek and Garlic 152

New England Chowder 154

PART FIVE

Raw Soups and Dessert Soups   157

Lavender-Infused Watermelon Soup 159

Spicy Strawberry Soup 161

Pineapple Ginger Soup with Apricot Puree 162

Raw Papaya Soup with Red Pepper Cream 164

Cantaloupe Rose Soup with Blueberry Cream 165

Raw Peaches and Cream Soup 166

Raw Chocolate Mint Soup with Raspberries 167

Creamy Brazil Nut Fig Soup with Kiwi Compote 168

Slushy Summer Fruit Soup 169

Danish Fruit Soup 170

Golden Gazpacho with Saffron 171

Raw Cucumber Mint Soup 172

Raw Cream of Tomato Soup 173

Raw Chopped Vegetable Soup with Shaved Fennel 174

Raw Mediterranean Onion Soup 176

Spicy Kale Soup with Pepitas 177

Savory Brazil Nut Soup with Jicama 178

Raw Corn Chowder 179

Raw Creamy Greens Soup 180

Raw Thai Coconut Soup 181

Chilled Avocado Soup with Cherry Tomato Salsa Fresca 183

PART SIX

Garnishes and Sides   185

Flavored Ice Cubes and Frozen Melon Balls 186

Red Oil 187

Basil Oil 188

Balsamic Reduction 189

Toasted Coconut 190

Sweet and Spicy Toasted Nori Sheets 191

Candied Pepitas 192

Tapenade 193

Roasted Garlic Spread 194

Vegan Crème Fraîche 195

Raw Crème Fraîche 196

Red Pepper Coulis 197

Crostini 198

Pita Chips 199

Herbed Croutons 200

Vegetable Chips 201

Crispy Sunchokes 202

Krispy Kale 203

Guacamole 204

CONTENTS

Caramelized Onions   205

Pesto Magnifico   206

Tofu Feta   207

Tempeh Bacon   208

Herbed Bread Sticks   209

Cosmic Corn Bread   211

Conversion Chart   *212*

Appendices:

    A: Preparation Basics   *213*

    B: Seasonal Growing Charts *231*

    C: Supplemental Information *235*

    D: Additional Resources   *243*

Contributor Bios   *249*

Acknowledgments   *251*

About the Author   *253*

The 10-Day Vegan Fusion Culinary
    Immersion   *255*

Index   *257*

Foreword by
Dr. Neal Barnard

In our research studies, we have seen the power of vegan diet. Our participants lose weight, improve their cholesterol and blood pressure, and in many cases reduce or even eliminate the need for medications.

And now, you can put this powerful way of eating to work right at home. With these wonderful recipes you will get the very best of plant-based nutrition. And not only will your health rebound, but your taste buds will be delighted as well.

When you try a vegan diet on for size, you will be struck by the fact that it is not in the least bit limiting. Just the opposite—it is liberating. As you page through this wonderful book, you'll see what I mean. The enormous range of delicious soups served as appetizers, main dishes, or even desserts is stunning.

As you learn about these delicious creations, I have one request: don't keep them a secret. A meal prepared from any one of these marvelous recipes would make the most loving gift you could imagine. The practical tips and savory tastes in this volume are made to share. They will transform the way your friends and family members think about food. In the process they may well transform their health, too.

Neal Barnard, MD
President, Physicians Committee for Responsible Medicine

Welcome to *Soup's On!*

I am super excited to introduce you to the fourth book in the 30-Minute Vegan Series . . . *Soup's On!* I love sharing with people how to prepare soups because it is one of the simplest and most rewarding types of meal to prepare. While you may think of cooking soups as being very time consuming, virtually all these recipes were all created to fall within the thirty-minute time frame. These recipes also were selected so that you will be able to enjoy gourmet soups year-round . . . from the coldest winter night, to the hottest summer afternoon. There is truly a soup for every season!

In my Vegan Fusion culinary immersions and workshops I offer around the world, I always start off with soups. In fact, in my ten-day immersion, we spend the entire first day making soups. Pretty much everyone has had a soup before, so it makes for a wonderful entry point to the world of healthy and delicious vegan cuisine.

My goal is for you to be a rock star soup creator. In these pages you will learn all that you need to know to create hundreds and even thousands of soups and stews, with more flavor and variety than you ever thought possible from vegan cuisine. Don't quite believe it? In *Soup's On!* you'll learn template cooking, which will show you how to expand upon one recipe to create countless variations. I will be sharing the tips and tricks I have developed over the last twenty years, which I share in all of my classes.

Vegan Fusion

The style of my cuisine is Vegan Fusion. This means that I often combine ingredients from different culinary traditions in the same dish or menu. Quinoa is a

South American grain, yet it complements a dish of Caribbean beans or Italian minestrone just as well as any rice. I also find that wheat-free tamari, a by-product of the miso-making process and a soy sauce used extensively in Asian cuisine, creates a layer of flavor and helps accentuate the flavor of other ingredients, regardless of the ethnicity of the dish. You will be amazed when you begin experimenting with different spice blends and adding them to dishes to create a wide range of ethnic cuisine with the toss of your hands.

Vegan Fusion cuisine also represents a return to the natural methods of growing food and utilizes organic ingredients whenever possible. Organic food is grown without the use of chemical fertilizers and pesticides, most of which have not been fully tested for their long-term effects on humans. For maximum food safety, go organic. Please see Appendix C for more information on organics.

I also recommend using a minimum of processed and packaged ingredients. This is much better for your health and the reduction in packaging is good for the planet.

Eating locally grown foods whenever possible ensures optimal flavor and freshness and saves all the resources involved in shipping over long distances. Growing foods in your own garden or participating in community-supported agriculture programs (CSAs) are the best option if you have the opportunity. It's very rewarding to see something grow from seed to plant. Farmers' markets are the next best choice. Get to know the people growing your food! Many of the recipes in *Soup's On!* can be adapted to include whatever ingredients are fresh and available.

Recipes for Peace

To me, the time we spend inside the kitchen can serve as a metaphor for life outside the kitchen. Many of the skills we can develop while cooking—being present with what we are doing, cultivating the qualities of mindfulness and gratitude—can overflow into all other aspects of our lives.

Preparing food can be a special and healing time for you to connect with nature in your own kitchen. It can be a time when you leave all of your cares at the door and focus on creating delicious meals. Besides being so much fun, getting creative in the kitchen and enjoying the fruits of your labor is one of life's greatest treasures.

I strongly encourage you to view meal preparation as a joy and privilege, rather than a chore. Cultivate calmness and infuse love into what you do and all of your guests will notice the difference. Most of us appreciate the food that is lovingly prepared by our grandmother and can tell the difference between that and other meals that may not be prepared with the same loving intention.

Do what you need to do to make your time in the kitchen special—play your favorite music, bring in flowers or candles, and let the inspiration flow. Food is art, and the palate is there for you to create your own culinary masterpiece!

It is my sincere wish that you experience the joy that comes through creating world-class plant-based cuisine. It will be of the greatest benefit to your health and the health of the planet.

With deep thanks and aloha,

Mark

Want to Know More?

Our company, Vegan Fusion, promotes the benefits of vegan foods for our health, the preservation of our planet, and to create a more peaceful world. In addition to our award-winning cookbooks, we offer workshops, chef trainings and immersions, and vegan culinary retreats around the world. We also offer consulting services and can assist in menu and recipe development with this innovative global cuisine. For inspiration surrounding the vegan lifestyle, to check out our online culinary course, and to sign up for our free online newsletter, please visit our website: www.veganfusion.com. For more information on Vegan Fusion Culinary Immersions, please see page 255.

How to
Use This Book

S oup's On! is divided into sections based on the different techniques involved in vegan soup creation. In this way, you can consider the book a soups preparation training manual, just as much as a cookbook. This is the approach I take in my cooking classes and it will allow you to grasp the basic techniques underlying the recipes, so you can create countless versions of the recipes provided.

In "Part 1: The Art of Soup Creation," I introduce my award-winning Template Recipe format. We will explore the basics of soup stock creation and the different ingredients used to create the flavorful base for our soups.

Part 2 contains soups that are vegetable based and do not require blending.

In Part 3, we will be adding grains, legumes (including soy-based foods, such as tofu and tempeh), and pasta to our vegetable-based soups to create heartier soups.

In Part 4, we take the leap into the blended creamy soup. Various ingredients, such as nuts, seeds, starchy vegetables, and plant-based milks, are introduced that create that "I can't believe it's vegan!" effect.

In Part 5, we explore the art of the raw soup. No cooking required!

"Part 6: Garnishes and Sides" introduces recipes that will enhance your soup experience in countless ways.

The recipes in each section are listed roughly from lighter to heavier. Enjoy the heavier recipes in the colder winter and autumn months. The lighter recipes will provide a perfectly satisfying meal on the warmer spring and summer days. You will particularly enjoy the raw soups in the warmer months and climates.

It's True—Soups in Thirty Minutes!

Virtually all the recipes can be completed in less than thirty minutes, including preparation and cooking time. Even though this is the case, I still do recommend cooking the soups at a lower temperature for slightly longer time periods, to really bring the dishes up to their highest culinary potential. Sometimes the flavor is further enhanced when soups are allowed to sit for a few hours and are then gently reheated.

The clock starts ticking once the ingredients have been gathered and are ready for use. The time doesn't include searching through the cabinets for tools or ingredients. The addition of ingredients that are listed as "optional" will also add to the preparation time. Read through the recipe carefully, perhaps even twice. Make sure you have everything you need and gather it before you begin. Remember that with practice, everything becomes easier. The more you make a recipe, the faster you will get and the more likely you will be able to fit it into the thirty-minute time frame.

Use these recipes as a starting point for creating your own versions and specialties based on your preferences and whatever ingredients are fresh and available. Look over the suggested variations to give you ideas on how you can experiment with the recipes. I'm a strong believer of creative expression in the kitchen; don't just try to stick to the recipe. If you love garlic, add more garlic. If you like it hot, up the quantity of chiles. For instance, the quantity "pinch" is often listed next to such ingredients as crushed red pepper flakes. Let your preference be your guide in how big a pinch you will add. Never let one or two missing ingredients stop you from making a recipe. There is always something you can substitute; be creative! For more on this, see the section on my Template Recipe format, page 20.

Specialty Ingredients

Although most of the ingredients used in *Soup's On!* can be purchased at your supermarket, some items may require a trip to the natural foods or ethnic market. Please do not be intimidated if you cannot stock up on all of them, as there is usually a way to substitute with what you do have on hand.

Here is a list of less common ingredients that are included in the main portion of a recipe or in one of its variations:

Amaranth: An ancient grain of the Aztecs, amaranth is nutrient rich and high in protein.

Anasazi beans: In the same family as pinto beans, these purple and white beans are said to be one of the main crops of Native Americans.

Berbere spice mix: A spice blend used in Ethiopian cuisine. See page 93 for a homemade version.

Beyond Meat: A relatively new product on the market; currently a chicken-free version is available in several flavors. Indistinguishable from the animal product, this is a recommended brand in terms of flavor and because, unlike seitan, it is gluten-free. If Beyond Meat is not available at your local store, see if you can find chicken-style seitan.

Brown rice pasta: Tinkyada brand is recommended.

Burdock root: A nutrient rich root vegetable popular in Asian cuisine.

Capers: A peppercorn-size flower bud of a Mediterranean bush, *Capparis spinosa*, native to the Mediterranean and parts of Asia. Capers are usually sun dried and pickled in vinegar brine to bring out their lemonlike flavor. Imparts a tangy, salty flavor to dishes.

Chinese cuisine spices: Five-spice powder, a blend of spices, is common in Chinese and other Asian cuisines. The blend typically contains cinnamon, star anise, cloves, fennel, and Szechuan pepper. Szechuan peppercorns have a slightly lemon flavor and accentuate the heat of other spices, such as chiles, that are used in a dish.

Chipotle chile powder: One of my all-time favorite ingredients. It consists of smoked jalapeño peppers. It imparts a smoky heat to dishes. A little goes a long way.

continues

Specialty Ingredients continued

Coconut milk: Available in most supermarkets; look for the organic variety of full-fat coconut milk, for optimal flavor. Low-fat coconut milk is an acceptable alternative for those wishing to cut down on fat.

Coconut oil, organic: One of my go-to oils to use for higher-heat sautéing.

Culinary-grade lavender flowers: See page 160.

Flaxseeds, either ground or whole, or Ener-G egg replacer: See page 76.

Liquid smoke: Purified water that has been infused with smoke. It adds a unique, smoky flavor to dishes. Choose those brands without artificial additives. Only a small amount is necessary.

Milks, nondairy (soy, rice, hemp, oat, and almond): An abundance of dairy-free milks are available in the market today, something for everyone's individual taste preferences. The soy milks tend to have the creamiest flavors when added to the recipes. Look for organic, unsweetened, whenever possible.

Mirin: A Japanese rice cooking wine with low alcohol content. It adds a sweet and tangy flavor to dishes. Use sparingly.

Miso paste: A salty paste made by fermenting soybeans, grains, and other beans. Purchase unpasteurized, for maximum nutritional benefits. See page 34.

Nutritional yeast: A plant-based culture consisting of up to 50 percent protein. The Red Star variety is a source of B vitamins, including B_{12}. It imparts a nutty and cheesy flavor to dishes. Go for the large flake variety, if possible.

Organic sugar substitutes: These include raw coconut nectar: see page 227.

Orzo: A delicate, rice-shaped, semolina-based Italian pasta.

Pearled couscous: A toasted, pearl-shaped pasta.

Polenta: A coarse Italian cornmeal.

Specialty Ingredients continued_____

Quinoa: Botanically a seed, though commonly referred to as the ancient grain of the Inca, quinoa is high in protein and may be used to replace rice in any of the recipes in the book.

Quinoa flakes: See page 76.

Raw apple cider vinegar or coconut vinegar

Culinary-grade rose water: See page 160.

Salts: Consider purchasing gourmet salts, such as Celtic or Himalayan, which are higher in mineral content than are most commercial salts. You can also experiment with smoked salts, which add an additional depth of flavor to your dishes.

Sea vegetables: These mineral rich foods have been consumed in Japan and around the world since ancient times. They will impart the flavor of the sea to your soups. They are rich in iodine, essential for proper thyroid function, and are also good sources of folic acid and magnesium, vital for heart health. As always, look for the organic varieties, without added coloring. Varieties to explore include wakame, kombu, nori, kelp, dulse, alaria, laver, hijiki, and sea lettuce.

Some varieties of sea vegetables used in *Soup's On!*:

Arame: A species of kelp high in calcium, protein, iron, iodine, and other vitamins and minerals.

Kombu: A wide and flat seaweed, kombu is a good source of calcium, folate, and magnesium. A key ingredient in the Dashi soup stock (page 28), we also add it to beans while cooking, to bring out the flavor of the bean and increase digestibility.

Nori: A highly nutritious red algae that's shredded, dried, and pressed like paper, providing calcium, iron, and other vitamins and minerals.

Wakame: Part of the kelp family, this green seaweed is popular in Asia and is used in soups, salads, and noodle dishes. It's high in calcium, niacin, thiamine, and B vitamins.

continues

Specialty Ingredients continued

Smoked paprika: A smoky version of the commonly available paprika. Some varieties are spicier than others, so adjust your quantities accordingly.

Tamarind paste: The tangy and slightly sweet pulp from the pod of a large tropical tree that is used in several cuisines from around the world, including Asian and South American.

Teff: The world's smallest grain used as the primary ingredient in Ethiopian flat bread called *injera*.

Tempeh: A cultured soy product high in protein; I recommend Turtle Island brand (see page 215).

Thai food essentials: Kaffir lime leaf, lemongrass, galangal root, and Thai basil are ingredients that are an integral component in Thai cuisine. Find them at the natural foods store or an ethnic market to add the greatest authenticity to your Thai soups.

Tofu, silken firm variety, organic

Truffle oil: Truffles are a highly sought-after edible fungi in the mushroom family that grow underground around tree roots. Truffle oil is available in different varieties, including oil that is infused with black or white truffles, each with its own unique flavor.

Vegan butter: Try Earth Balance, use sparingly.

Vegan cheese: Try Daiya or Follow Your Heart.

Vegan mayonnaise: Try Vegenaise, or make your own (page 226).

Vegan sausages: Tofurky and Field Roast have good products.

Wheat-free tamari: A by-product of the miso-making process, this is the recommended soy sauce for all the recipes in the book.

Specialty Ingredients continued_____

White spelt flour or gluten-free flour mix: Bob's Red Mill has a wonderful gluten-free baking mix that can replace the flour called for in the recipes in a one-to-one ratio. For gluten-free baking, you will also want to pick up xanthan gum or guar gum, as a specialty product. These are substances to replace the gluten in other flours that can contribute elasticity to the recipes. I include a recipe for a gluten-free flour mix on page 223. For that recipe you can pick up sorghum flour, brown rice flour, and tapioca flour.

Prep

Throughout the book, I introduce many of the techniques of vegan natural food preparation. These techniques are also highlighted in the preparation basics section in Appendix A. For a more thorough exploration, including tips for stocking your kitchen, as well as for an extensive resource guide, please check out the first book in the 30-Minute Vegan series, *The 30-Minute Vegan.*

Keys to Success in a 30-Minute Kitchen: Guidelines for the Efficient Chef

Preparing food is an art form. As with any art form, the more you practice, the more skilled you will become. These tips will help you have great success in the kitchen and will enable you to enjoy yourself. If you're having a good time, this good juju will be imparted to the food and everyone will enjoy it!

1. Read each recipe thoroughly. Look up words and ingredients you are unfamiliar with. Understand the process involved. Understand when multitasking is necessary, rather than waiting for each step to be complete before moving on to the next step.

2. Before beginning any preparation, create a clean work area. A clean and un-cluttered work area allows for a clearer, less cluttered mind, which will greatly improve your efficiency and help you develop a deeper culinary in-tuition. Gathering the ingredients in the recipe before you begin ensures that you have everything you need and you know what you will be using as a substitute, and eliminates time spent searching through cabinets. Gather your measuring spoons and cups, tools, and appliances. Preparing food in a clean and organized space is always easier.

3. Having the proper tools is essential to being able to whip food up quickly. It may increase your cooking time if you don't have such tools as a garlic press, zester, citrus juicer, or blender. Work up to a fully stocked kitchen.

4. Although the recipes are designed to taste their best by following the exact measurements, eventually you will learn to discover acceptable approxima-tions. At some point you will be able to look at two different cloves of garlic and know that, chopped, one is about 1 teaspoon, and the other is about 1 tablespoon. In cases like these, don't worry too much about measuring everything with ultimate precision. With baking, however, measurements need to be precise because leavening is involved.

5. Some herbs, such as parsley, cilantro, or dill, don't need to be plucked from the thin part of their stems before mincing or chopping. Just keep them bundled together and chop into the whole bunch at once. The thin parts of the stems generally have the same flavor, and once minced, basically taste the same.

6. Cut stacks of veggies rather than each individual piece. Don't separate cel-ery stalks when you can cut into the whole bunch at once. The same goes for heads of lettuce and cabbage. Stack tomato, potato, or onion slices and cut them simultaneously.

7. You don't need to peel carrots, cucumbers, potatoes, zucchini, or beets un-less specified; just wash them well. This is not only quicker, but also helps preserve the nutritional content of the food.

8. All the cooked soup recipes call for adding vegetable stock or water. You can save on cooking time by heating the stock or water in a separate pot while you gather the other ingredients. In this way you will save the time it takes to bring the stock up to a cooking temperature.

9. Most blenders have cup and fluid ounce measurements right on the pitcher; no need to dirty more measuring cups.

10. One of the most important tips to help cut down on preparation time is to set aside an hour or so on one of your least busy days for advance prepping. Having prepped ingredients on hand makes it easier to create meals on the go. You can cut vegetables and store them in a glass container in the fridge. You can also cook a squash, grain, or pot of beans. You can then use these foods in recipes over the next few days. Consider preparing a pot of rice in the morning and using it for the evening meal.

Useful Kitchen Gear for Soup Preparation

In addition to the usual culprits of kitchen gear (measuring cups, spoons, bowls, spatulas, etc.), here are a few items you may wish to have to make your soup creation more fun and enjoyable:

Heavy-bottomed stockpot and 3-quart pot—stainless steel preferred

Strong blender, such as a Vitamix (see Appendix D)

Immersion blender—use to create creamy blended soups. Works best with blended soups that do not contain nuts.

Microplane zester

Sprout bags, for creating plant milk (see page 245)

Mandoline, for thinly slicing vegetable chips (see page 201)

Spiralizer, for creating amazing julienne strips and veggie "noodles" to garnish your raw soups (see page 158)

Shelf Life/Storage of Prepared Foods

As for the shelf life of the dishes, I generally recommend enjoying the food the day it is prepared and for the next day or two after that. Some recipes, such as some of the garnishes and side dishes, may last a bit longer. Please check daily to ensure freshness. Store leftovers in a glass container in the refrigerator.

Health for Life

When developing the recipes for *Soup's On!* I was looking to create the best-tasting soups possible, while keeping an eye on the overall healthiness of the dishes. Many people turn to soups when they are looking to heal, or to give their digestive system a rest, and enjoy a light and simple meal. The raw food soups in particular are loaded with nutrients that have not been altered through the heating process.

With this in mind, I have reduced the use of processed oils in the recipes, especially when heating the oils by sautéing, which many believe is potentially damaging to our health. For those wishing to enhance the flavor of the dishes by sautéing in oil, using some high-heat oil, such as coconut, will bring out more flavor in the recipes. I mention this as a variation in the recipes where I feel it will benefit the flavor.

Another option is to add a small amount of a high-quality oil to the soup and stir well just before serving, so you eliminate the high-heat dilemma and still receive the flavor. Those wishing to completely eliminate processed oils, especially when sautéing, should use the water sauté method discussed on page 217.

Gluten-Freedom

Virtually all the recipes in this book are gluten-free. Gluten is a protein that is found in wheat and other cereal grains that is responsible for its elasticity. More and more people are being diagnosed with celiac disease (extreme gluten intolerance)—or are simply cutting gluten out of their diet for overall health. Some recipes, such as those with vegan sausage, or seitan, do contain gluten and can be easily adapted to gluten-free. On the recipes that do include a gluten product, I have noted what to use as a gluten-free replacement.

I have used spelt flour in the few recipes that do call for flour. Spelt is an ancient variety of wheat, which does contain gluten, though in a form that many with wheat allergies can tolerate. Those with celiac disease are unable to tolerate gluten in any form. For a gluten-free flour mix, please see page 223. For the gluten intolerant, please remember to use gluten-free tamari as the soy sauce, and to purchase a gluten-free variety of nutritional yeast—two common ingredients used in the book.

Some Other Healthful Considerations

Low Sodium: If you wish to reduce your sodium intake, please use a low-sodium soy sauce, add salt to taste instead of following the recipe's recommendation, and/or replace the sea salt with kelp granules. Not all salts are created equal. The recipes were developed using a mineral rich sea salt. Some sea salts are higher in sodium than others, and the coarseness of the salt will also determine the amount of sodium in a measured amount. (One teaspoon of coarsely ground salt will contain less sodium than 1 teaspoon of finely ground salt.)

Soy Free: Those with soy allergies may use chopped portobello mushrooms whenever tofu or tempeh is called for in the recipe. You can eliminate the soy sauce, or replace the soy sauce called for in the recipes with coconut aminos, a coconut-based sauce available at your local natural foods store.

Sugar Free: Refined white sugar is implicated in many illnesses. In some of the fruit-based soup recipes I list organic coconut nectar, which is derived from the coconut palm (see page 227), as an ingredient alternative to white sugar. Please see the sweetener chart on page 227 for some healthful alternatives to white sugar and visit your local natural foods store to discover several natural sweeteners on the market.

A Note About Raw Foods

Raw food cuisine is on the cutting edge of the culinary scene, with many raw food restaurants, books, and online communities sprouting up all the time (no pun intended). Raw food advocates report more energy and greater health and mental clarity by preserving vital nutrients, many of which are destroyed in the heating process. This is why I have devoted an entire section to raw soups—so you can experience for yourself the joys of live food cuisine.

Sidebars and Symbols

Throughout the pages you will see the following sidebars and symbols:

If You Have More Time: These recipes and variations of recipes take longer than thirty minutes. Give them a try when you have more time to explore them!

Chef's Tips and Tricks: We share the secrets that make your life in the kitchen easier and more enjoyable.

♥ Indicates a recipe that is 95 percent or more raw, or can be easily adapted to raw. See page 157 for information on raw foods.

This variation provides a gluten-free alternative to a recipe that contains a gluten product. **All other recipes are gluten-free by nature.**

This recipe or variation may take longer than thirty minutes if you count baking, refrigerating, or freezing time. Some recipes may take longer than thirty minutes until you are comfortable with the steps of the recipe. With practice you will find yourself preparing them at a much quicker pace.

Chef's Tips and Tricks

Serving Sizes

As soups may be enjoyed both as an appetizer course or a main course, there is some variability in the serving size. All the cooked soups, except the vegetable stocks, can be prepared in a 3-quart pot and have an 8- to 10-cup yield. (The Versatile Miso Soup with Pickled Ginger is an exception and makes two servings.) The raw soups will typically fit in a large blender and are less than 7 cups. If a recipe is said to serve 6 to 8, the lower number would be if the soup were enjoyed as a main course, the higher number would indicate appetizer portions.

Chef's Tips and Tricks

Vegan Wines and Beer

Many commercially available beers and wines are filtered with animal product ingredients such as isinglass (from fish bladder), gelatin, egg whites, or seashells. Most Guinness beer, for instance, uses isinglass in the refining process. The Guinness Extra Stout made in North America does not contain isinglass and is therefore suitable for vegans. Please check with the company to insure that your beverage is vegan. You can also visit www.Barnivore.com—a website with a comprehensive vegan beer and wine guide.

PART ONE

THE ART OF SOUP CREATION

Soups have allegedly been part of the human menu plan since 6000 BC, where Stone Soup, or Stone Age Soup more likely, was probably all the rage. We are fortunate that things have changed a bit on the culinary scene since then. The plant kingdom today provides a remarkable array of vegetables, fruits, herbs, grains, legumes, seeds, and nuts for us to create outrageously delectable and satisfying soups.

One of my favorite things about preparing soups is the ability to use whatever ingredients are on hand to create an amazing dish. There are many who advocate eating seasonally and locally grown foods for optimal flavor and nutrition, and to conserve the resources involved in shipping foods over long distances. Soups provide the perfect medium because there are so many options to incorporate whatever is fresh and local. This is something that you can do year-round, to experience for yourself the cycle of seasonal produce in your community. Visit your local farmers' market to see what is in season and check out the index of *Soup's On!* to see which recipes include them. When developing the recipes, I wanted to include as many vegetables as possible that you are likely to find in the market, so you will always have a recipe to turn to throughout the year.

Of course, with the advent of the modern-day market and shipping, we have a world of produce at our fingertips. The distinction of seasonal eating based on availability is becoming a thing of the past. Popular summer foods, such as strawberries, corn, and watermelon, are available in the cold winter months, and you can feast on winter squash and pumpkins in the heat of the summer.

Please see the seasonal growing charts on page 231 to learn about which fruits and vegetables are grown during which part of the year.

Soup Terms

What is the difference between a soup and a stew? Generally, soups have more liquids than stews, though one person's watery stew is another person's soup. Here are some other common words you will hear in the soup world:

Bouillon: A broth typically made with mirepoix (celery, onions, and carrots) and aromatic herbs.

Consommé: A type of clear soup that is traditionally animal product based and involves a long process of simmering.

Puree: A vegetable soup thickened with a starch, such as potatoes or flour.

Bisque: A pureed soup that is traditionally animal product based and thickened with cream.

Chowder: A thickened soup or stew typically made with milk or cream.

The Template Recipe:
How a Hundred Recipes Turn into Thousands of Recipes

How can I show you how to prepare thousands of soups with one hundred recipes? The answer is a style of recipe development that will help you exponentially expand your creativity in the kitchen. It's called a Template Recipe format, and I've taught it to students in my workshops, immersions, and online trainings. It's something I would like to share with you now, before we dive into the recipes of the book.

To view recipes as a template, you look at a recipe in the most general form possible and break it down into its component parts. By changing the component parts, you create an entirely new recipe. Some recipes lend themselves to this template approach more than others do. The Creamy Broccoli Soup with Shiitake Mushrooms (page 137) is a perfect example of a Template Recipe.

First, instead of viewing it as "broccoli soup," we view it as a "creamy vegetable soup." This way we can know that if we are out of broccoli, this soup can still be an option for us to prepare.

The component parts are the following:

Base: In this case, vegetable stock or water, onion, celery, and garlic
Main vegetable component: Broccoli
Creaminess component: Macadamia nuts
Herb/spice component: Cilantro, crushed red pepper flakes
Vegetables added after blending component: Mushrooms and corn

Once we have broken down the recipe into its parts, we can alter any or all of them to create a new recipe. The interesting thing about this is that even when we leave every other part of the recipe the same, altering one component creates a new flavor profile for the entire dish.

Using this method, our broccoli soup recipe suddenly becomes hundreds of recipes:

- Change the base by experimenting with different types of vegetable stock.
- Change the main veggie component by replacing the broccoli with cauliflower, zucchini, asparagus, or any combination of vegetables you desire.
- To create creaminess, you can replace the macadamia nuts with cashews, sunflower seeds, pumpkin seeds, Brazil nuts, hazelnuts, blanched almonds—any of which can be raw or toasted. You can also replace them with coconut milk, soy milk, rice milk, almond milk, or other plant-based milks.
- The herb component can be altered by replacing the cilantro with any herb or herb combination of your choosing, such as basil, dill, or parsley. You can add Mexican spices, such as chili powder and cumin; Indian spices, such as curry powder; or Italian spices, such as oregano, thyme, or rosemary.

Once your soup is blended, you can then add any vegetables of your choosing. Replace the mushrooms and corn with chopped broccoli, asparagus, red bell pepper, or any combination.

Using this flexible recipe, the possibilities are endless!

As you follow the recipes in the book, keep this idea of a Template Recipe in mind and pay close attention to the variations that are suggested. This will allow you to greatly expand your soup repertoire.

Soup Stock

Soup stock is at the foundation of any good soup or stew. It adds a depth and layer of flavor to your dish that you cannot attain with water alone. You have four options when considering a base for your soups.

1. **Use *Soups On!* stock recipes.** I provide five basic soup stock recipes to follow if you wish to create a stock based on specific ingredients.

2. **Use commercially available soup stocks.** These typically come in liquid form in aseptic packages, or as powdered mixes, or condensed bouillon cubes or pastes. Read the labels carefully to make sure that you are purchasing a vegan brand. Be aware of those with high sodium content and any artificial flavorings.

3. **Create your own stock with vegetable trimmings.** For a simple soup stock, save the clippings and scraps of vegetables used in preparing other recipes. Place them in a large, heavy-bottomed stockpot over low heat with water to cover and simmer until all the veggies are completely cooked. Cook until the liquid is reduced to about 75 to 50 percent of its original volume. The veggies' flavor will be imparted to the broth. Experiment with different vegetables and herbs until you discover your favorite combinations. In general, you are looking to create a relatively neutral stock that can be used for all of your soup needs. Strain well, and add salt and pepper to taste.

   Try using trimmings from potatoes, celery, carrots, tomatoes, onions, parsley, mushrooms, parsnip, zucchini, leeks, corn cobs, and garlic. Many avoid using vegetables that become bitter, such as bell peppers, radishes, turnips, broccoli, cauliflower, and Brussels sprouts. As far as herbs go, the only one I use freely is parsley. You can use a few stalks of other herbs, such as thyme, oregano, dill, basil, or marjoram. Keep in mind that too much of these herbs can overpower the stock. The stock may be frozen and defrosted

for future use. You can even pour broth into ice cube trays, freeze, and use as needed.

If you find that you do not have many trimmings to use, you can keep a bag or small bucket in the freezer to save the trimmings. Once you have enough accumulated to fill a stockpot, 6 to 8 cups, get your soup stock going.

4. **Use water as the base.** Water can be used as the base of your soups, though it will typically not be as flavorful as those soups made with vegetable stocks. The water can be in the form of pot liquor, which is the liquid that remains in a pot after vegetables are steamed or boiled, provided that the liquid does not have a bitter or overpowering flavor.

When creating the recipes for *Soup's On!* I was confronted with the dilemma of realizing that using a soup stock will enhance the flavor of the dish and also that many people will not wish to go through the effort or expense of purchasing or creating stocks. There are also so many different varieties and flavors of stocks available that it would be challenging to create an accurate recipe for everyone to follow.

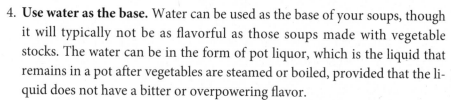

Chef's Tips and Tricks

Before You Begin: Sodium Levels

Given the variability in flavor of the different soup stocks on the market, all the recipes in *Soup's On!* were developed with water as the base. In several recipes, I used a wheat-free tamari soy sauce to create a base flavor in the absence of the stock. If you do use a stock instead of water, feel free to reduce or even eliminate the tamari. If you use a stock that already contains any salt or soy sauce, it is very important to reduce or eliminate the salt and/or soy sauce that a recipe may contain.

Chef's Tips and Tricks

Before You Begin

Please remember these four things while preparing the recipes to create the most optimal flavor:

1. **Chop as you go.** Be sure to start adding vegetables to the pot in the order in which they are listed in the recipe as soon as you are done chopping them. There is no need to wait until you chop everything before adding it to the soup. The longer the veggies are in the pot, the more flavorful your soup will become. This will also make it easier for you to fit recipes into the thirty-minute time frame. Of course, if a recipe specifies to add an ingredient at a specific time, such as after the rest of the soup is blended or after a grain has cooked, please follow the instructions.

2. **Use a vegetable stock instead of water.** Remember to reduce or eliminate the use of additional salt or soy sauce if you are using a stock that contains sodium.

3. **Cook for longer periods of time.** Most soups require closer to forty-five minutes to reach their full flavor potential. Cook over medium or even low heat instead of the high or medium-high temperatures listed in the recipes.

4. **Sauté vegetables in oil before adding the stock.** Sautéing the base ingredients, such as onion, celery, and garlic, for a few minutes with a high-temperature oil, such as coconut oil, before adding the stock, will deepen the flavor of the recipes.

Basic Vegetable Stock

Here is a simple go-to stock to create with some of the more popular stock ingredients. Chop the vegetables as small as possible to have the flavor come out with less cooking time. While times are given to fit into the thirty-minute time frame, it is recommended to cook for forty-five to sixty minutes over a lower temperature, for optimal results.

MAKES 12 CUPS STOCK

14 cups cold water

2 large onions, chopped small

5 garlic cloves, crushed

4 large celery stalks, chopped small

1 large potato, chopped small

1 large carrot, chopped small

10 sprigs parsley

1 large zucchini, chopped small

1 large parsnip, chopped small (optional)

3 bay leaves

½ teaspoon black peppercorns

1 corn cob (optional)

1. Place the cold water in a large stockpot over high heat. Begin chopping the vegetables and placing them in the pot as you go. Add bay leaves and peppercorns.
2. Cook for 25 minutes, stirring occasionally.
3. Strain well before using.

Variations

- If you wish for deeper flavor, you can sauté the onion, garlic, and celery in 2 tablespoons of oil, stirring frequently, before adding the water and remaining vegetables.
- See page 22 for various vegetables, herbs, and spices that can go into the stock.
- For a **No-Bones Broth**, add ½ cup of arame (see page 9) along with the vegetables. The arame will add an abundance of minerals to your stock and is the perfect vegan substitute for animal product–based "healing" broths. Enjoy while fasting on liquids or any other time you wish to give your digestive system a rest. Thanks go to Cindy Edwards for the suggestion to include this recipe!

Mushroom Stock

The addition of mushrooms gives this stock a deeper flavor than the Basic Vegetable Stock has. Remember again to chop the vegetables as small as possible to have the flavor come out with less cooking time. As with the Basic Vegetable Stock, it is recommended to cook for forty-five to sixty minutes over a lower temperature for optimal results.

MAKES 12 CUPS STOCK

14 cups water

1 large onion, chopped small

3 large celery stalks, chopped small

1 large carrot, chopped small

6 garlic cloves (optional)

1 large leek, sliced thinly, rinsed and drained well

4 cups chopped mushrooms (try button, cremini, portobello, shiitake, or a combination)

8 sprigs parsley (about ¼ cup)

1 large apple, cored and quartered (optional)

1. Place the cold water in a large stockpot over high heat. Begin chopping the ingredients and placing them in the pot as you go.
2. Cook for 25 minutes, stirring occasionally.
3. Strain well before using.

Roasted Vegetable Stock

Roasting of the vegetables and the addition of wine give this stock the richest and deepest flavor. Although this stock does take longer than thirty minutes from start to finish, the time you spend chopping the vegetables will be well under this time frame. Experiment with adding different vegetables and changing the type of wine to create a myriad of ultimate soup stocks.

MAKES 11 TO 12 CUPS STOCK

1 medium-size onion, chopped small

1 leek, sliced thinly, rinsed and drained well

2 medium-size carrots, chopped small

1 medium-size zucchini, chopped small

10 cremini or button mushrooms, quartered (leave stems on)

2 medium-size tomatoes, quartered

6 garlic cloves

2 tablespoons olive oil

14 cups cold water

3 large celery stalks, chopped small

3 bay leaves

10 to 12 sprigs flat-leaf parsley

10 to 12 black peppercorns

5 sprigs thyme

5 sprigs marjoram

1 cup red or white wine

1. Preheat the oven to 450°F. Place the onion, leek, carrots, zucchini, mushrooms, tomatoes, and garlic on a large baking sheet or in a baking dish. Add the oil and toss well. Bake for 35 minutes, stirring occasionally and checking to make sure the veggies are not burning.
2. Meanwhile, place the cold water in a large stockpot over medium heat. Add all the remaining ingredients, except the wine, and stir well.
3. When the vegetables are done roasting, transfer them to the stockpot. Deglaze the baking sheet (see page 205) by pouring the wine onto the sheet and scraping off as much as possible of the cooked vegetables that stuck to the pan. Add to the stockpot.
4. Increase the heat to medium-high and cook for 45 minutes, stirring occasionally.
5. Strain well before using.

Dashi

Dashi is a popular stock in Japanese cuisine that typically contains the sea vegetable kombu, an edible form of kelp, as well as fish flakes. This simple stock uses the sea vegetable arame (see page 9) to add the flavor of the sea. Use this vegan dashi in all of your Asian soups, including Versatile Miso Soup with Pickled Ginger (page 34), Adzuki Bean Soup with Enoki Mushrooms (page 116), and Hot Pot with Soba Noodles, Seared Shiitake Mushrooms, and Baby Bok Choy (page 80). For optimal results, cook for at least forty-five minutes.

MAKES 12 CUPS DASHI

14 cups cold water

3 (6-inch) strips kombu (see page 9)

½ cup arame (see page 9)

6 large shiitake mushrooms, fresh or dried (optional)

1. Place the water in a large stockpot over high heat. Add the remaining ingredients and stir well.
2. Cook for 30 minutes, stirring occasionally.
3. Strain well before using.

Basic Tamari Stock

I am expecting to win the Julia Child Award for this recipe, so please let me know what you think. This simple stock can provide a base flavor for your soups in the absence of a more complex stock. Tamari is a soy sauce that is the by-product of the miso-making process. Because there is sodium in the tamari, please adjust the quantity of salt added to any recipe in which you used this stock as a base. Keep in mind that different soy sauces have different flavors.

MAKES 5 CUPS STOCK

5 cups water

2 to 3 tablespoons wheat-free tamari or other soy sauce

1. Place the water and tamari in a 3-quart pot over medium-high heat.
2. Cook for 3 minutes, or until just warm.

Chef's Tips and Tricks

To Cover or to Uncover?

I typically always cook soups without a lid. I like to be able to see how the soup is progressing and easily give it a loving stir every now and then. Cooking with the lid off allows the water or stock to evaporate more quickly, creating a thicker, more flavorful base. Some also suggest that cooking with a lid on creates condensation that then finds its way back into the soup, diluting its flavor. Proponents of lid-on cooking suggest that fewer nutrients escape through the steam if you leave the lid on and that the soup will cook faster. Perhaps this is a perennial debate that will perplex philosophical cooks until the end of time.

To Freeze or Not to Freeze?

I am not a big fan of freezing soups, mainly because I like to enjoy my food as fresh as possible. I do understand that freezing is a popular way for people to conserve time and to save themselves from throwing out leftover food. For the busy cook, you can prepare a soup on your least busy day, freeze it, and defrost as needed during the week. For best results, place the soup in a glass container and allow it to cool completely, either at room temperature or in the refrigerator with the lid slightly open, before closing the lid and placing it in the freezer. Some soups freeze better than others. Those with potatoes and greens are generally not as good when defrosted. Others will need a little sprucing up, either with additional vegetable stock added to achieve your desired consistency, and/or with salt or tamari to taste. You can also add some chopped fresh herbs or veggies to defrosted soups to liven them up a bit.

PART TWO

VEGETABLE-BASED SOUPS

In this section we are going to explore the most simple form of soup creation—the one-pot soup. This basically involves adding chopped vegetables and seasonings to your stock and cooking until done. Recipes that demonstrate this technique are the Mayan Tomato and Corn Soup, the Szechuan Hot and Sour Vegetable Soup, and the Versatile Miso Soup with Pickled Ginger.

We will then go a step further and introduce such techniques as toasting spices (Peasant Vegetable with Toasted Spice Soup), sautéing (Fried Green Tomato Soup au Gratin), roasting (Roasted Root Vegetable Soup and Roasted Beet Borscht), broiling (Broiled Zucchini with Saffron), and grilling (Truffled Wild Mushroom Consommé with Grilled Baby Asparagus). Each of these techniques will add a deepening flavor to the soups.

Coconut lovers will be happy to see that we will be introducing the use of coconut milk as part of the stock, as in the Jamaican Jerk Plantain Stew and Thai Coconut Soup with Lemongrass.

After preparing several recipes from this section, you will get a glimpse of the amazing diversity possible with simple vegan soups. So, let's get cooking!

Versatile Miso Soup with Pickled Ginger

No book on soups would be complete without the ubiquitous miso soup—the picture of simplicity, and one of the healthier choices in the dining world. So many variations are possible, depending upon the type of miso used and the assortment of vegetables added. Enjoy on its own or topped with Sweet and Spicy Toasted Nori Sheets (page 191).

SERVES 2

2 ½ cups vegetable stock (page 27) or water

¼ cup diced extra-firm tofu

2 tablespoons diced carrot or daikon radish

2 tablespoons dried arame

2 tablespoons miso paste (see Chef's Tips and Tricks)

3 tablespoons plus 1 teaspoon wheat-free tamari or other soy sauce, or to taste

¼ cup diced cucumber

1 tablespoon finely chopped pickled ginger

2 tablespoons finely chopped green onion

Pinch of crushed red pepper flakes (optional)

1 teaspoon toasted sesame oil (optional)

1. Heat the vegetable stock over medium-high heat in a small pot.
2. Add the tofu, carrot, and arame and cook for 7 minutes.
3. Place the miso paste in a small bowl or measuring cup. Remove about 1 cup of liquid from the pot and add it to the bowl. Stir well with a fork or whisk until the miso is dissolved. Return the mixture to the pot.
4. Add the remaining ingredients, and stir well before serving.

Variations

- Experiment with different types of miso, such as red, white, or chickpea.
- Add 1 cup of assorted chopped vegetables, such as bok choy, spinach, or broccoli, along with the tofu. Cook until the veggies are just tender, before adding the remaining ingredients.
- Add ½ toasted nori sheet, crumbled, before serving.
- Add ½ avocado, peeled, pitted, and cubed, before serving.
- Replace the arame with any other sea vegetable, such as sea lettuce, wakame, or hijiki.

Chef's Tips and Tricks:
Miso Madness

High in protein, vitamins, and minerals, miso paste is most commonly made with soybeans, though countless varieties of miso paste are available. Be sure to purchase the unpasteurized varieties. Avoid boiling, for optimal nutrition.

Cleansing Burdock Soup
with Ginger and Dandelion Greens

This is the soup to go to when you are feeling under the weather. Most of the ingredients have medicinal qualities that have been touted for centuries—and this is medicine that tastes great! Experiment with different varieties of miso, using the darker colors in the colder months, and remember not to boil the miso! Top with Krispy Kale (page 203).

SERVES 6 TO 8

6 cups vegetable stock (page 25) or water

2 burdock roots, sliced thinly (1 cup) (see page 7)

2 tablespoons peeled and minced fresh ginger

¾ cup thinly sliced shiitake mushrooms

1 cup diced carrot

⅛ to ¼ teaspoon cayenne pepper

3 tablespoons wheat-free tamari or other soy sauce

1 bunch dandelion greens, sliced into 1-inch slices (2 cups) (see Chef's Tips and Tricks)

½ cup loosely packed, thinly sliced green onion

3 tablespoons miso paste

½ teaspoon sea salt, or to taste

1. Place the vegetable stock in a 3-quart pot over medium-high heat. Add all the remaining ingredients, except the dandelion greens, green onion, miso paste, and sea salt, and cook for 15 minutes, stirring occasionally.
2. Add the dandelion greens and green onion and cook for 5 minutes, stirring occasionally.
3. Place the miso paste in a small bowl with 1 cup of liquid from the soup and whisk until the miso dissolves. Return the mixture to the pot. Mix well, add the sea salt, and enjoy.

Variations

- Add 1 cup of your favorite vegetables, chopped small, along with the carrots. Try parsnip, broccoli, or cauliflower.
- Replace the ginger with garlic.
- Replace the dandelion with greens of your choosing, such as kale, chard, or collards.
- For a heartier soup, add 12 ounces (1¾ cups) of shelled edamame beans and cook for 10 minutes.

> **Chef's Tips and Tricks:** *Dandelion Greens and Other Wild Greens*
>
> Explore your produce section to discover some of the lesser-used though equally tasty, and in some instances more nutritious, green veggies. Dandelion greens in particular are quite high in iron and calcium and are a super addition to soups that call for greens. Other wild greens include sorrel, stinging nettles, mustard greens, and watercress. When choosing watercress, select the younger, more tender leaves for optimal flavor.

Truffled Wild Mushroom Consommé
with Grilled Baby Asparagus

Here we have a sophisticated and satisfying soup made with truffles, a highly prized fungus that imparts a distinct flavor and strong aroma to dishes. A little bit goes a long way. Most people's experience with truffles is through truffle oil, which is used in this dish. Experiment with different varieties of mushrooms and see how the flavor of the soup changes. Garnish with a drizzle of Red Oil (page 187) and top with toasted chopped hazelnuts (see page 215).

SERVES 6 TO 8

GRILLED ASPARAGUS

2 tablespoons freshly squeezed
   lemon juice
1 tablespoon olive oil
Pinch of sea salt
Pinch of ground black pepper
1 small bunch asparagus, trimmed
   to 4-inch spears

CONSOMMÉ

1 tablespoon oil (try coconut)
2 teaspoons herbes de Provence
   (see Chef's Tips and Tricks)
½ cup diced shallot
¾ cup thinly sliced leek, rinsed
   and drained well
1½ cups thinly sliced wild
   mushrooms (try chanterelle
   and/or morel, or a cultivated
   mushroom such as shiitake)
½ cup white wine
6 cups vegetable stock (page 25)
   or water
1 teaspoon truffle oil
2 tablespoons freshly squeezed
   lemon juice
½ cup seeded and diced red bell
   pepper
2 teaspoons sea salt, or to taste
¼ teaspoon ground black pepper
Pinch of cayenne pepper

Chef's Tips and Tricks

Herbes de Provence

A staple of French cuisine that typically contains dried thyme, rosemary, marjoram, basil, savory, and bay leaf, herbes de Provence may also include lavender flowers. Thyme usually imparts the dominant flavor of the mixture.

continues

continued

1. Prepare the asparagus: Preheat a grill. Place the lemon juice, olive oil, salt, and pepper in a shallow dish and mix well. Add the asparagus and toss well. (See Variations for stove-top directions.)

2. Prepare the soup: Place the oil in a 3-quart pot over medium-high heat. Add the herbes de Provence, shallot, leek, and mushrooms and cook for 3 minutes, stirring frequently. Add the white wine and stir well. Add the vegetable stock and cook for 20 minutes, stirring occasionally.

3. Meanwhile grill the asparagus until just tender, about 5 minutes, depending upon the heat of your grill. Chop into 1-inch pieces and add to the soup. (You can also add the asparagus marinade ingredients to the soup for additional flavor.)

4. Add the remaining ingredients, and stir well before serving.

Variations

- Grill the bell pepper whole, along with the asparagus. Seed, dice, and add to the soup.
- If no grill is available, you can sauté the asparagus or roast it in a preheated 375°F oven until just tender, about 10 minutes.
- Broiling the asparagus is another option. Broil on HIGH BROIL until tender, about 5 minutes. You can broil the bell pepper, halved and seeded, along with the asparagus. Dice and add to the soup.
- Replace the asparagus with other grilled vegetables, such as broccoli rabe, zucchini, or baby bok choy.
- Experiment with different varieties of mushrooms, such as portobello or cremini.
- For a low-oil version, use the water sauté method discussed on page 217.

Chef's Tips and Tricks

Truffle Oil

Some oils sold as truffle oil are actually made with synthetic chemicals that mimic the aroma and flavor of truffles. Steer clear of brands that say "truffle essence" or "truffle aroma." Look for labels that say "infused with truffles" and/or those with small amounts of truffles in the jar, for the real deal. Store truffle oil in the refrigerator and use within a few months, for optimal flavor.

Mayan Tomato and Corn Soup

This soup is inspired by a dish we had at the Mayan Center in Belize during a Vegan Fusion Culinary Immersion, where I was introduced to jipijapa palm, similar to the heart of palm used in this recipe. Fortunately, doomsayers' 2012 ending of the Mayan calendar was incorrect and I get to share this recipe with you. Make sure to purchase sustainably harvested heart of palm (see Chef's Tips and Tricks). Serve with a dollop of Vegan Crème Fraîche (page 195) and a side of Cosmic Corn Bread (page 211).

SERVES 6 TO 8

4½ cups vegetable stock (page 25) or water

1 cup diced yellow onion

4 large garlic cloves, pressed or minced

1 teaspoon seeded and diced jalapeño pepper

1 cup chopped tomato (½-inch pieces)

2 cups fresh or frozen corn

1 tablespoon tomato paste

1 (14.5-ounce) can diced fire-roasted tomatoes, or an additional 1½ cups fairly tightly packed chopped tomato (½-inch pieces)

¼ cup freshly squeezed lime juice

¾ cup chopped heart of palm (½-inch pieces)

3 tablespoons finely chopped fresh cilantro

2 teaspoons chili powder

1 teaspoon ground cumin

2 teaspoons sea salt, or to taste

¼ teaspoon ground black pepper

¼ teaspoon cayenne pepper

¼ teaspoon chipotle chile powder, or to taste

1. Place the vegetable stock in a 3-quart pot over medium-high heat. Add the onion, garlic, jalapeño, and tomato and cook for 10 minutes, stirring occasionally.
2. Lower the heat to low, add the corn, and cook for 10 minutes, stirring occasionally.
3. Add the remaining ingredients and mix well before serving.

Variations

- Add 1½ tablespoons of olive oil before serving.
- Add 1 cup of cubed and roasted tofu or tempeh cubes (see page 215).
- Replace the hearts of palm with artichoke hearts.
- You can sauté the onion, garlic, and jalapeño in 1 tablespoon of oil for 3 minutes, stirring frequently, before adding the vegetable stock.
- For a fuller-bodied soup, remove 1½ cups of the liquid and tomatoes from the pot, transfer to a blender, and carefully blend well. Return the mixture to the pot. You can also blend ½ cup of chopped cashews with 2 cups of the soup and return the mixture to the pot.

continues

continued

Chef's Tips and Tricks

Heart of Palm

Heart of palm is a flavorful delicacy that is harvested from a variety of palm tree in the tropics. Many companies are criticized for destroying the rain forest so as to grow palm plantations to meet rising demand. Some companies, such as Native Harvest, sustainably harvest the heart of palm and support indigenous communities.

Seeding Tomatoes

Many chefs like to seed their tomatoes before using in recipes. This removes the liquid portion or juice of the tomato as well, which can benefit the consistency of certain dishes, especially salads. If you have more time and wish to seed your tomatoes, one method is to slice the tomato in half along its equator. Using a small spoon, scoop out the seeds and juice of the tomato and discard. You can also remove the entire inner portion of the tomato, if you wish. A quicker method involves gently squeezing the tomato once it is halved, to remove the seeds and juice. The advantage of the first method is that the tomato will better retain its shape and will allow for easier dicing and chopping.

French Onion Soup

Recipe courtesy of *The 30-Minute Vegan's Taste of Europe*

The humble onion forms the base of this delectable soup. I say "humble," though *ancient* is also an apt description. Cultivated since the Bronze Age, onions have been a favorite food of humans for over seven thousand years. The key to success in this dish is to cook the onions long enough for them to caramelize a bit, when the natural sweetness is released. If you have the classic ovenproof bowls, now is certainly the time to use them, as they contribute greatly to the experience.

SERVES 6 TO 8

FRENCH ONION SOUP

2 tablespoons olive oil or vegan butter

2 large yellow onions, sliced thinly (4 cups)

1 teaspoon sea salt, or to taste

½ teaspoon ground black pepper

¾ cup red wine (French Côtes de Rhône, Granache, or Syrah varietal recommended), or 1 cup sherry

1 tablespoon balsamic vinegar

6 cups vegetable stock (see Chef's Tips and Tricks)

3 sprigs thyme

2 bay leaves

5 sprigs flat-leaf parsley

1 cup grated vegan mozzarella-style cheese, or ½ cup nutritional yeast, to taste

FRENCH ONION SOUP CROUTONS

½ baguette

2 tablespoons olive oil

¼ teaspoon sea salt

¼ teaspoon ground black pepper

1. Prepare the onion soup: Place the olive oil in a large pot over medium-high heat. Add the onions, salt, and pepper and cook for 5 minutes, stirring constantly. Add the wine and vinegar and cook for 10 minutes, stirring frequently and adding small amounts of vegetable stock, if necessary, to prevent sticking.

2. Lower the heat to medium, add the vegetable stock and herbs to the pot, and cook for 15 minutes, stirring occasionally.

3. Meanwhile, prepare the croutons: Set the oven to BROIL. Slice the baguette into ½-inch slices and place on a well-oiled baking sheet. Baste with olive oil and sprinkle with salt and pepper. Broil for 5 minutes, or until the bread is crispy.

4. To serve, remove the bay leaves and thyme, pour the soup into oven-safe bowls, add a baguette slice, and sprinkle the top with vegan cheese. Broil until the cheese melts, about 3 minutes. If you do not have oven-safe bowls, simply top with the cheese or nutritional yeast before serving.

continues

continued

Variations

- Add three pressed or minced garlic cloves to the soup and/or on top of the bread before broiling.
- Add 1 tablespoon of Italian spice mix (page 223) to the bread.
- Add 1 sliced portobello mushroom along with onions.
- Add 1 tablespoon of smoked paprika along with the onions.
- For gluten-free croutons, use gluten-free bread.

Chef's Tips and Tricks

The vegetable stock is quite important in this dish. If you have more time, make your own stock (see page 25). If you are using a store-bought brand, I recommend using organic vegetable (vegan) bouillon cubes (one for every 2 cups of water).

Broiled Zucchini Soup with Saffron

Saffron, the stigma of the crocus flower that is hand harvested, is one of the world's most costly spices. Well worth the price, a little goes a long way: it imparts a unique flavor and a distinctive yellow color to dishes and is common in European, Indian, and Middle Eastern cuisine. Broiling veggies is a quick way to greatly bring out the flavors. Top with Vegan Crème Fraîche (page 195) and toasted slivered almonds (see page 213).

SERVES 6 TO 8

1 cup chopped red onion (½-inch pieces)

4 large garlic cloves, pressed or minced

4 cups chopped zucchini (½-inch pieces)

1½ cups fresh or frozen corn

¾ cup seeded and diced red bell pepper

1 tablespoon oil (try coconut or olive)

2 teaspoons paprika

2 teaspoons sea salt, or to taste

½ teaspoon ground black pepper

5 cups vegetable stock (see page 25) or water

3 large shiitake mushrooms, diced (1 cup)

½ teaspoon saffron strands

2 tablespoons freshly squeezed lemon juice

1 tablespoon minced fresh dill

1 tablespoon wheat-free tamari or other soy sauce

½ teaspoon smoked paprika (optional)

Pinch of crushed red pepper flakes

1. Preheat the oven to HIGH BROIL. Place the onion, garlic, zucchini, corn, and bell pepper in a bowl and mix well. Add the oil, paprika, 1 teaspoon of the salt, and the black pepper and stir well.

2. Transfer to a well-oiled baking sheet or casserole dish. Broil for 15 minutes, stirring a few times to ensure even cooking. Be careful when you open the oven; it gets pretty hot in there!

3. Meanwhile, place the vegetable stock, mushrooms, and saffron threads in a 3-quart pot over medium heat.

4. When the vegetables are done broiling, add them to the pot along with the remaining ingredients, including additional salt to taste, and stir well before serving.

Variations

- Add one 15-ounce can of chickpeas, rinsed and drained well, along with the mushrooms.
- You can sauté the mushrooms in 1 tablespoon of oil for 2 minutes, stirring frequently, before adding the vegetable stock.
- Add 1 cup of diced vegetables, such as carrot, cabbage, or potato, along with the vegetable stock.

Thai Coconut Soup with Lemongrass

Lemongrass and Kaffir lime are the quintessential ingredients to create the flavors of Thai cuisine that we know and love. This dish would especially benefit from additional cooking time, to allow these ingredients to do their magic and infuse fully into the soup. If you do wish to fit this recipe into the thirty-minute time frame, add each vegetable once you are done chopping it; do not wait until all the vegetables are chopped before adding them to the pot. Compare this soup to its raw counterpart, Raw Thai Coconut Soup (page 181). Garnish with Red Pepper Coulis (page 197).

SERVES 6 TO 8

4 cups vegetable stock (see page 25) or water

2 (15-ounce) cans coconut milk

3 (6-inch) lemongrass stalks (see Chef's Tips and Tricks)

1 tablespoon peeled and minced fresh ginger, or 1 (1-inch) piece of galangal root, sliced (see page 10)

2 garlic cloves, pressed or minced

2 teaspoons seeded and diced hot chile pepper (see the Scoville scale on page 57)

5 large Kaffir lime leaves, or 3 tablespoons freshly squeezed lime juice

3 large shiitake mushrooms, sliced thinly (1 cup)

1 cup thinly sliced carrot

1 cup small broccoli florets

¾ teaspoon sea salt, or to taste

2 tablespoons wheat-free tamari or other soy sauce

¾ cup snow peas, sliced in half lengthwise

2 tablespoons finely chopped fresh cilantro

1 tablespoon freshly squeezed lime juice (omit if using lime juice instead of the Kaffir lime leaves)

¼ cup diced green onion

1 tablespoon chiffonaded Thai basil (optional)

1. Place the vegetable stock and coconut milk in a 3-quart pot over medium-high heat. Crush the lemongrass (see Chef's Tips and Tricks) and place in the pot along with the ginger, garlic, chile pepper, Kaffir lime leaves, shiitake mushrooms, and carrot, and stir well.

2. Cook for 10 minutes, stirring occasionally. Add the broccoli florets and cook for 10 minutes, stirring occasionally. If you have more time, and for best results, allow to cook for an additional 10 minutes, to allow more of the lemongrass and Kaffir lime leaves to permeate the dish.

3. Add the remaining ingredients and stir well. Remove the lemongrass, Kaffir lime leaves, and galangal, if using, before serving.

continues

Thai Coconut with Lemongrass *continued*

Variations

- Replace the broccoli, carrot, and snow peas with vegetables of your choosing. Try with cauliflower, kale, tomatoes, and cabbage.
- Add 1 cup of cubed extra-firm tofu along with the carrot.
- If you wish, you can blend the Kaffir lime leaves, lemongrass (be sure to chop into 1-inch pieces first), ginger, and about 1½ cups of coconut milk until very creamy and then add to the pot with the vegetable stock.

Chef's Tips and Tricks

Working with Lemongrass

Cut both the very bottom and the top portion off the lemongrass stalk, leaving a stalk about 4 inches long. Peel off and discard the very outer leaf if it is brown or faded. Place on a clean, dry cutting board. Using a heavy measuring cup, clean jar, or the side of a large chef's knife, carefully crush and place in the soup. Be sure to remove before serving.

Ragout of Spring/Summer Vegetables

Ragouts are stews that are commonly served as a main dish. This version makes use of the bounty of veggies available in the spring and summertime. Serve with rice or quinoa and top with a dollop of Pesto Magnifico (page 206).

SERVES 6 TO 8

1 tablespoon oil (try coconut)

1 cup thinly sliced leek, rinsed and drained well

½ cup diced shallot

½ cup thinly sliced fennel bulb

½ cup white wine (sauvignon blanc recommended)

1½ cups vegetable stock (see page 25) or water

2 cups sliced fingerling potato (½-inch slices)

1 cup thinly sliced carrot

2½ teaspoons sea salt, or to taste

2½ cups soy, rice, or almond milk (see page 222)

1½ cups chopped asparagus (½-inch pieces)

1 cup fresh or frozen green peas

1½ cups halved cherry tomatoes

1 tablespoon freshly squeezed lemon juice

2 tablespoons nutritional yeast, or ¾ cup grated vegan Cheddar- or mozzarella-style cheese (optional)

2 tablespoons finely chopped tarragon, or 3 tablespoons finely chopped fresh flat-leaf parsley

Black sesame seeds, for garnish

Fresh fennel leaves, for garnish

1. Place the oil in a 3-quart pot over medium-high heat. Add the leek, shallot, and fennel and cook for 3 minutes, stirring frequently and adding small amounts of water, if necessary, to prevent sticking. Add the wine and cook for 1 minute, stirring frequently.

2. Add the vegetable stock, potato, carrot, and salt and cook for 10 minutes, stirring occasionally. Add the soy milk, asparagus, and peas and cook for 5 minutes, stirring occasionally.

3. Add all the remaining ingredients, except the tarragon and cook for 5 minutes, stirring occasionally. Add the tarragon and stir well. Garnish with black sesame seeds and fennel leaves before serving.

Variations

- For a ragout extraordinaire, add ½ teaspoon of saffron threads along with the vegetable stock.
- For an oil-free version, use the water sauté method discussed on page 217.
- Add 1 cup of tightly packed arugula just before serving.
- Add 2 tablespoons of vegan butter along with the lemon juice.
- Add three pressed or minced garlic cloves along with the shallot.
- Replace the shallot with 1 cup of diced yellow onion.
- Add ¼ teaspoon of truffle oil along with the lemon juice.
- Add 2 tablespoons of chiffonaded fresh basil along with the tarragon.

Fried Green Tomato Soup au Gratin

A popular dish in the Southern United States, fried green tomatoes involve breading and deep-frying. This healthier soup version is just as satisfying, especially with the grated vegan cheese. Enjoy with a dollop of Vegan Crème Fraîche (page 195) and top with Tempeh Bacon (page 208).

SERVES 6 TO 8

1½ tablespoons oil (try coconut)

1½ cups diced yellow onion

5 garlic cloves, pressed or minced

2 teaspoons seeded and diced jalapeño pepper

4 cups seeded and chopped green tomato (½-inch pieces)

4 cups vegetable stock (see page 25) or water

2 tablespoons freshly squeezed lime juice

2½ teaspoons chili powder

1½ teaspoons ground cumin

¼ teaspoon chipotle chile powder (optional)

2 teaspoons sea salt, or to taste

¼ teaspoon ground black pepper

2½ tablespoons finely chopped fresh cilantro

Grated vegan cheese or nutritional yeast

1. Place a 3-quart pot over high heat. Pour in the oil. Add the onion, garlic, and jalapeño pepper and cook for 5 minutes, stirring frequently and adding small amounts of water or stock, if necessary, to prevent sticking. Add the tomato and cook for 7 minutes, stirring frequently.
2. Lower the heat to medium-high and add all the remaining ingredients, except the cilantro and vegan cheese. Cook for 10 minutes, stirring frequently.
3. Add the cilantro and mix well. Top each serving liberally with vegan cheese or with 1 to 2 tablespoons of nutritional yeast.

Variations
- Add 1 cup of corn along with the vegetable stock.
- You can blend all or part of the soup just before serving.
- If green tomatoes are not available, you can use slightly underripe red tomatoes.

Szechuan Hot and Sour Vegetable Soup

Szechuan is a province in China and its cuisine is notoriously hot. Very hot. Chiles, along with garlic, are common ingredients. If you wish to create a sweet-and-sour version of this soup, add 1 cup of apricot preserves and sweeten to taste. Serve with a drizzle of Red Oil (page 187) and Basil Oil (page 188).

SERVES 6 TO 8

6 cups vegetable stock (see page 25) or water

¼ cup plus 2 tablespoons rice vinegar

3 tablespoons wheat-free tamari or other soy sauce, or to taste

1 cup thinly sliced yellow onion

½ cup thinly sliced celery

5 garlic cloves, pressed or minced

1 tablespoon seeded and diced hot chile pepper (see the Scoville scale on page 57)

2 cups small broccoli florets

¾ cup thinly sliced carrot (diagonally cut)

½ cup seeded and chopped red bell pepper

½ cup bamboo shoots or sliced water chestnuts

½ teaspoon sea salt, or to taste

½ to ¾ teaspoon Chinese five-spice powder (optional; see page 7)

¼ teaspoon crushed red pepper flakes, or to taste

¼ teaspoon ground Szechuan pepper (optional; see page 7)

½ cup snow peas, cut in half widthwise

¼ cup thinly sliced green onion

1. Place the vegetable stock in a 3-quart pot over medium-high heat. Add all the remaining ingredients, except the snow peas and green onion, and cook for 15 minutes, stirring occasionally.
2. Add the snow peas and cook for 5 minutes, stirring occasionally.
3. Add the green onion and stir well before serving.

Variations

- For a thicker broth, you can dissolve ¼ cup of arrowroot in ¼ cup of cold water. Add to soup once all the vegetables are cooked. Cook for 5 minutes, stirring frequently.
- Add 1 tablespoon of sesame oil along with the green onion.
- Add 1 tablespoon peeled and minced fresh ginger along with the garlic.
- You can sauté the onion and garlic in 1 tablespoon of sesame oil for 3 minutes before adding the remaining ingredients.
- Add ½ cup of diced extra-firm tofu along with the carrot.

Four Mushroom and Baby Spinach Soup

Why four mushrooms and not two or three? They all looked so amazing at the market, I couldn't decide which ones to go for. Actually, having the assortment makes for a richer, more complex flavor. For variety, replace the spinach with kale, chard, or collards. Top with Vegan Crème Fraîche (page 195) and Candied Pepitas (page 192).

SERVES 6 TO 8

6 cups vegetable stock (see page 25) or water

1 bay leaf (optional)

1 cup thinly sliced yellow onion (sliced into half-moons)

½ cup thinly sliced celery

4 garlic cloves, pressed or minced

1 cup diced carrot

2 cups chopped cremini mushrooms

2 cups chopped portobello mushroom (½-inch pieces)

½ cup chopped oyster mushrooms

½ cup thinly sliced shiitake mushrooms

1½ cups chopped tomato (½-inch pieces), or 1 (14.5-ounce) can diced fire-roasted tomatoes

2 teaspoons sea salt, or to taste

½ teaspoon ground black pepper

¼ teaspoon ground nutmeg

Pinch of crushed red pepper flakes

3 cups chopped baby spinach, rinsed and drained well

1 tablespoon freshly squeezed lemon juice

3 tablespoons chiffonaded fresh basil

1. Place a 3-quart pot over medium-high heat.
2. Place all the ingredients, except the spinach, lemon juice, and basil, in the pot and cook for 20 minutes, stirring occasionally.
3. Add the remaining ingredients and cook for 5 minutes, stirring occasionally. Remove the bay leaf, if using, before serving.

Variations

- You can sauté the onion, celery, and garlic in 1 tablespoon of oil for 3 minutes over high heat, stirring frequently, before adding the vegetable stock.
- Experiment with different varieties of dried or fresh mushrooms, such as chanterelle, wood ear, button, or morel.
- Add 2 tablespoons of finely chopped fresh flat-leaf parsley, 1 teaspoon of dried oregano, 1 teaspoon of dried marjoram, ½ teaspoon of minced fresh rosemary, and ½ teaspoon of fresh thyme along with the basil.
- Replace the basil with fresh cilantro and add 1 tablespoon of chili powder and 1 teaspoon of toasted ground cumin (see page 213).
- Replace the basil with fresh cilantro and add 1 tablespoon of curry powder and 1 teaspoon each of cumin seeds and brown mustard seeds.
- Replace 1½ cups of the vegetable stock with coconut milk or soy or rice milk.

Roasted Brussels Sprouts
and Red Cabbage Soup

Brussels sprouts are up there on top of the list for healthy green veggies to include in your lifestyle. Roasting them brings out the best flavor possible. Because they range in size, be sure to cut into pieces small enough to fit on your spoon. The addition of red cabbage is a popular combo in German cuisine. Top with Caramelized Onion (page 205) and Tempeh Bacon (page 208).

SERVES 6 TO 8

3½ cups quartered or halved Brussels sprouts, outer leaves removed if brown

1½ tablespoons olive or coconut oil

2 tablespoons freshly squeezed lemon juice

2½ teaspoons sea salt, or to taste

½ teaspoon ground black pepper

5 cups vegetable stock (see page 25) or water

1¼ cups diced yellow onion

½ cup thinly sliced celery

5 garlic cloves, pressed or minced

1 teaspoon caraway seeds (optional)

1 cup diced potato

¾ cup diced carrot

½ cup diced shiitake mushrooms

Pinch of cayenne pepper

1½ cups shredded red cabbage (½-inch pieces)

1 tablespoon minced fresh dill

2 teaspoons wheat-free tamari or other soy sauce (optional)

2 teaspoons raw apple cider vinegar

1. Preheat the oven to 450°F. Place the Brussels sprouts, oil, lemon juice, a liberal pinch of salt and black pepper, and 1 tablespoon or so of water on a baking sheet and toss well. Roast for 15 minutes, being careful not to burn.

2. Meanwhile, place the vegetable stock in a 3-quart pot over medium-high heat. Add all the remaining ingredients, including the additional salt, and except the red cabbage, dill, tamari, and vinegar, and cook for 15 minutes, stirring occasionally.

3. Add the cabbage and Brussels sprouts and cook for 8 minutes, stirring occasionally. Add the dill, tamari, if using, and vinegar, and stir well before serving.

Variations

- You can sauté the onion and garlic in 1 tablespoon of oil for 3 minutes over high heat, stirring frequently, before adding the vegetable stock.
- Replace 1 cup of the vegetable stock with a vegan stout beer (see page 17).
- Replace the Brussels sprouts with an equal amount of chopped veggies, such as parsnip, carrot, and Jerusalem artichoke.

New Orleans Corn and Bell Pepper Soup (Maque Choux)

Where Cajun meets Native American, you can take a virtual trip to the Big Easy, with this veggie soup version of a traditional southern Louisiana dish. Serve over rice, grits, or quinoa, and top with Vegan Crème Fraîche (page 195) or Chipotle Mayonnaise (see page 195).

SERVES 6 TO 8

2 cups vegetable stock (see page 25) or water

¼ cup white wine (optional)

3 bay leaves

1 cup diced yellow onion

5 garlic cloves, pressed or minced

2 teaspoons seeded and diced jalapeño pepper

1 tablespoon plus 2 teaspoons paprika

2 teaspoons dried oregano

1 teaspoon dried thyme

⅛ teaspoon cayenne pepper, or to taste

½ teaspoon smoked paprika (optional)

3 cups chopped tomato (½-inch pieces), or 2 (14.5-ounce) cans diced fire-roasted tomatoes

2 cups seeded and diced bell pepper (try green, red, or a combination)

1½ tablespoons wheat-free tamari or other soy sauce (optional)

3 cups fresh or frozen corn

2 cups soy milk

3 tablespoons finely chopped fresh flat-leaf parsley

1. Place the vegetable stock in a 3-quart pot over medium-high heat. Add all the remaining ingredients, except the corn, soy milk, and parsley, and cook for 10 minutes, stirring occasionally.
2. Add the corn and cook for 8 minutes, stirring occasionally.
3. Add the soy milk and parsley, remove the bay leaves, and stir well before serving.

Variations

- You can sauté the onion, garlic, and chile pepper in 1 tablespoon of oil for 3 minutes over high heat, stirring frequently, before adding the vegetable stock.
- Replace the corn with diced zucchini and yellow squash (try gold bar).
- Add 1 cup of chopped arugula along with the corn.
- Add 1 cup of cubed and roasted tofu or tempeh (see page 215).
- Replace the parsley with fresh cilantro or 1½ tablespoons of fresh dill.

Peasant Vegetable and Toasted Spice Soup

With a potentially politically incorrect name, Peasant Soup is made with whatever vegetables are available, typically left in larger pieces. Toasting the spices brings their flavor up to the next level. Serve with Vegan Crème Fraîche (page 195) and Red Pepper Coulis (page 197).

SERVES 6 TO 8

2 teaspoons brown mustard seeds

2 teaspoons fennel seeds

2 teaspoons cumin seeds

4½ cups vegetable stock (see page 25) or water

2 bay leaves

1 cup chopped yellow onion (½-inch pieces)

½ cup sliced celery

6 garlic cloves

1 cup sliced carrot (½-inch slices)

1 cup chopped potato (½-inch pieces)

1 cup sliced parsnip (½-inch slices)

1¼ cups chopped tomato, or 1 (14.5-ounce) can diced fire-roasted tomatoes

¼ cup sliced fennel

1 cup chopped zucchini (½-inch pieces)

1 cup chopped green cabbage (½-inch pieces)

2 teaspoons sea salt

¼ teaspoon ground black pepper

Pinch of crushed red pepper flakes

1 tablespoon freshly squeezed lemon juice

1 tablespoon balsamic vinegar

2 tablespoons wheat-free tamari or other soy sauce (optional)

1 teaspoon smoked paprika (optional)

1 tablespoon nutritional yeast (optional)

3 tablespoons finely chopped fresh flat-leaf parsley

1. Place a 3-quart pot over high heat. Place the mustard seeds, fennel seeds, and cumin seeds in the pot and cook for 2 minutes, stirring constantly.
2. Lower the heat to medium-high, add the vegetable stock, bay leaves, onion, celery, garlic, carrot, potato, parsnip, tomato, and fennel, and cook for 15 minutes, stirring occasionally.
3. Add the zucchini and the remaining ingredients, except the parsley, and cook for 5 minutes, stirring occasionally.
4. Add the parsley, stir well, and remove the bay leaves before serving.

Variations

- You can sauté the onion, celery, and garlic in 1 tablespoon of oil for 3 minutes, stirring frequently, before adding the vegetable stock.
- Add 2 cups of chopped spinach, kale, or chard.
- Experiment with different vegetables, such as turnip, rutabaga, or yellow summer squash, especially the gold bar variety.
- For an Indian twist, add 1 tablespoon of curry powder and 1 teaspoon of ground cumin, and replace the parsley with fresh cilantro.

51

Indian Chutney Stew with Tamarind

Gracing the tables of Indian restaurants from Bombay to Brooklyn, chutneys are condiments with a variety of Indian spices and ingredients, oftentimes sweet, salty, and spicy at the same time. Tamarind, the tangy and slightly sweet pulp from the pod of a large tropical tree, adds a distinctive flavor to this dish. Because commercially available tamarind varies in flavor and intensity, start with a smaller quantity and add more if necessary. Top with Herbed Croutons (page 200) or serve with Herbed Bread Sticks (page 209).

SERVES 6 TO 8

5 cups vegetable stock (see page 25) or water

1½ cups chopped tomato (½-inch pieces), or 1 (14.5-ounce) can diced fire-roasted tomatoes

1 tablespoon tomato paste

1 to 3 teaspoons tamarind paste (see page 10)

1 tablespoon curry powder

1 teaspoon garam masala (see page 104)

½ teaspoon ground coriander (optional)

½ teaspoon ground cumin (optionally toasted; see page 213)

1 cup diced yellow onion

3 garlic cloves, pressed or minced

1 tablespoon peeled and minced fresh ginger

1 teaspoon seeded and diced hot chile pepper (see the Scoville scale on page 57)

¾ cup diced shiitake mushroom

1½ cups chopped zucchini (½-inch pieces)

1½ cups chopped yellow summer squash (½-inch pieces) (try the gold bar variety)

1 cup sliced carrot

¼ cup raisins or dried currants

2 teaspoons sea salt, or to taste

¼ teaspoon ground black pepper

1½ tablespoons pure maple syrup or sweetener of choice (optional)

1½ tablespoons, wheat-free tamari or other soy sauce (optional)

2 to 3 tablespoons finely chopped fresh cilantro

1. Place the vegetable stock in a 3-quart pot over medium-high heat.
2. Add all the remaining ingredients, except the cilantro, and cook for 20 minutes, stirring occasionally.
3. Add the cilantro and stir well before serving.

continues

continued

Variations

- Replace the shiitakes with other mushrooms, such as cremini, portobello, or button.
- Replace the yellow summer squash with potato, broccoli, or additional zucchini.
- Add 1½ cups of cubed and roasted tofu (see page 215).
- Add one 15-ounce can of chickpeas, rinsed and drained well, or 1½ cups of cooked.
- You can sauté the onion, garlic, and ginger in 1 tablespoon of oil for 3 minutes over high heat, stirring frequently, before adding the vegetable stock.

Portuguese Kale and
Potato Soup (Caldo Verde)

Get ready to experience comfort food, Portuguese style. Although *caldo verde* commonly contains sausage or other animal products, this version uses liquid smoke to create additional flavor. If you wish for a heartier stew, try the variation that follows, which adds high-quality vegan sausage. Top with Vegan Crème Fraîche (page 195) and Red Pepper Coulis (page 197).

SERVES 6 TO 8

6 cups vegetable stock (see page 25) or water

1¼ cups diced yellow onion

½ cup thinly sliced celery

6 large garlic cloves, pressed or minced

1½ cups chopped potato (½-inch pieces)

¾ cup sliced carrot

½ cup thinly sliced shiitake mushrooms

½ cup seeded and chopped green bell pepper

2 tablespoons nutritional yeast (optional)

1½ tablespoons paprika

2 teaspoons sea salt, or to taste

¼ teaspoon ground black pepper

¼ to ½ teaspoon liquid smoke, or 1 teaspoon smoked paprika

Pinch of cayenne pepper

2 tablespoons freshly squeezed lemon juice

3 cups tightly packed shredded kale

1. Place the vegetable stock in a 3-quart pot over medium-high heat. Add all the remaining ingredients, except the lemon juice and kale, and cook for 15 minutes, stirring occasionally.
2. Add the lemon juice and kale and cook for 8 minutes, stirring occasionally.

Variations

- Add 7 ounces of vegan sausage (1½ cups sliced; see page 10), or 1½ cups of cubed and roasted tofu or tempeh (see page 215) along with the kale.
- Add 1 cup of fresh or frozen corn along with the kale.
- You can sauté the onion and garlic in 1 tablespoon of oil for 3 minutes over high heat, stirring frequently, before adding the vegetable stock.

Irish Cabbage and Potato Stew

Containing two of the most memorable ingredients in Irish cuisine, keep this recipe in mind to warm you on those cold Irish nights (something you can experience twelve months a year!). Be sure to add the vegetables to the pot as you chop them, to fit this recipe into the thirty-minute time frame. Top with a dollop of Vegan Crème Fraîche (page 195) and serve with Cosmic Corn Bread (page 211).

SERVES 6 TO 8

4½ cups vegetable stock (see page 28) or water

2 bay leaves

1¼ cups diced yellow onion

½ cup thinly sliced celery

4 garlic cloves, pressed or minced

1 cup sliced cremini or button mushrooms

¾ cup sliced carrot

¾ cup sliced parsnip or additional carrot

2½ cups chopped potatoes (½-inch pieces)

1½ cups vegan dark stout beer, (see page 17), or additional vegetable stock or water

2 cups shredded green cabbage (½-inch pieces)

½ cup shredded red cabbage or additional green cabbage (½-inch pieces)

¼ cup tomato paste

2 teaspoons sea salt, or to taste

½ teaspoon ground black pepper

1 tablespoon wheat-free tamari or other soy sauce (optional)

Pinch of cayenne pepper or crushed red pepper flakes

3 tablespoons finely chopped fresh flat-leaf parsley

1. Place the vegetable stock in a 3-quart pot over medium-high heat. Add the bay leaves, onion, celery, garlic, mushrooms, carrot, parsnip, and potato and cook for 15 minutes, stirring occasionally.

2. Add all the remaining ingredients, except the parsley, and cook for 10 minutes, stirring occasionally.

3. Add the parsley, remove the bay leaves, and stir well before serving.

Variations

- Sauté the onion and celery in 1 tablespoon of oil for 3 minutes over high heat, stirring frequently, before adding the vegetable stock.
- For the full Irish stew effect, add 1 cup of chopped vegan sausage, roasted tofu, tempeh cubes (see page 215), or chopped Tempeh Bacon (page 208) or beans, such as kidney or navy.
- Add 1½ cups of finely chopped kale along with the cabbage, and more vegetable stock, if necessary, to reach desired stew consistency.
- Add 2 tablespoons of nutritional yeast along with the salt.
- Add 1 tablespoon of dark miso paste along with the parsley (see page 34).
- Replace the parsley with 1½ tablespoons of minced fresh dill.

Jamaican Jerk Plantain Soup

A superspicy blend of hot chile peppers, such as Scotch bonnet, and herbs, including allspice and cinnamon, jerk seasonings are popular throughout the Caribbean. Here we are soupifying the blend by adding vegetable stock, as well as coconut milk and plantains, two favorite ingredients in the tropics. Feel free to add more chile pepper if you want it hotter. Don't let the long ingredients list put you off—the flavors make it worth your while. Enjoy topped with Caramelized Onions (page 205) or Krispy Kale (page 203).

SERVES 6 TO 8

1½ tablespoons oil (try coconut)

1 cup thinly sliced yellow onion

4 garlic cloves, pressed or minced

2 teaspoons peeled and minced fresh ginger (optional)

½ to 1 teaspoon seeded and diced habanero or Scotch bonnet pepper (see Chef's Tips and Tricks)

1½ cups seeded and sliced green or red bell pepper

2 teaspoons dried thyme

1 teaspoon ground allspice

2 teaspoons sea salt, or to taste

½ teaspoon ground black pepper

½ teaspoon ground cinnamon

¼ teaspoon ground nutmeg

¼ teaspoon ground cloves

3 cups vegetable stock (see page 25) or water

2 (15-ounce) cans coconut milk

1 bay leaf (optional)

1 cup thinly sliced carrot

2 cups chopped plantains or underripe bananas (½-inch pieces) (see Chef's Tips and Tricks)

3 tablespoons freshly squeezed lime juice

1 tablespoon wheat-free tamari or other soy sauce (optional)

½ cup thinly sliced green onion

1. Place a 3-quart pot over high heat. Pour in the oil. Add the onion, garlic, ginger, if using, and habanero pepper, and cook for 3 minutes, stirring frequently and adding small amounts of water or stock, if necessary, to prevent sticking.
2. Lower the heat to medium-high, add all the remaining ingredients, except the plantains, lime juice, tamari, and green onion, and cook for 5 minutes, stirring frequently.
3. Add the plantains and cook for 10 minutes, stirring occasionally. Add the lime juice, tamari, if using, and green onion and stir well.
4. Remove the bay leaf, if using, before serving.

Variations
- For more of a vegetable-based soup, replace the plantains with assorted chopped vegetables, such as potatoes, sweet potatoes, broccoli, or asparagus.

continues

continued

- Replace the plantains with 1 cup of cubed and roasted tofu (page 215) plus 2 cups of chopped spinach or kale.
- Replace the carrot and bell pepper with other vegetables, such as peas, chopped tomato, or eggplant.

Chef's Tips and Tricks

How Hot Do You Like It? The Scoville Scale

There are many flavorful peppers to sample, ranging from mild to inferno. The heat of the peppers is determined by the amount of capsaicin they contain. They are rated using Scoville units, a method developed by Wilbur Scoville in 1912. The scale is from 0 being the mildest to 10 having the highest heat. Try them all and see how hot you can take it. To avoid burning your fingers while chopping, wear rubber gloves!

From cool to hot: Sweet bells/pimiento, cherry, ancho, jalapeño/chipotle/poblano, serrano, cayenne, habanero, Scotch bonnet, and Red Savina habanero.

Working with Plantains

Plantains are often referred to as "cooking bananas." They are common in the cuisines of the tropics, including Africa, South and Central America, and the Caribbean. They are much larger and starchier than the common banana and are not eaten raw. Unripe plantains are hard and green. As a plantain ripens, it is easier to peel. It will become softer and yellow. As it continues to ripen, black spots will appear. A fully ripe plantain is black. This recipe works best with slightly ripe plantains. To peel them, cut off the very bottom and top, then carefully make a slit along the side with a knife. Peel off the skin completely. You can then slice the fruit. The less ripe the plantain, the longer it takes to cook. You want them to be just tender, and not starchy.

Tropical Coconut Yam Soup

Nothing says the tropics quite like coconuts, and the coconut yam combination is an all-time favorite of the region. Experiment with different vegetables and herbs. If you wish for a thicker consistency, carefully blend 2 to 3 cups of the soup when done and return the mixture to the pot. Try topping with Crispy Sunchokes (page 202) or Krispy Kale (page 203).

SERVES 6 TO 8

3½ cups vegetable stock (see page 25) or water

2 (15-ounce) cans coconut milk

3 cups chopped garnet yam or other sweet potato (⅓-inch pieces)

1¼ cups diced yellow onion

1 tablespoon plus 1 teaspoon peeled and minced fresh ginger

1 teaspoon seeded and diced hot chile pepper (see the Scoville scale on page 57)

¾ cup seeded and diced red bell pepper

1½ cups chopped zucchini (½-inch pieces)

2 tablespoons wheat-free tamari or other soy sauce (optional)

2 tablespoons freshly squeezed lime juice

3 tablespoons finely chopped fresh cilantro

2 teaspoons sea salt, or to taste

¼ teaspoon ground black pepper

Pinch of crushed red pepper flakes (optional)

2 tablespoons chiffonaded fresh mint

1. Place the vegetable stock and coconut milk in a 3-quart pot over medium-high heat. Add the yams, onion, ginger, and chile pepper and cook for 12 minutes, stirring occasionally.
2. Add the bell pepper and zucchini and cook until the yams are just soft, about 5 minutes, stirring occasionally.
3. Add the remaining ingredients, and stir well before serving.

Variations

- You can sauté the onion, ginger, and hot pepper in 1 tablespoon of oil, stirring frequently, before adding the vegetable stock.
- If you are able to find purple Okinawan sweet potatoes for this recipe, you will be exceedingly happy.
- Replace some or all of the yam with assorted chopped vegetables, such as carrot, broccoli, zucchini, or your favorites.
- Replace the cilantro with minced fresh basil or flat-leaf parsley or 1 tablespoon of minced fresh dill.
- Add 1 tablespoon of curry powder, for more of an Indian flair.

continues

continued

- Add 1 tablespoon of chili powder and 1 teaspoon of ground cumin, to take it in a Mexican direction.
- Replace the coconut milk with soy, rice, or almond milk (see page 222).
- For a lighter soup, replace one can of coconut milk with an equivalent amount of vegetable stock or water.
- For a thicker soup, before adding the cilantro, carefully transfer 2 cups of liquid and vegetables from the pot to a blender. Blend well and return the mixture to the pot.

Chef's Tips and Tricks

The Great Yam-Sweet Potato Debate

Many garnet and jewel "yams" are actually a variety of sweet potato. Yams are a botanically different species and are common in Africa. They are starchier and drier than sweet potatoes. Unless you are at an international market, what you are purchasing as a "yam" is likely a variety of sweet potato that has softer and moister flesh when cooked as compared to what is sold as a sweet potato.

Ragout of Fall Vegetables

Celebrating the bounty of the fall harvest, this is a heartier version of the ragout when compared to the spring veggie version. Lots of variations are possible, depending upon which vegetables are abundant at the market. Top with Vegan Crème Fraîche (page 195) and Vegetable Chips (page 201).

SERVES 6 TO 8

1½ tablespoons oil (try coconut)

1 cup diced yellow onion

½ cup thinly sliced celery (optional)

5 garlic cloves, pressed or minced

4 cups vegetable stock (see page 25) or water

2 cups peeled, seeded, and chopped butternut squash (½-inch pieces)

1½ cups chopped potato (½-inch pieces)

1 cup chopped parsnip (½-inch pieces)

1 cup chopped turnip (½-inch pieces), or additional chopped parsnip

2 cups thinly sliced kale

1 cup thinly sliced cabbage

1 tablespoon balsamic vinegar

1 tablespoon wheat-free tamari or other soy sauce

2 teaspoons sea salt, or to taste

¼ teaspoon ground black pepper

Pinch of crushed red pepper flakes

1½ teaspoons red wine vinegar

3 tablespoons finely chopped fresh flat-leaf parsley

1. Place the oil in a 3-quart pot over medium-high heat. Add the onion, celery, and garlic and cook for 3 minutes, stirring frequently.
2. Add all the remaining ingredients, except the red wine vinegar and parsley, and cook for 18 minutes, stirring occasionally.
3. Add the red wine vinegar and parsley, and stir well before serving.

Variations

- For an oil-free version, use the water sauté method discussed on page 217.
- Replace the turnip with rutabaga.
- Replace the potato with sweet potato.
- Add more Italian herbs, such as 1 tablespoon of chiffonaded fresh sage, 1 teaspoon of minced fresh rosemary, and 1 teaspoon each of finely chopped fresh thyme and oregano.
- Create a **Mexican Ragout** by adding 1 tablespoon of chili powder, 2 teaspoons of ground cumin, and ¼ teaspoon of chipotle chile powder. Replace the parsley with fresh cilantro.

Ratatouille Stew with Grilled Broccoli Rabe

With origins in the French Mediterranean town of Nice, ratatouille is a hearty tomato-based stew that can be made with whatever vegetables are fresh and available. Don't fret if no grill is available; see the variations for alternative cooking methods for the broccoli rabe. Top with Vegan Crème Fraîche (page 195) and serve this as a main course along with rice or quinoa.

SERVES 6 TO 8

BROCCOLI RABE MARINADE

2 tablespoons freshly squeezed lemon juice

1½ tablespoons olive oil

Pinch of sea salt

Pinch of ground black pepper

1 bunch broccoli rabe (2 cups after grilling and chopping; see directions)

RATATOUILLE STEW

1 tablespoon oil

1 cup diced yellow onion

½ cup diced celery

4 large garlic cloves, pressed or minced

3 cups cubed eggplant (⅓-inch cubes)

¼ cup red wine (optional)

2 teaspoons sea salt, or to taste

4 cups vegetable stock (see page 25) or water

½ cup diced carrot

¼ cup thinly sliced fennel

1 (14.5-ounce) can diced fire-roasted tomatoes, or 2 cups chopped tomato (½-inch pieces)

¼ cup tomato paste

1 tablespoon balsamic vinegar

1 tablespoon capers

1 teaspoon dried oregano

½ teaspoon dried thyme

¼ teaspoon ground black pepper

Pinch of crushed red pepper flakes

2 tablespoons chiffonaded fresh basil

2 tablespoons finely chopped fresh flat-leaf parsley

continues

Ratatouille Stew with Grilled Broccoli Rabe *continued*

1. Prepare the broccoli rabe: Preheat a grill. Place the lemon juice, oil, salt, and pepper in a shallow dish and mix well. Add the broccoli rabe and toss well.
2. Prepare the stew: Place the oil in a 3-quart pot over medium heat. Add the onion, celery, garlic, and eggplant, red wine, if using, and 1 teaspoon of salt and cook for 3 minutes, stirring constantly. Lower the heat to medium-high, add all the remaining Ratatouille Stew ingredients, except the basil and parsley, and cook for 15 minutes, stirring occasionally. Lower the heat to medium or medium-low, if necessary, to prevent boiling over.
3. Meanwhile grill the broccoli rabe until just tender (about 5 minutes, depending upon the heat of your grill). Chop into 1-inch pieces and add to the soup.
4. Add the basil and parsley and mix well before serving.

Variations

- Add 1 tablespoon of Herbes de Provence (see page 36), along with the onion.
- Add 1 cup of chopped zucchini or yellow summer squash (try gold bar) along with the carrot.
- Replace half of the eggplant with zucchini.
- Replace the broccoli rabe with asparagus.
- Replace the broccoli rabe with broccoli. Steam for 5 minutes before grilling.
- If no grill is available, you can sauté the broccoli rabe in 1 tablespoon of oil until just tender. You can also toss the broccoli rabe in the marinade and either roast at 375°F for 10 minutes or broil on HIGH BROIL for 5 minutes.

Chef's Tips and Tricks

Herbes de Provence

Create your own blend of this classic French herb combination. Feel free to leave out an ingredient or two (or three) if necessary. You can even experiment with different quantities of the same ingredients based upon your personal preference. Combine all of the following in a bowl and mix well: 2 tablespoons dried thyme, 2 tablespoons dried summer savory, 2 tablespoons dried marjoram, 1 tablespoon dried rosemary, 1 tablespoon dried tarragon, 1 tablespoon dried oregano, 1 tablespoon dried basil, 1 tablespoon dried sage, 2 teaspoons crushed lavender flowers, 2 teaspoons fennel seed.

Roasted Root Vegetable Soup

Roasting root vegetables is a simple technique that has a big payoff in terms of enhancing their flavor. You can create a multitude of versions of this recipe by altering the vegetables according to what is available at your local market. Look to enjoy this soup in the cooler months of autumn and winter. Top with Vegan Crème Fraîche (page 195) or Tofu Feta (page 207).

SERVES 6 TO 8

2 cups diced tomatoes

1½ cups chopped yellow onion (½-inch pieces)

5 large garlic cloves, chopped

1 cup chopped carrot (½-inch pieces)

1 cup chopped parsnip (½-inch pieces)

1 cup chopped sweet potato (½-inch pieces)

½ cup chopped fennel

¾ cup seeded and diced red bell pepper (optional)

1 tablespoon olive oil

2 tablespoons balsamic vinegar

1 tablespoon sea salt, or to taste

½ teaspoon ground black pepper

5 cups vegetable stock (see page 25) or water

¾ cup diced celery

1½ tablespoons Italian Spice Mix (see page 223), or 1 teaspoon dried thyme plus 2 teaspoons each dried oregano and dried marjoram

1 tablespoon wheat-free tamari or other soy sauce (optional)

2 tablespoons chiffonaded fresh basil

1 tablespoon finely chopped fresh flat-leaf parsley

1. Preheat the oven to 450°F. Place the tomato, onion, garlic, carrot, parsnip, sweet potato, fennel, and bell pepper, if using, in a bowl and mix well. Add the oil, balsamic vinegar, 1 teaspoon of the salt, and the black pepper and stir well.
2. Transfer to a well-oiled baking sheet or casserole dish. Roast for 20 minutes, stirring a few times to ensure even cooking.
3. Meanwhile, place the vegetable stock, celery, and dried herbs in a 3-quart pot over medium heat.
4. When the vegetables are done roasting, add to the pot along with the remaining ingredients, including additional salt to taste, and stir well before serving.

Variations
- Replace any of the carrot, parsnip, or sweet potato with an equivalent amount of your favorite root vegetable, such as beet, Jerusalem artichoke, rutabaga, celeriac, kohlrabi, potato, or turnip.
- Be bold and add some chopped Brussels sprouts with your root veggies.
- Replace the basil with fresh cilantro.
- Add 1 teaspoon of fresh oregano, ½ teaspoon of fresh thyme, and ¼ teaspoon of minced fresh rosemary.

63

 Roasted Beet Borscht

From Moscow with love. This is the dish that has rocked the Catskill Mountain community in New York so much that the region is officially referred to as the Borscht Belt. There are countless versions, some blended, some not. Try it both ways to compare. For the full effect, serve with a large dollop of Vegan Crème Fraîche (page 195).

SERVES 6 TO 8

5 cups chopped beet (½-inch pieces), cleaned well

1½ tablespoons oil

¼ cup water

2½ teaspoons sea salt

¼ teaspoon ground black pepper

6 cups vegetable stock (see page 25) or water

2 bay leaves

1¼ cups diced yellow onion

½ cup thinly sliced celery

4 large garlic cloves, pressed or minced

½ teaspoon caraway seeds (optional)

1 cup diced potato

½ cup diced carrot

Pinch of cayenne pepper

2 teaspoons red wine vinegar

2 teaspoons balsamic vinegar

2 tablespoons nutritional yeast (optional)

1 cup shredded green cabbage (½-inch pieces)

1½ tablespoons minced fresh dill

1. Preheat the oven to 450°F. Place the beet, oil, water, and a pinch of salt and black pepper on a baking sheet and toss well. Bake in the oven for 20 minutes.

2. Meanwhile, place the vegetable stock in a 3-quart pot over medium-high heat. Add all the other ingredients, except the vinegars, the nutritional yeast, the cabbage, and the dill, and cook for 15 minutes, stirring occasionally.

3. Add the vinegars, the nutritional yeast, if using, the cabbage, dill, the beets, and the remaining salt and black pepper and cook for 5 minutes, stirring occasionally. Remove the bay leaves before serving.

Variations

- You can pass on roasting the beet and just add it to the soup along with the onion. No additional cooking time is required.
- Replace the dill with fresh cilantro.
- It would be a stretch to consider it a borscht, but you can replace the beet with root vegetables of your choosing, such as parsnip, carrot, and yam.
- You can blend all or half of the soup, for a creamier borscht.

African Peanut Soup

Inspired by a traditional West African soup made with yams, this version has a creamy coconut base and is made with sweet potatoes. Be sure to purchase organically grown peanuts and peanut butter. Add the vegetables as you chop them, to fit this dish into a thirty-minute time frame. Garnish with Red Pepper Coulis (page 197) and serve over quinoa or rice.

SERVES 6 TO 8

3 cups vegetable stock (see page 25) or water

2 (15-ounce) cans coconut milk

1 cup diced yellow onion

½ cup diced celery

4 large garlic cloves, pressed or minced

1 teaspoon seeded and diced hot chile pepper (see the Scoville scale on page 57)

4 cups chopped sweet potato (½-inch pieces)

1½ cups chopped tomato (½-inch pieces), or 1 (14.5-ounce) can diced fire-roasted tomatoes

2 teaspoons sea salt, or to taste

¼ teaspoon ground black pepper

Pinch of cayenne pepper

1 tablespoon wheat-free tamari or other soy sauce (optional)

1 tablespoon Berbere spice mix (see page 93; optional)

¾ cup creamy or crunchy peanut butter

2 tablespoons finely chopped fresh cilantro

½ cup roasted unsalted peanuts, for garnish

1. Place the vegetable stock in a 3-quart pot over medium-high heat. Add all the remaining ingredients, except the peanut butter, cilantro, and peanuts, and cook for 15 minutes, stirring occasionally.

2. Remove about 1 cup of the liquid and place it into a small bowl. Add the peanut butter and stir until creamy. Return the mixture to the pot, stir well, and cook for 5 minutes, stirring occasionally.

3. Add the cilantro, stir well, and garnish with peanuts before serving.

Variations

- You can sauté the onion, celery, and garlic in 1 tablespoon of oil before adding the vegetable stock.
- Replace the peanut butter with almond butter or other nut butter.
- For a lighter soup, replace one can of coconut milk with an equivalent amount of vegetable stock or water.
- Add 2 cups of chopped spinach, chard, or kale once the peanut butter is added.

PART THREE

SOUPS AND STEWS WITH GRAINS, LEGUMES, AND PASTA

In this section we begin to enhance our vegetable-based soups with the inclusion of legumes (including soybean-based foods, such as tofu or tempeh), grains, and pasta. These recipes tend to be heartier soups that may serve as a meal unto themselves, especially when served with a large salad as a side dish. You may find yourself gravitating toward these dishes in the colder months, though many of them will provide the perfect opportunity for you to enjoy the bounty of the spring and summer harvest.

Visit the bulk food section of your local natural food store and stock up on some of these essentials that are featured in *Soup's On!* The legumes we will introduce include black beans, pinto beans, lima beans, red beans, cannellini beans, red and green lentils, split peas, and black-eyed peas. Remember to allow your legumes to thoroughly cook before adding any salt. The salt can prevent them from becoming tender.

Pastas include orzo, Israeli couscous, soba noodles, and rice noodles. Grains include rice, barley, polenta, quinoa, and wild rice. We use grains processed into flours to create a roux, as in the Veggie Gumbo and Veggie Coq au Vin. Flours are also part of the Tibetan Noodle Soup (Thenthuk) and the Matzo Ball Soup.

Tofu is featured in the Coconut Curry Veggie Soup with Tofu, as well as the North African Tagine with Broiled Tofu. Tempeh graces the recipes in the Cha-Cha Chili with Tempeh and the popular BBQ Tempeh and Roasted Corn Stew.

In your culinary voyage, you will explore several cuisines from around the world, including India (Himalayan Dal with Curried Chickpeas), Greece (Greek Lentil Soup with Grilled Red Peppers), Peru (Andean Incan Stew with Quinoa), Vietnam (Vietnamese Pho Real Bowl), Brazil (Brazilian Black Bean Soup with Baked Plantain), and even Ethiopia (Ethiopian Stew). Happy travels!

Fire-Roasted Tomato and Rice Soup with Spinach

Fire-roasted tomatoes add a depth of smoky flavor to the classic Italian tomato, rice, and spinach soup that has its origins in Florence. Try grilling your own tomatoes (see page 216) for the most vibrant flavor. Drizzle with Basil Oil (page 188) and top with Herbed Croutons (page 200) or top with Tofu Feta (page 207) and serve with Crostini (page 198) and Tapenade (page 193).

SERVES 6 TO 8

1¼ cups diced yellow onion

¾ cup diced celery

4 large garlic cloves, pressed or minced

1 teaspoon dried oregano

½ teaspoon dried thyme

2 (14.5-ounce) cans diced fire-roasted tomatoes (3½ cups)

4 cups vegetable stock (see page 25) or water

½ cup uncooked white basmati rice

2 teaspoons sea salt, or to taste

¼ teaspoon ground black pepper

Pinch of crushed red pepper flakes

2 cups chopped spinach, lightly packed, rinsed, and drained well

1 teaspoon wheat-free tamari or other soy sauce (optional)

1 tablespoon nutritional yeast (optional)

2 tablespoons chiffonaded fresh basil

2 tablespoons finely chopped fresh flat-leaf parsley

1. Place the vegetable stock in a 3-quart pot over medium-high heat.
2. Add the onion, celery, garlic, oregano, thyme, tomatoes, vegetable stock, and rice and cook for 15 minutes, stirring occasionally.
3. Add the remaining ingredients and cook for 5 minutes, stirring occasionally.

Variations

- Add ½ cup of chopped fennel and/or 1 cup of sliced mushrooms along with the onion.
- Replace the spinach with other greens, such as kale, chard, or mustard greens.
- Replace the basmati rice with wild rice, brown rice, or quinoa. See chart on page 219 for cooking times.
- You can sauté the onion, celery, garlic, oregano, and thyme in 1½ tablespoons of oil for 3 minutes, stirring frequently, before adding the remaining ingredients.
- For a fuller-bodied soup, you can carefully blend 2 cups of the soup (or give it a few quick buzzes with an immersion blender) before adding the spinach. Return the mixture to the pot and mix well before adding the remaining ingredients.

Andean Incan Stew with Quinoa

While botanically a seed, quinoa, native to the Andes Mountains, is considered the mother grain of the ancient Inca, due to its high nutrient content. Its light and nutty flavor, combined with its quick cooking, make it a favorite for thirty-minute vegan meals. To bring out the full flavor of this soup, sauté the vegetables in oil according to the variations, and allow an additional ten minutes of cooking time to allow the stew to thicken. Serve with Vegan Crème Fraîche (page 195) or Guacamole (page 204), and top with toasted sunflower seeds (see page 213).

SERVES 6 TO 8

5 cups vegetable stock (see page 25) or water

1¼ cups diced yellow onion

4 large garlic cloves, pressed or minced

½ cup diced celery

1 cup chopped potato (½-inch pieces)

1 teaspoon seeded and diced hot chile pepper (see the Scoville scale on page 57), or crushed red pepper flakes, to taste

¾ cup diced carrot

½ cup uncooked quinoa (see Chef's Tips and Tricks)

1 cup chopped tomato (½-inch pieces)

2 teaspoons sea salt, or to taste

½ teaspoon ground black pepper

¾ cup fresh or frozen corn

1½ cups well-rinsed and finely chopped kale or spinach

2 tablespoons finely chopped fresh cilantro

3 tablespoons thinly shredded purple cabbage, for garnish (optional)

1. Place the vegetable stock in a 3-quart pot over medium-high heat.
2. Add all the remaining ingredients, except the corn, kale, cilantro, and purple cabbage and cook until the potato is just tender and the quinoa is cooked, about 15 minutes, stirring occasionally. Add the corn and kale and cook for 5 minutes, stirring occasionally.
3. Add the cilantro and mix well. Garnish with purple cabbage, if using, before serving. Viva Peru!

Variations

- Experiment with different varieties of potato and sweet potato, such as Peruvian purple, Yellow Finn, or garnet.
- Replace the carrot, corn, and tomato with vegetables of your choosing, such as chopped zucchini, broccoli, or romanesco.
- Add 1½ cups of thinly sliced vegan sausage along with the potatoes.
- You can sauté the onion, garlic, and celery in 1½ tablespoons of oil for 3 minutes, stirring frequently, before adding the remaining ingredients.

continues

continued

Chef's Tips and Tricks

Rinsing Quinoa

It is recommended to rinse quinoa well through a fine-mesh sieve or sprout bag to remove the saponins, a nontoxic but soapy substance that can cause bitterness. Drain very well before adding to recipes. Some brands do come prerinsed.

⏱ Wonton Soup

What soup book would be complete without a wonton soup recipe? These little dumplings are popular in several regional cuisines throughout China. Be sure to purchase a vegan brand of wonton wrapper, as several varieties contain egg. We will be cooking the wontons in a separate pot of water before adding them to the soup. Although this soup does take longer than thirty minutes to prepare, you can prepare the wontons in advance and add to the soup just before serving. Having a wonton-making helper will also speed things up!

SERVES 6 TO 8

WONTONS

1 tablespoon sesame oil

½ cup diced shallot

2 garlic cloves, pressed or minced

1 teaspoon seeded and diced hot chile pepper (see the Scoville scale on page 57), or a pinch of crushed red pepper flakes

½ cup diced shiitake mushrooms

1 cup minced cabbage

½ cup crumbled extra-firm tofu

2 teaspoons wheat-free tamari or other soy sauce

2 teaspoons rice vinegar

1½ teaspoons toasted sesame oil

¼ teaspoon sea salt, or to taste

⅛ teaspoon liquid smoke (optional)

16 vegan wonton skins

SOUP

7 cups vegetable stock (see page 25) or water

1½ tablespoons peeled and minced fresh ginger

3 tablespoons wheat-free tamari or other soy sauce, or to taste

1 teaspoon toasted sesame oil

2 cups thinly sliced spinach, rinsed and drained well

½ cup thinly sliced green onion

1. Prepare the wontons: Place the sesame oil in a small sauté pan over medium-high heat. Add the shallot, garlic, and chile pepper and cook for 1 minute, stirring constantly. Add the mushrooms, cabbage, and tofu and cook for 5 minutes, stirring frequently, and adding small amounts of water, if necessary, to prevent sticking. Add the remaining ingredients, except the wonton wrappers, and cook for 5 minutes, stirring frequently. Remove from the heat.

2. Bring a large pot of water to a boil over high heat. Lay out the wonton skins on a clean, dry surface. Place about 1 tablespoon of filling on

continues

continued

the center of each wrapper. Pull up the sides and seal tightly, creating a purse effect. Set aside until all the wontons are wrapped.

3. Prepare the soup: Place the vegetable stock in a 3-quart pot over medium heat. Add the ginger, tamari, and toasted sesame oil, and stir well.
4. Lower the heat of the large pot of water to a low simmer. (Boiling water will have a tendency to cause the wontons to break apart.) Carefully place the wontons in the pot and cook for 5 minutes. Depending upon the size of the pot, you may want to cook them in two batches. Using a slatted spoon, carefully transfer the cooked wontons to a large plate until all of the wontons are cooked.
5. Place the cooked wontons and spinach in the soup pot and cook for 1 minute. You can also place a few wontons directly into each serving bowl and top off with the soup. Garnish each serving with green onion.

Variations
- Replace the cabbage with bok choy, kale, or spinach
- Replace the tofu with an equal amount of diced seitan or tempeh.
- Add to the wonton filling 2 teaspoons of peeled and minced fresh ginger along with the garlic.

Vietnamese Pho Real Bowl

Pho (pronounced *fuh*) is a classic Vietnamese broth containing a plethora of veggies and rice noodles. This dish contains the star-shaped star anise, voted the coolest-looking spice on the planet. Although this dish can easily fit in the thirty-minute time frame, keep in mind that the longer the star anise and cinnamon sit, the more their flavor will infuse into the soup. Go all out and serve with a condiment platter that can include fresh basil leaves, mint leaves, cilantro leaves, mung bean sprouts, jalapeño slices, and fresh lime wedges.

SERVES 6 TO 8

6 cups vegetable stock (see page 25) or water

3 tablespoons wheat-free tamari or other soy sauce

3 whole star anise

1 cinnamon stick

½ cup thinly sliced shallot

1 tablespoon peeled and minced fresh ginger

2 teaspoons seeded and diced hot chile pepper (see the Scoville scale on page 57), or a pinch of crushed red pepper flakes

1 cup thinly sliced shiitake mushrooms

¾ cup thinly sliced carrot

1 teaspoon sea salt, or to taste

1 tablespoon mirin (see page 8; optional)

8 ounces beef- or chicken-style seitan, with marinade (see page 216)

3 ounces uncooked thin rice noodles

1 cup thinly sliced napa cabbage

1½ teaspoons freshly squeezed lime juice

¼ cup thinly sliced green onion

3 tablespoons coarsely chopped fresh cilantro

1. Place the vegetable stock in a 3-quart pot over medium-high heat. Add all the remaining ingredients, except the rice noodles, cabbage, lime juice, green onion, and cilantro. Cook for 15 minutes, stirring occasionally.

2. Add the rice noodles and cabbage and cook for 7 minutes, stirring occasionally. Add the lime juice, green onion, and cilantro and stir well. Remove the star anise and cinnamon stick before serving

Variations

- For a gluten-free version, replace the seitan with cubed and roasted tofu.
- Add 1 cup of small broccoli florets, sugar snap peas, or snow peas.
- Add 2 tablespoons of chiffonaded Thai basil instead of, or in addition to, the cilantro.
- Add 2 tablespoons of miso paste (see page 34) and stir until dissolved just before serving.

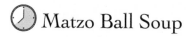 Matzo Ball Soup

There is no way I could do a soup cookbook that did not include a matzo ball soup recipe, without generations of Jewish guilt being cast upon me. The broth is indistinguishable from the one I grew up enjoying before my vegan days. The matzo balls are held together with ground quinoa and flaxseeds, which makes them denser than the traditional egg-infused ones.

SERVES 6 TO 8

MATZO BALLS

Makes 12 matzo balls

¼ cup ground flaxseeds or egg replacer (see Chef's Tips and Tricks)

1 cup seltzer water or water

1 cup matzo meal

¼ cup quinoa flakes or flour (see Chef's Tips and Tricks)

1½ teaspoons sea salt

¼ teaspoon ground black pepper

¼ teaspoon dried dill (optional)

SOUP

1 tablespoon coconut or other oil

1½ cups thinly sliced yellow onion

1 cup sliced celery (¼-inch slices)

4 garlic cloves, pressed or minced

7 cups vegetable stock (see page 25) or water

1¼ cups sliced carrot (½-inch slices)

1 cup sliced mushrooms (try cremini or button)

2 teaspoons sea salt, or to taste

½ teaspoon ground black pepper

1½ tablespoons minced fresh dill

1. Prepare the matzo balls: Place water in a large pot and bring to a boil over high heat. Meanwhile, place the ground flaxseeds in a bowl with ¾ cup plus 2 tablespoons of the seltzer water and stir well. Add the remaining matzo ball ingredients and mix well. Form into a loaf. Add a small amount of additional seltzer water, if necessary, to hold the loaf together. You are looking for a slightly moist consistency, just enough to have all the ingredients come together. Transfer to a clean, dry cutting board. Pinch off twelve equal portions to form balls about 1 inch in diameter.

2. Place the matzo balls in the boiling water. Lower the heat to medium-high. After a few minutes, the matzo balls will rise to the top. Cook for an additional 45 minutes.

3. Meanwhile, prepare the soup: Place the oil in a 3-quart pot over medium-high heat. Add the onion, celery, and garlic and cook for 5 minutes, stirring frequently and adding small amounts of water, if necessary, to prevent sticking.

4. Lower the heat to medium, add the vegetable stock, carrot, mushrooms, salt, and pepper, and cook for 20 minutes, stirring occasionally.

5. When the matzo balls are done cooking, transfer them to the pot of soup, add the dill, and cook for 5 minutes, stirring occasionally. Serve one or two matzo balls per serving of soup.

continues

Matzo Ball Soup *continued*

Chef's Tips and Tricks

Quinoa Flakes

Quinoa flakes come from the quinoa grain. They will create a lighter matzo ball. If you are unable to locate the flakes, you can make your own flour, using the whole quinoa grain. To make quinoa flour, place uncooked quinoa in a strong blender and blend until a powdery consistency is attained.

Flaxseeds or Egg Replacer

Ground flaxseeds may be used to replace the eggs in many recipes calling for eggs. You can purchase them already ground, or for optimal freshness, grind your own. Place the whole seeds in a coffee grinder or strong blender and process until powdery fine. Store in a glass container in the freezer for up to a week. Use 1 tablespoon of ground seeds and 3 tablespoons of water to replace one egg.

Ener-G Egg Replacer is a commercially available egg substitute that is made with potato and tapioca flours. Follow the package instructions for use.

Variations

- Add 2 tablespoons of finely chopped fresh flat-leaf parsley along with the dill in the soup.
- Add 2 teaspoons wheat-free tamari or other soy sauce and 2 tablespoons of nutritional yeast to the soup along with the dill.
- You can add more veggies to the soup if you would like a heartier soup. Add 1½ cups of chopped cabbage, kale, parsnip, or your faves.

French Bouillabaisse

Recipe courtesy of *The 30-Minute Vegan's Taste of Europe*

A traditional French stew that typically includes several varieties of seafood and traces its origins back to 600 BC, when ancient Greeks were chillaxing in the harbor town of Marseille in the Provence region of France. This innovative version uses the sea vegetable arame to create the flavor of the sea. If you have more time, you can prepare a bouquet garni (see Chef's Tips and Tricks).

SERVES 4 TO 6

14 ounces extra-firm tofu

¼ cup freshly squeezed lemon juice

1 cup white wine (French rosé, or California-style chardonnay recommended)

1 tablespoon oil (try coconut)

¾ cup diced shallots

¾ cup thinly sliced celery

¼ cup finely chopped or thinly sliced fennel

3 garlic cloves, pressed or minced

½ teaspoon seeded and diced hot chile pepper (see the Scoville scale on page 57)

1 cup diced shiitake mushrooms

3 cups vegetable stock (see page 25) or water

2 bay leaves

¼ cup arame (see page 9)

½ teaspoon saffron strands

2 teaspoons fresh thyme

2 tablespoons finely chopped fresh flat-leaf parsley

1 cup chopped tomato (½-inch pieces)

1¾ teaspoons sea salt, or to taste

¼ teaspoon ground black pepper

Finely chopped fresh flat-leaf parsley, for garnish

1. Slice the tofu into three cutlets and stack them on top of one another. Slice the cutlets three times widthwise and four times lengthwise. Place the cubes in a shallow dish with the lemon juice and ½ cup of the wine. Allow it to sit for 10 minutes, gently stirring occasionally to ensure even coating.

2. Meanwhile, place a large pot over medium-high heat. Pour in the oil. Add the shallots, celery, fennel, garlic, chile pepper, and shiitake mushrooms and cook for 3 minutes, stirring constantly. Lower the heat to medium, add the remaining ½ cup of wine and the vegetable stock, bay leaves, arame, and saffron, and stir well. Add the thyme and parsley and cook for 10 minutes, stirring occasionally.

3. Add the tofu and its marinade and cook for 10 minutes, gently stirring occasionally. Add the tomato, salt, and black pepper and stir well. Remove the bay leaves, garnish with parsley, and *bon appétit*!

Variations

- Roast the tofu for 15 minutes in a preheated 400°F oven before adding to the bouillabaisse (see page 215).

continues

French Bouillabaisse *continued*

- You can used dried shiitake instead of fresh. Soak three or four dried shiitake in 1 cup of boiling water until they are soft enough to chop, about 10 minutes. Use the soak water to replace some of the vegetable stock.
- If you have more time, allow the soup to cook for an additional 20 minutes on low heat, for added flavor.

Chef's Tips and Tricks

Bouquet Garni

Use sprigs of thyme instead of the loose leaves, and tie together the bay leaf, parsley, and thyme with a piece of culinary string. Remove before serving.

Un-Chicken Noodle Soup

Not quite what Grandma used to make, this soup uses Beyond Meat chicken-style strips, or chicken-style seitan, a wheat product that takes on the texture and flavor of the animal product it aims to replace. If you have more time, and for those special holidays, add matzo balls (see page 75).

SERVES 6 TO 8

5 cups vegetable stock (see page 25) or water

2 bay leaves

1¼ cups diced yellow onion

½ cup thinly sliced celery

4 garlic cloves, pressed or minced

¼ teaspoon minced fresh rosemary (optional)

1 cup thinly sliced carrot (sliced into half-moons)

1 cup thinly sliced parsnip

½ cup chopped mushrooms (try cremini)

8 ounces chopped Beyond Meat chicken-style strips, or chicken-style seitan and broth (see page 7)

2 tablespoons wheat-free tamari or other soy sauce, or to taste (optional)

1 teaspoon sea salt, or to taste

¼ teaspoon ground black pepper

Pinch of crushed red pepper flakes

2 to 3 ounces uncooked thin rice noodles

1 tablespoon minced fresh dill

1. Place the vegetable stock in a 3-quart pot over medium-high heat. Add the bay leaves, onion, celery, garlic, rosemary, if using, carrot, parsnip, and mushrooms and cook for 10 minutes, stirring occasionally.
2. Add all the remaining ingredients, except the dill, and cook for 8 minutes, stirring occasionally.
3. Add the dill, stir well, and remove the bay leaves before serving.

Variations

- You can sauté the onion, celery, and garlic in 1 tablespoon of oil for 3 minutes, stirring frequently, before adding the vegetable stock.
- For a gluten-free version, replace the seitan with marinated and roasted tofu (see page 215).
- Replace the dill with 2 tablespoons of finely chopped fresh flat-leaf parsley or basil.
- Add 1 cup of chopped cabbage and 1 cup of chopped spinach or kale.

Hot Pot with Soba Noodles, Seared Shiitake Mushrooms, and Baby Bok Choy

The fondue of the soup world, this dish is a variation of the traditional hot pot, popular throughout Asia, where diners serve themselves by dipping vegetables into a hot broth. Here you will be preparing the soup completely before serving. Get creative with the veggies and the types of pasta. For a festive presentation, serve in a large hot pot in the center of the table and allow guests to serve themselves in small bowls.

SERVES 6 TO 8

TOFU MARINADE

1 tablespoon wheat-free tamari or other soy sauce

1 tablespoon toasted sesame oil

1 tablespoon water

7 ounces extra-firm tofu, cut into ½ inch-cubes

BROTH

6 cups vegetable stock (see page 25) or water

1 teaspoon toasted sesame oil

2 tablespoons peeled and minced fresh ginger

3 garlic cloves, pressed or minced

¾ cup thinly sliced carrot (diagonally cut)

3 tablespoons arame (see page 9)

5 teaspoons wheat-free tamari or other soy sauce, or to taste

Pinch of crushed red pepper flakes

3 ounces uncooked soba noodles

¼ cup diced green onion

SEARED SHIITAKE AND BOK CHOY

2 tablespoons mirin (see page 8), sherry, or white wine

1 tablespoon toasted sesame oil

1 tablespoon wheat-free tamari or other soy sauce

4 large shiitake mushrooms

3 baby bok choy, sliced in half lengthwise

1. Prepare the tofu: Preheat the oven or toaster oven to 400°F. Place all the tofu marinade ingredients on a small baking sheet or in a casserole dish and mix well to coat the tofu. Bake for 20 minutes. Remove from the oven and set aside.

2. Meanwhile, prepare the broth: Place all the broth ingredients, except the soba noodles and green onion, in a 3-quart pot over medium-high heat and cook for 8 minutes, stirring occasionally. Add the soba noodles and cook for 8 minutes, stirring occasionally.

continues

continued

3. While the broth, then the soba noodles, are cooking, prepare the seared shiitake mushrooms and bok choy: Place a sauté pan over high heat. Combine the mirin, the toasted sesame oil, and the tamari in a small bowl and mix well. Dip the shiitakes in the liquid and place in the sauté pan. Cook until slightly browned, about 3 minutes on each side, pressing down firmly with a spatula and adding small amounts of water or vegetable stock, if necessary, to prevent sticking. Transfer to a cutting board, slice into thin strips, and add to the broth. Repeat with the bok choy, trimming off the very bottom and slicing into ½-inch pieces before adding to the broth.

4. Add the tofu and green onion to the broth and mix well before serving.

Variations

- You can cook the soba noodles in a separate pot according to the package instructions. Place directly in individual serving bowls and top off with the soup.
- Replace the soba with udon, somen, or rice noodles.
- Add 1 cup of chopped vegetables, such as broccoli, snow peas, or zucchini.
- Add ¾ cup of enoki mushrooms and cook for 5 minutes before serving
- You can also grill the shiitakes and bok choy instead of searing (see page 216).

Veggie Gumbo

Inspired by a recent trip to New Orleans, this is a vegan version of a Cajun classic, passed down from generation to generation in the Boudet clan. Traditional gumbo is a cross-cultural dish with elements of French, German, Spanish, and West African influence. Serve over rice or quinoa and top with Vegan Crème Fraîche (page 195) and Red Pepper Coulis (page 197).

SERVES 6 TO 8

6½ cups vegetable stock (see page 25) or water

2 bay leaves

1 cup diced yellow onion

½ cup diced celery

¾ cup diced shiitake mushrooms

2 tablespoons paprika

2 teaspoons dried oregano

1 teaspoon dried thyme

½ teaspoon smoked paprika or chipotle chile powder (optional)

⅛ teaspoon cayenne pepper

2½ teaspoons sea salt, or to taste

½ teaspoon ground black pepper

1 tablespoon wheat-free tamari or soy sauce (optional)

2 tablespoons arame (see page 9; optional)

1½ cups sliced okra (very bottom removed; ½-inch slices)

1¼ cups seeded and diced red bell pepper

2 cups finely chopped curly kale

1 tablespoon freshly squeezed lemon juice

3 tablespoons flour (try gluten-free)

1½ tablespoons olive oil

¼ cup thinly sliced green onion

3 tablespoons finely chopped fresh flat-leaf parsley

1. Place the vegetable stock in a 3-quart pot over medium-high heat. Add all the remaining ingredients, except the kale, lemon juice, flour, olive oil, green onion, and parsley, and cook for 15 minutes, stirring occasionally. Add the kale and lemon juice and cook for 5 minutes, stirring occasionally.

2. Meanwhile, create a roux by placing a small sauté pan over high heat. Place the flour in the pan and cook until the flour turns golden brown, about 3 minutes, stirring constantly. Be careful not to let it burn. Remove it from the heat. Allow it to cool for 5 minutes. Add the olive oil and stir well.

3. Add the roux to the soup and stir well. Cook until the soup thickens slightly, about 5 minutes, stirring occasionally.

4. Add the green onion and parsley and stir well. Remove the bay leaves before serving.

Variations

- Replace the kale with other greens, such as chard, collards, spinach, or a combination.
- Add ¼ teaspoon each of ground cloves and allspice along with the other spices.
- Replace the smoked paprika, if using, with ¼ teaspoon of liquid smoke.
- Add ½ cup of white wine along with the onion.

Israeli Couscous Soup with Sun-Dried Tomatoes

A toasted pearl-shaped pasta, Israeli couscous is larger than common North African couscous and tends to hold its form when added to soups. Purchase the spelt or whole wheat varieties, if possible. Top with a spoonful of Tapenade (page 193) or diced kalamata olives and serve with Pita Chips (page 199).

SERVES 6 TO 8

15 to 18 sun-dried tomatoes
  (½ cup diced)

1 tablespoon ground cumin

1 teaspoon ground coriander
  (optional)

6 cups vegetable stock (see page 25)
  or water

1 cup diced yellow onion

½ cup diced celery

6 garlic cloves, pressed or minced

¼ teaspoon crushed red pepper
  flakes

1 (15-ounce) can chickpeas, rinsed
  and drained well, or 1½ cups
  cooked (see page 220)

½ cup uncooked pearled couscous

2 tablespoons tomato paste

2 teaspoons wheat-free tamari or
  other soy sauce (optional)

1 tablespoon capers (optional)

2 teaspoons sea salt, or to taste

½ teaspoon ground black pepper

1 teaspoon balsamic vinegar
  (optional)

1½ cups thinly sliced baby spinach,
  rinsed and drained well

3 tablespoons finely chopped fresh
  flat-leaf parsley

1. Place the sun-dried tomatoes in a small bowl and cover with hot water. Soak until soft. Drain well, dice, and measure out ½ cup for this recipe.

2. Meanwhile, place the cumin and coriander, if using, in a 3-quart pot over medium-high heat. Cook for 1 minute, stirring constantly. Add the vegetable stock, onion, celery, garlic, crushed red pepper flakes, and chickpeas and cook for 10 minutes, stirring occasionally.

3. Add all the remaining ingredients, including the sun-dried tomatoes, and except the spinach and parsley, and cook for 8 minutes, stirring occasionally. Add the spinach and cook for 5 minutes, stirring occasionally.

3. Add the parsley, and stir well before serving.

Variations

- For a gluten-free version, replace the couscous with quinoa or white basmati rice. If using other types of rice, see page 219 for cooking times, and add additional vegetable stock, if necessary, to reach your desired consistency.

continues

Israeli Couscous Soup with Sun-dried Tomatoes *continued*

- Sauté the onion, celery, and garlic in 1 tablespoon of oil over high heat for 3 minutes, stirring constantly and adding small amounts of water or stock, if necessary, to prevent sticking, before adding the remaining ingredients.
- Replace the chickpeas with navy beans or great northern beans.
- Add 1 cup of diced mushrooms along with the onion.
- Add 2 tablespoons of chiffonaded fresh basil, 1 teaspoon of dried oregano, and ½ teaspoon of minced fresh rosemary along with the parsley.
- Replace the parsley with 1 ½ tablespoons of minced fresh dill.

Black-Eyed Peas and Collards Stew

A favorite in the Southern United States, the black-eyed peas–collard greens combo is traditionally eaten on New Year's Day to ensure an abundant year. Enjoy it year-round and feel the power! Top with Vegan Crème Fraîche (page 195) and chopped Tempeh Bacon (page 208).

SERVES 6 TO 8

5 cups vegetable stock (see page 25) or water

1½ cups diced yellow onion

¾ cup thinly sliced celery

4 large garlic cloves, pressed or minced

1 teaspoon seeded and diced hot chile pepper (see the Scoville scale on page 57; optional)

1 cup diced potato

1 cup thinly sliced carrot

1½ cups chopped tomato (½-inch pieces), or 1 (14.5-ounce) can diced fire-roasted tomatoes

1 (15-ounce) can black-eyed peas, rinsed and drained well, or 1½ cups cooked (see page 220)

½ teaspoon liquid smoke

2 cups stemmed and sliced collards

1 teaspoon sea salt, or to taste

¼ teaspoon ground black pepper

Pinch of cayenne pepper

2 tablespoons freshly squeezed lemon juice

1 tablespoon nutritional yeast (optional)

2 tablespoons finely chopped fresh flat-leaf parsley

2 tablespoons wheat-free tamari or other soy sauce, or to taste (optional)

1. Place the vegetable stock in a 3-quart pot over medium-high heat. Add the onion, celery, garlic, chile pepper, if using, potato, carrot, tomato, black-eyed peas, and liquid smoke and stir well. Cook for 5 minutes, stirring occasionally.
2. Slice the collards in half lengthwise and then into ½-inch-wide ribbons, add to the soup, and cook for 10 minutes, stirring occasionally.
3. Add the remaining ingredients, stir well, and cook for 5 minutes, stirring occasionally, before serving.

Variations

- Replace the black-eyed peas with other beans, such as black, pinto, or cannellini.
- Replace the collards with kale, spinach, chard, dandelion greens, mustard greens, or a combo. Add along with the parsley.
- Replace the carrot with parsnip or beet.
- Try sautéing the onion, celery, and garlic in 1 tablespoon of oil for 3 minutes, stirring frequently, before adding the remaining ingredients.

Caribbean Red Bean and Rice Soup

Coconut rice and beans was a staple meal for me while traveling through Central America. I'm pretty sure it's a national dish somewhere, or at least should be. This is a soup version of that iconic dish. For a thicker soup, cook for an additional ten or fifteen minutes. Numerous variations are possible by changing up . . . you guessed it . . . the beans and the rice. See below for some suggestions. Top with Red Pepper Coulis (page 197) or Krispy Kale (page 203).

SERVES 6 TO 8

4½ cups vegetable stock (see page 25) or water

1 (15-ounce) can coconut milk

½ cup uncooked white basmati rice

1½ cups diced yellow onion

½ cup diced celery

4 large garlic cloves, pressed or minced

1½ teaspoons finely chopped fresh thyme, or ½ teaspoon dried

1 cup diced carrot

1 (15-ounce) can red kidney beans, rinsed and drained well, or 1½ cups cooked (see page 221)

1 cup fresh or frozen corn

2 tablespoons finely chopped fresh flat-leaf parsley

2 teaspoons sea salt, or to taste

¼ teaspoon ground black pepper

¼ teaspoon crushed red pepper flakes

2 teaspoons wheat-free tamari or other soy sauce (optional)

¼ cup plus 2 tablespoons toasted coconut, for garnish (optional; see page 213)

6 fresh flat-leaf parsley leaves, for garnish (optional)

1. Place the vegetable stock and coconut milk in a 3-quart pot over medium-high heat. Add the rice and stir well.
2. Add the onion, celery, garlic, and thyme and cook for 10 minutes, stirring occasionally.
3. Add the carrot and beans and cook for 5 minutes, stirring occasionally. Add the remaining ingredients, except the toasted coconut and parsley leaves, if using, and stir well.
4. Garnish each dish with toasted coconut and a parsley leaf before serving.

Variations
- Add 2 teaspoons of freshly squeezed lime juice along with the parsley.
- Replace the white basmati with other types of rice, or grains such as quinoa or millet (see page 218).
- Replace the beans with your favorite, including black or pinto beans, or black-eyed peas.
- Replace the crushed red pepper flakes with 1 teaspoon of seeded and diced hot chile pepper (see the Scoville scale on page 57).

continues

continued

- Replace the coconut milk with soy, rice, or hemp milk.
- You can sauté the onion, celery, and garlic in 1 tablespoon of oil for 3 minutes, stirring frequently, before adding the vegetable stock.
- For a heartier soup, add an additional ¾ cup beans.

Chef's Tips and Tricks

Substituting Dried Herbs for Fresh

In general you may substitute dried herbs for fresh herbs in a one-to-three ratio. For instance, 1 teaspoon of dried herb is equivalent in flavor to 1 tablespoon of fresh herb. This is only true if the dried herbs are extremely fresh, otherwise you will need to increase the amount of dried herb used to achieve the same amount of flavor.

Orzo Minestrone with Broiled Fennel

Predating the Roman Empire, minestrone can be made with whatever vegetables and legumes are fresh and available. This version is a unique twist on the classic Italian soup and uses orzo, or risoni, which is a delicate, rice-shaped, semolina-based Italian pasta. Top with Vegan Crème Fraîche (page 195) and a drizzle of Balsamic Reduction (page 189).

SERVES 6 TO 8

ORZO ITALIANO

5 cups vegetable stock (see page 25) or water

2 bay leaves

1 cup diced yellow onion

½ cup thinly sliced celery

4 garlic cloves, pressed or minced

1 teaspoon dried oregano (optional)

½ teaspoon dried thyme (optional)

¼ teaspoon minced fresh rosemary (optional)

¾ cup diced shiitake mushrooms

1 (14.5-ounce) can diced fire-roasted tomatoes, or 1½ cups chopped tomato (½-inch pieces)

1 (15-ounce) can chickpeas or cannellini beans, rinsed and drained well

1 tablespoon wheat-free tamari or other soy sauce (optional)

2 teaspoons sea salt, or to taste

¼ teaspoon ground black pepper

Pinch of crushed red pepper flakes

¾ cup uncooked orzo

2 tablespoons finely chopped fresh flat-leaf parsley

1 tablespoon chiffonaded fresh basil

2 teaspoons minced fresh sage (optional)

1 tablespoon balsamic vinegar

BROILED FENNEL

1½ cups chopped fennel (½-inch pieces)

1 tablespoon freshly squeezed lemon juice

2 teaspoons olive oil

Pinch of sea salt

1. Prepare the orzo: Place the vegetable stock in a 3-quart pot over medium heat. Add all the remaining Orzo Italiano ingredients, except the orzo, parsley, basil, sage, and balsamic vinegar, and cook for 10 minutes, stirring occasionally.

2. Add the orzo and cook for 10 minutes, stirring occasionally.

3. Meanwhile, prepare the fennel: Preheat the oven to HIGH BROIL. Combine the Broiled Fennel ingredients on a small baking sheet and toss well. Broil until the fennel is just golden brown, about 5 minutes.

4. Add the fennel to the pot along with the parsley, basil, sage, if using, and balsamic vinegar and stir well.

5. Remove the bay leaves before serving.

continues

continued

Variations

- Add 1½ cups of assorted chopped vegetables, such as carrot, parsnip, and zucchini.
- Add ½ cup of red wine along with the vegetable stock.
- Add 1 cup of cubed and roasted tofu along with the beans (see page 215).
- You can sauté the onion, celery, and garlic in 1 tablespoon of oil for 3 minutes over high heat, stirring frequently, before adding the vegetable stock.
- You can grill the fennel instead of broiling it. Slice the fennel bulb into ½-inch slices and grill, basting periodically with olive oil, until char marks appear and the fennel is tender, about 4 minutes on each side, depending on the temperature of the grill.
- For a gluten-free version, replace the orzo with a small brown rice pasta.

Persian Lima Bean and Dill Soup

The lima bean–dill combo is a favorite throughout Central Asia. I am not sure where or when lima beans got a bad rap, but this dish will open your eyes to this delightfully creamy and buttery bean. Top with Red Pepper Coulis (page 197) and drizzle with Basil Oil (page 188).

SERVES 6 TO 8

5 cups vegetable stock (see page 25) or water

1¼ cups diced yellow onion

½ cup diced celery

3 garlic cloves, pressed or minced

½ teaspoon ground cumin

1¼ cups diced carrot

½ cup diced turnip or additional carrot

10 ounces frozen lima beans (2 cups)

1 cup fresh or frozen corn

1½ teaspoons sea salt, or to taste

¼ teaspoon ground black pepper

Pinch of cayenne pepper

1 cup Vegan Crème Fraîche (page 195)

1½ tablespoons minced fresh dill

3 tablespoons chopped fresh chives, for garnish

1. Place the vegetable stock in a 3-quart pot over medium-high heat.
2. Add the onion, celery, garlic, cumin, carrot, turnip, if using, and lima beans and cook for 15 minutes, stirring occasionally.
3. Add the corn, salt, pepper, and cayenne to the soup and mix well. Lower the heat to medium, add the Vegan Crème Fraîche, and cook for 10 minutes, stirring occasionally. Add the dill and stir well. Garnish with chives before serving.

Variations

- For a lighter soup, you can leave out the Vegan Crème Fraîche.
- Replace the Vegan Crème Fraîche with Raw Crème Fraîche (page 196)
- Replace the lima beans with fava beans, black-eyed peas, chickpeas, or your favorite.
- Replace the dill with 2 tablespoons of fresh cilantro, basil, or flat-leaf parsley.
- Replace the carrot and turnip with zucchini and seeded bell pepper.
- You can sauté the onion, celery, garlic, and cumin in 1½ tablespoons of oil for 3 minutes, stirring frequently, before adding the remaining ingredients.

Three Sisters Soup

Named after the three most revered crops of the Native Americans—corn, beans, and squash—this simple soup is a way for you to connect with the peoples who walked this land before us. No need to peel the squash as long as it is washed well. Serve with Cosmic Corn Bread (page 211) and top with Vegan Crème Fraîche (page 195) and a drizzle of Balsamic Reduction (page 189) or Red Pepper Coulis (page 197).

SERVES 6 TO 8

5 cups vegetable stock (see page 25) or water

1¼ cups diced yellow onion

½ cup thinly sliced celery

4 large garlic cloves, pressed or minced

1 teaspoon seeded and diced jalapeño pepper

1¾ cups seeded and chopped butternut squash (½-inch pieces)

1 tablespoon chili powder

1 (15-ounce) can pinto beans, rinsed and drained well, or 1½ cups cooked (see page 221)

1 cup fresh or frozen corn

1 tablespoon wheat-free tamari or other soy sauce (optional)

1 tablespoon nutritional yeast (optional)

2 teaspoons sea salt, or to taste

¼ teaspoon ground black pepper

Pinch of cayenne pepper

2 tablespoons finely chopped fresh cilantro

1. Place the vegetable stock in a 3-quart pot over medium-high heat. Add the onion, celery, garlic, jalapeño, squash, chili powder, and beans and cook for 10 minutes, stirring occasionally.
2. Add the corn, tamari, if using, nutritional yeast, if using, salt, black pepper, and cayenne and cook for 5 minutes, stirring occasionally.
3. Add the cilantro, and stir well before serving.

Variations

- For a thicker soup, you can carefully transfer 2 to 3 cups of the soup to a blender, blend until creamy, and return it to the pot.
- You can sauté the onion, celery, and garlic in 1 tablespoon of oil for 3 minutes, stirring frequently, before adding the vegetable stock.
- Replace the beans with your favorite, such as anasazi, kidney, great northern, or gigante.
- Experiment with different types of squash or replace with potato, sweet potato, eggplant, or zucchini.
- Replace the cilantro with 1 tablespoon of fresh dill or 2 teaspoons each of minced fresh sage, marjoram, and flat-leaf parsley.
- Add 1 cup each of seeded and diced red bell pepper and corn.

Ethiopian Stew

Ethiopian cuisine is perhaps my favorite, and the experience of dining in a traditional Ethiopian restaurant is not to be missed. Large portions of food are served on a platter of *injera* bread (made with teff—see Chef's Tips and Tricks), and pieces of the *injera* are rolled up to use instead of forks or spoons. To get the full effect of this recipe, visit an ethnic market to pick up the Berbere spice mix, or if you have time, you can make your own blend (see see Chef's Tips and Tricks). If you are unable to locate teff, you can replace it with quinoa or amaranth (see page 218). Serve with Herbed Bread Sticks (page 209).

SERVES 6 TO 8

5½ cups vegetable stock (see page 25) or water

1 cup thinly sliced yellow onion

4 garlic cloves, pressed or minced

2 tablespoons Berbere spice mix (see Chef's Tips and Tricks)

1½ cups chopped carrot (½-inch pieces)

1 cup chopped sweet potato, yam, or potato (½-inch pieces)

½ cup uncooked red lentils

¼ cup uncooked teff, quinoa, or amaranth (see Chef's Tips and Tricks)

1½ cups chopped green cabbage

2 cups stemmed and sliced collard greens (cut in half lengthwise, then into ½-inch slice)

2 teaspoons sea salt, or to taste

½ teaspoon ground black pepper

1 tablespoon wheat-free tamari or other soy sauce

1. Place the vegetable stock in a 3-quart pot over medium-high heat.
2. Add all the remaining ingredients, except the collard greens, salt, pepper, and tamari, and cook for 15 minutes, stirring occasionally.
3. Add the collards, salt, pepper, and tamari, and cook for 5 minutes, stirring occasionally.

Variations

- Replace the carrot with turnip, rutabaga, or parsnip.
- Replace the collards with spinach, kale, or chard.
- You can sauté the onion and garlic with 1 tablespoon of oil for 3 minutes, stirring frequently, before adding the remaining ingredients.

continues

continued

Chef's Tips and Tricks

Ethiopian Cuisine

Teff is the world's smallest grain and is used as the primary ingredient in Ethiopian flat bread called *injera*.

Berbere is a spice blend that consists of up to ten different spices common to Ethiopian cuisine. Purchase yours at an ethnic market. You can make your own by combining the following ingredients in a bowl and mixing well: 2 teaspoons of paprika, 2 teaspoons of dried ginger, 1 teaspoon of ground coriander, ½ teaspoon of ground allspice, ½ teaspoon of ground cinnamon, ½ teaspoon of fenugreek, ¼ teaspoon of ground nutmeg, ¼ teaspoon of ground cloves, and ¼ teaspoon of cayenne pepper.

Greek Lentil Soup with Grilled Bell Pepper

A staple food since Neolithic times, lentils are a nutritious, flavorful, and versatile ingredient to include in a well-rounded diet. They are a vital component in several cuisines from around the world, including Ethiopian, Iranian, Mediterranean, and Indian. The round shape is said to symbolize the life cycle. Several varieties are available, some taking longer to cook than others—experiment with them all! Red lentils are the fastest cooking. Serve with Tofu Feta (page 207) and Tapenade (page 193).

SERVES 6 TO 8

8 cups vegetable stock (see page 25) or water

¾ cup uncooked green lentils, rinsed and drained well

1 cup diced yellow onion

½ cup thinly sliced celery

6 to 10 garlic cloves

1 cup diced cremini mushrooms

1 tablespoon dried oregano, or 2 tablespoons minced fresh

2 large or 3 medium-size red bell peppers, quartered and seeded

1½ tablespoons olive oil

2¼ teaspoons sea salt, or to taste

½ teaspoon ground black pepper

2 cups well rinsed and thinly sliced baby spinach

Pinch of crushed red pepper flakes

2 teaspoons wheat-free tamari or other soy sauce (optional)

2 tablespoons chiffonaded fresh mint

2 tablespoons finely chopped fresh flat-leaf parsley

1. Preheat a grill. Place the vegetable stock in a 3-quart pot over medium-high heat. Add the lentils, onion, celery, garlic, mushrooms, and oregano and cook for 25 minutes, stirring occasionally.

2. Meanwhile, place the bell peppers in a small dish with the olive oil and ¼ teaspoon each of salt and black pepper. Grill the peppers directly on the grill, basting periodically with the olive oil mixture, until char marks appear on both sides and the peppers are just tender, about 8 minutes. Chop into ½-inch pieces and measure out 1¼ cups for this recipe.

3. After the lentils have cooked for 25 minutes, add the bell peppers and spinach and cook for 5 minutes, stirring occasionally. Add the remaining ingredients, and stir well before serving.

Variations

- Sauté the onion, celery, and garlic in 1 tablespoon of oil over high heat for 3 minutes, stirring constantly and adding small amounts of water or stock, if necessary, to prevent sticking, before adding the remaining ingredients.

continues

continued

- For a quicker soup, use red lentils and 1½ cups less water.
- Replace the mushrooms with shiitake, oyster, chanterelle, or button.
- Add 2 tablespoons of chiffonaded fresh basil and 1 teaspoon each of fresh thyme and marjoram along with the parsley.
- You can broil the peppers. To do so, preheat the oven to HIGH BROIL. Place the bell peppers on a small baking sheet with the olive oil and ¼ teaspoon each of salt and pepper, and toss well. Broil until the peppers are just soft and slightly charred, about 10 minutes, depending upon the temperature of the oven. Chop into ½-inch pieces and measure out 1¼ cups for this recipe.

Coconut Greens Soup with Polenta

Can you say "vegan soup decadence"? One sip of this creamy, rich, and velvety soup, and you will discover why coconut trees are referred to as the "tree of life." For an over-the-top experience, garnish with a drizzle of Basil Oil (page 188) and a sprinkle of toasted coconut (page 213).

SERVES 6 TO 8

3 cups vegetable stock (see page 25) or water

2 (15-ounce) cans coconut milk

½ cup thinly sliced shallot

1 tablespoon peeled and minced fresh ginger

2 teaspoons seeded and diced hot chile pepper (see the Scoville scale on page 57)

¾ cup thinly sliced shiitake mushrooms

½ cup uncooked polenta cornmeal

2 teaspoons sea salt, or to taste

¼ teaspoon ground black pepper

Pinch of crushed red pepper flakes

⅛ teaspoon ground nutmeg (optional)

1 tablespoon wheat-free tamari or other soy sauce

1½ cups small broccoli florets

1 cup chopped zucchini (½-inch pieces)

¾ cup seeded and diced red bell pepper

3 cups chopped spinach, kale, or rainbow chard, or a combination

2 tablespoons finely chopped fresh cilantro or flat-leaf parsley

1. Place the vegetable stock in a 3-quart pot over medium-high heat. Add all the remaining ingredients, except the broccoli, zucchini, bell pepper, spinach, and cilantro, and cook for 10 minutes, stirring frequently and being careful not to burn the polenta.
2. Add the broccoli and zucchini and cook for 5 minutes, stirring occasionally.
3. Add the red bell pepper and spinach and cook for 5 minutes, stirring occasionally.
4. Add the cilantro, and stir well before serving.

Variations

- You can use the prepackaged polenta (Food Merchants Organic). Chop into ½-inch cubes and add at the end of the recipe along with the greens.
- Replace the shiitake mushrooms with cremini or oyster.
- Replace the broccoli and bell pepper with veggies of your choosing, including cauliflower, carrot, romenesco broccoli, or gold bar squash.
- Replace the shallot with onion.
- For a lighter soup, replace one can of coconut milk with an equivalent amount of vegetable stock or water.
- Add five pressed or minced garlic cloves along with the ginger.

Coconut Curry Veggie Soup with Tofu

Experience true coconut bliss with this creamy tropical soup that has an Indian flair. Countless variations are possible, depending upon your selection of seasonal veggies. Remember that the firmer the vegetable, the longer the time it needs to cook. Softer veggies, such as zucchini or red bell pepper, will take less time to cook, so you can add them along with the broccoli. Serve over quinoa or rice and top with toasted coconut flakes (see page 213).

SERVES 6 TO 8

COCONUT VEGGIE SOUP

1 tablespoon curry powder

2 teaspoons ground cumin

1 teaspoon ground coriander

3 cups vegetable stock (see page 25) or water

2 (15-ounce) cans coconut milk

¾ cup thinly sliced yellow onion

4 garlic cloves, pressed or minced

1 tablespoon peeled and minced fresh ginger

3½ cups assorted chopped vegetables (try carrot, cauliflower, and potato)

2 teaspoons wheat-free tamari or other soy sauce (optional)

2 teaspoons sea salt, or to taste

¼ teaspoon ground black pepper

Pinch of crushed red pepper flakes

1 cup broccoli florets

3 tablespoons chopped fresh cilantro

BROILED TOFU

2 tablespoons wheat-free tamari or other soy sauce

1 tablespoon coconut or sesame oil

1 tablespoon water

14 ounces extra-firm or super-firm tofu, cut into ½-inch cubes

1. Prepare the soup: Place a 3-quart pot over high heat. Place the curry powder, cumin, and coriander in the pot and cook for 1 minute, stirring constantly. Lower the heat to medium-high, add all the remaining soup ingredients, except the broccoli and cilantro, and cook for 10 minutes, stirring occasionally. Add the broccoli and cook for 5 minutes, stirring occasionally.

2. Meanwhile, prepare the broiled tofu: Heat the oven to HIGH BROIL. Place the tamari, oil, and water on a small baking sheet and stir well. Add the tofu and stir until the tofu is evenly coated. Broil for 10 minutes, carefully stirring a few times to ensure even cooking. Add to the pot and cook for 5 minutes, stirring occasionally.

3. Add the cilantro, and stir well before serving.

Variations

- You can roast the tofu instead of broiling it (see page 215).
- You can omit the broiling process and add the cubed tofu along with the veggies.
- Add 1 cup of chopped greens, such as bok choy, nettles, dandelion greens, arugula, or spinach along with the cilantro.
- Try it with tricolored cauliflower—purple, yellow, and white.
- Replace the tofu with chickpeas or your favorite bean.

Tibetan Noodle Soup (Thenthuk)

Recipe courtesy of *The 30-Minute Vegan's Taste of the East*

Thenthuk is a hardy soup in which the "noodles" are actually small pieces of dough. It will definitely keep you warm and happy in the high Himalayas. Create your own designer *thenthuk* by adding what's fresh in your garden.

SERVES 6 TO 8

NOODLES

¾ cup white spelt flour

¼ teaspoon sea salt

3 tablespoons water

SOUP BASE

6 cups vegetable stock (see page 25) or water

1¼ cups diced yellow onion

4 garlic cloves, pressed or minced

2 teaspoons seeded and diced hot chile pepper, or 3 dried red chiles

1¼ cups chopped tomato (½-inch pieces)

2 cups small cauliflower florets

1 cup chopped cabbage (½-inch pieces)

3 tablespoons wheat-free tamari or other soy sauce

1 teaspoon sea salt, or to taste

2 cups chopped kale or spinach

2 tablespoons minced fresh cilantro

1. Make the "noodles": Place the flour and salt in a bowl and mix well. Add the water and mix well, forming it into a dough.
2. Place the vegetable stock in a 3-quart pot over medium-high heat. Add the remaining soup ingredients, except the kale and cilantro, and bring to a boil, stirring occasionally. Lower the heat to medium and cook until the cauliflower is just soft, about 8 minutes.
3. Pinch off small pieces of the dough, flatten with your fingers, and add them to the soup.
4. Cook for 5 minutes, stirring occasionally. Add the kale and cilantro, cook for 2 minutes longer, and mix well before serving.

Variations

- Replace the vegetables with potato, broccoli, squash, carrot, zucchini, or mushrooms.
- Try adding 1 cup of roasted tofu or tempeh cubes (see page 215).
- For a gluten-free noodle, use a gluten-free flour mix plus ¼ teaspoon of xanthan gum (see page 11).

BBQ Tempeh and Roasted Corn Stew

Who says vegans need to give up on the amazing flavors of a BBQ just because we leave out the animal products. A little bit of tempeh (see page 215) goes a long way to create a hearty and flavorful summer fun meal. If you have more time, and it's in season, go for fresh corn instead of frozen. Serve with Cosmic Corn Bread (page 211) and top with Vegan Crème Fraîche (page 195) and toasted pepitas (see page 213) and serve along with rice or quinoa.

SERVES 6 TO 8

TEMPEH MARINADE

1 tablespoon wheat-free tamari or other soy sauce

1 tablespoon coconut or olive oil

1 tablespoon water

1 tablespoon pure maple syrup (optional)

16 ounces tempeh, diced (see Chef's Tips and Tricks)

STEW

5 cups vegetable stock (see page 25) or water

1¼ cups diced yellow onion

¾ cup diced celery

4 large garlic cloves, pressed or minced

1 cup chopped tomato (½-inch pieces)

6 ounces tomato paste

3 tablespoons cornmeal

1 tablespoon chili powder

1 tablespoon molasses, brown sugar, or pure maple syrup

1 teaspoon sea salt, or to taste

¼ teaspoon ground black pepper

1 tablespoon wheat-free tamari or other soy sauce

¼ teaspoon liquid smoke

¼ teaspoon chipotle chile powder (optional)

Pinch of ground cloves (optional)

2 tablespoons finely chopped fresh flat-leaf parsley

continues

BBQ Tempeh and Roasted Corn Stew *continued*

ROASTED CORN

2 cups corn
½ tablespoon olive oil
Pinch of sea salt
Pinch of ground black pepper

1. Preheat the oven to 375°F. Prepare the tempeh marinade: Place all its ingredients on a small baking sheet or casserole dish and stir well, coating the tempeh evenly. Bake for 20 minutes.
2. Meanwhile, prepare the stew: Place the vegetable stock in a 3-quart pot over medium-high heat. Add the remaining stew ingredients, except the parsley, and cook for 10 minutes, stirring occasionally.
3. Add the tempeh to the pot and stir well.
4. Prepare the corn: Place the corn, oil, salt, and pepper on a small baking sheet and bake for 15 minutes. (You can use an additional baking sheet, or wait until the tempeh is finished, to save on pans.) Add to the pot along with the parsley and mix well.

Variations
- Replace the tempeh with extra-firm tofu or vegan sausages (see page 10).
- Add 1 cup of chopped carrot or seeded and chopped bell pepper along with the onion.
- Replace the parsley with fresh cilantro.
- You can sauté the onion, celery, and garlic in 1½ tablespoons of oil for 3 minutes, stirring frequently, before adding the remaining ingredients.

Indian Mulligatawny

Recipe courtesy of *The 30-Minute Vegan's Taste of the East*

Mulligatawny literally means "pepper water" in Tamil, though peppers are not a common ingredient in this curry-flavored soup. Surprisingly, the origin of mulligatawny soup, widely considered the national soup of India, is actually of Anglo-Indian origin. There are as many variations of this soup as there are temples in India. Top with Vegan Crème Fraîche (page 195) and Red Pepper Coulis (page 197)

SERVES 6 TO 8

2 tablespoons sesame oil

1 tablespoon curry powder

2 teaspoons ground cumin

1 cup diced yellow onion

3 large garlic cloves, pressed or minced

6 cups vegetable stock (see page 25) or water

½ cup uncooked red lentils

¼ cup uncooked white basmati rice

1½ cups diced potato

1¼ cups cored, peeled, and chopped apple

½ cup diced celery

¾ cup diced carrot

1½ cups soy creamer or coconut milk

2 teaspoons garam masala (see page 104)

Pinch of cayenne pepper, or to taste

1 teaspoon tamarind paste (see page 10), or 2 teaspoons freshly squeezed lime juice

1 tablespoon wheat-free tamari or soy sauce (optional)

2 tablespoons minced fresh cilantro

1 teaspoon sea salt, or to taste

Lemon wedges, for garnish

1. Place the oil in a 3-quart pot over medium-high heat. Add the curry and cumin and cook for 1 minute, stirring constantly. Add the onion and garlic and cook for 2 minutes, stirring frequently. Add the stock, lentils, and rice, and bring to a boil.
2. Lower the heat to medium, add the potato, apple, celery, and carrot, and cook for 20 minutes, stirring occasionally. The rice and lentils should be thoroughly cooked.
3. Add the remaining ingredients, mix well, and garnish with a lemon wedge before serving.

Variations
- Try adding 2 cups of chopped kale, spinach, collard greens, or Swiss chard.
- Replace the rice with quinoa or another variety of rice (see page 219).

Greek Fasolada Soup with Cannellini Beans

Get your protein on with *fasolada*, the Greek version of the bean stew found in menus throughout Central Asia, Europe, and the Middle East. Serve over rice or quinoa and top with Tofu Feta (page 207) and a drizzle of Balsamic Reduction (page 189).

SERVES 6 TO 8

5 cups vegetable stock (see page 25) or water

1 cup diced yellow onion

½ cup thinly sliced celery

4 garlic cloves, pressed or minced

1¼ cups diced potato

½ cup diced carrot

½ cup seeded and chopped bell pepper

½ cup diced shiitake mushrooms

1 (15-ounce) can cannellini beans, rinsed and drained well, or 1½ cups cooked (see page 220)

6 ounces tomato paste

1 tablespoon dried oregano

1 teaspoon dried thyme

1 teaspoon sea salt, or to taste

¼ teaspoon ground black pepper

Pinch of crushed red pepper flakes

1½ cups chopped rinsed and well-drained spinach

2 teaspoons balsamic vinegar

2 tablespoons wheat-free tamari or other soy sauce (optional)

1 tablespoon nutritional yeast (optional)

1. Place the vegetable stock in a 3-quart pot over medium-high heat. Add all the remaining ingredients except the spinach, balsamic vinegar, and tamari and yeast, if using, and cook for 15 minutes, stirring occasionally.
2. Add the remaining ingredients and cook for 7 minutes, stirring occasionally.

Variations

- You can sauté the onion and garlic in 1 tablespoon of oil for 3 minutes over high heat, stirring frequently, before adding the vegetable stock.
- Replace the dried oregano with 2 tablespoons of fresh, and the dried thyme with 2 teaspoons of fresh.
- Replace the cannellini beans with fava, gigante, navy, or your favorites.

Himalayan Dal with Curried Chickpeas

Dal is a lentil (pulse) -based dish that is served throughout the Indian subcontinent and surrounding areas. You can find it everywhere—on the menu of roadside stands and in five-star restaurants. Cooking the chickpeas separately gives them an added crunch that you miss if you cook them directly in the soup. Top with Vegan Crème Fraîche (page 195) and Candied Pepitas (page 192).

SERVES 6 TO 8

DAL

2 teaspoons cumin seeds, or
  1 teaspoon ground cumin

1 teaspoon brown mustard seeds

1 teaspoon curry powder

1 teaspoon coriander seeds, or
  ½ teaspoon ground coriander
  (optional)

½ teaspoon garam masala (see
  Chef's Tips and Tricks; optional)

1¼ cups diced yellow onion

1 tablespoon peeled and minced
  fresh ginger

4 garlic cloves, pressed or minced

7 cups vegetable stock (see page 25)
  or water

¾ cup uncooked red lentils

1 cup chopped carrot (½-inch
  pieces)

1 cup chopped tomato (½-inch
  pieces)

2 tablespoons freshly squeezed
  lemon juice

2 cups chopped, rinsed, and well-
  drained spinach

2 teaspoons sea salt, or to taste

¼ teaspoon ground black pepper

Pinch of cayenne pepper

2 tablespoons finely chopped fresh
  cilantro

Cilantro leaves, for garnish

CURRIED CHICKPEAS

1 tablespoon toasted sesame oil

2 teaspoons curry powder

1 (15-ounce) can chickpeas, rinsed
  and drained well, or 1½ cups
  cooked (see page 220)

1 teaspoon sea salt, or to taste

1. Prepare the dal: Place a 3-quart pot over high heat. Add the cumin, mustard seeds, curry powder, coriander, if using, and garam masala, if using, and cook for 1 minute, stirring constantly. Add the onion, ginger, and garlic, and stir well.

2. Lower the heat to medium-high, add the vegetable stock, lentils, and carrot, and cook for 20 minutes stirring occasionally. Add the chopped cilantro, and stir well.

3. Meanwhile, prepare the curried chickpeas: Place a small sauté pan over medium-high heat. Add the sesame oil and curry powder and stir well. Carefully add the chickpeas and salt and cook until the chickpeas are slightly crispy and browned, stirring frequently and adding small amounts of water or vegetable stock, if necessary, to prevent sticking.

4. To serve, top each bowl with chickpeas and a few leaves of cilantro.

continues

Himalayan Dal with Curried Chickpeas *continued*

Variations

- Replace 1 cup of the vegetable stock with coconut milk.
- You can sauté the spices in 1 tablespoon of oil for 1 minute over high heat, stirring constantly, before adding the onion.
- Replace the carrot with zucchini, broccoli, cauliflower, or your favorite veggie.
- Replace the red lentils with mung beans, split mung beans, or green or yellow lentils, and add more stock as needed. See page 221.
- For a thicker soup, you can carefully blend about half of the soup just before adding the cilantro. Return the mixture to the pot and mix well before serving.

Chef's Tips and Tricks

Garam Masala

From the Hindi words *garam*, meaning "hot" and *masala*, meaning "spices," this is one of India's popular spices. In this case, the "hot" refers to pungency, and not necessarily hot as in spicy hot. The ingredients and quantities vary widely throughout different regions in India. You can make your own by whisking all of the following ingredients together: 2 tablespoons of ground coriander, 1 tablespoon of ground cumin, 1 tablespoon of ground black pepper, 1 tablespoon of ground ginger, 1 teaspoon of ground cardamom, 1 teaspoon of ground cinnamon, 1 teaspoon of ground cloves, 1 teaspoon of ground nutmeg, ¼ teaspoon of cayenne pepper, and ¼ teaspoon of ground turmeric (optional). Store in a glass container.

Polish Vegan Sausage and Sauerkraut Stew

Craving the kielbasa but looking for a healthier alternative? Check out this classic Polish stew, done vegan style. Serve with Vegan Crème Fraîche (page 195) and Herbed Croutons (page 200).

SERVES 6 TO 8

4½ cups vegetable stock (see page 25) or water

2 bay leaves

1 cup diced yellow onion

½ cup thinly sliced celery

4 garlic cloves, pressed or minced

1 cup diced potato

1 cup shredded cabbage (optional)

¾ cup thinly sliced carrot

½ cup seeded and diced red bell pepper

1 tablespoon paprika

1½ teaspoons sea salt, or to taste

¼ teaspoon ground black pepper

Pinch of cayenne pepper

⅛ teaspoon liquid smoke, or ½ teaspoon smoked paprika (optional)

7 ounces vegan sausage (see page 10), sliced (1½ cups)

1 cup sauerkraut, rinsed and drained well

2 tablespoons finely chopped fresh flat-leaf parsley

1 tablespoon minced fresh dill

1. Place the vegetable stock in a 3-quart pot over medium-high heat. Add all the remaining ingredients, except the sausage, sauerkraut, parsley, and dill, and cook for 10 minutes, stirring occasionally.
2. Add the sausage and sauerkraut and cook for 10 minutes, stirring occasionally. Add the parsley and dill, and stir well before serving.

Variations

- You can sauté the onion, celery, and garlic in 1 tablespoon of oil for 3 minutes over high heat, stirring frequently, before adding the vegetable stock.
- For a gluten-free version, replace the vegan sausage with an equivalent amount of cubed and roasted tofu or tempeh (see page 215).
- Replace the cabbage with kale, spinach, or chard.

Tofurky and Rice Soup

A favorite of vegans (and turkeys) during the holiday season, Tofurky is a soy-based food that can now be enjoyed year-round. This soup uses the slices that are available in different flavors. The white basmati rice is a favorite for quick and easy cooking. Feel free to replace it with a longer-cooking rice, especially wild rice for a true celebratory feast. Top with Krispy Kale (page 203) or Crispy Sunchokes (page 202).

SERVES 6 TO 8

6 cups vegetable stock (see page 25) or water

1¼ cups diced yellow onion

½ teaspoon dried thyme

¾ cup thinly sliced celery

4 large garlic cloves, pressed or minced

½ cup uncooked white basmati rice

1 cup chopped carrot (½-inch pieces)

1 cup quartered cremini mushrooms

2 (5.5-ounce) packages Tofurky, cut into ½-inch slices

1 teaspoon sea salt, or to taste

¼ teaspoon ground black pepper

¼ teaspoon crushed red pepper flakes

2 tablespoons finely chopped fresh flat-leaf parsley

1 tablespoon finely chopped fresh sage

½ teaspoon smoked paprika, or ¼ teaspoon chipotle chile powder (optional)

1 tablespoon wheat-free tamari or other soy sauce

1 tablespoon freshly squeezed lemon juice

1. Place the vegetable stock in a 3-quart pot over medium-high heat.
2. Add the onion, thyme, celery, garlic, basmati rice, carrot, and mushrooms and cook for 15 minutes, stirring occasionally.
3. Add the remaining ingredients and cook for 5 minutes, stirring occasionally.

Variations

- Replace the basmati rice with wild rice, brown rice, or quinoa (see chart on page 219 for cooking times).
- You can sauté the onion, thyme, celery, and garlic in 1½ tablespoons of oil for 3 minutes, stirring frequently, before adding the stock.
- Add 1 tablespoon of fresh marjoram.
- For a gluten-free version, replace the Tofurky with cubed and roasted tofu (see page 215).

Spanish Rice and Artichoke Heart Stew

Here we have a soup version of the classic Spanish dish called paella. With origins in the Valencia region of Spain, paella is traditionally a seafood-based stew. This vegan version with saffron and artichoke hearts is guaranteed to deliver. For a full-blown fiesta, top each serving with a dollop of Vegan Crème Fraîche (page 195) or Tofu Feta (page 207), a drizzle of Balsamic Reduction (page 189), and a spoonful of Tapenade (page 193).

SERVES 6 TO 8

5 cups vegetable stock (see page 25) or water

½ teaspoon saffron threads (see page 42)

2 tablespoons arame (see page 9; optional)

1¼ cups diced yellow onion

4 large garlic cloves, pressed or minced

½ cup diced shiitake mushrooms

½ cup uncooked white basmati rice

1 tablespoon paprika

1 teaspoon smoked paprika, or ¼ teaspoon liquid smoke

Pinch of cayenne pepper

1 (14.5-ounce) can diced fire-roasted tomatoes, or 1½ cups chopped tomato (½-inch pieces)

1 (15-ounce) can chickpeas, rinsed and drained well, or 1½ cups cooked (see page 220)

1½ teaspoons sea salt, or to taste

3 tablespoons freshly squeezed lemon juice

2 teaspoons, wheat-free tamari or other soy sauce (optional)

½ cup chopped artichoke hearts

3 tablespoons finely chopped fresh flat-leaf parsley

Lemon wedges, for garnish

1. Place the vegetable stock, saffron, and arame in a 3-quart pot over medium-high heat. Add all the remaining ingredients, except the artichoke hearts, parsley, and lemon wedges, and cook for 15 minutes, stirring occasionally.
2. Add the artichoke hearts and cook for 5 minutes, stirring occasionally.
3. Add the parsley and stir well.
4. Garnish each dish with lemon wedges before serving.

Variations

- You can sauté the onion and garlic in 1½ tablespoons of oil for 3 minutes, stirring frequently before adding the remaining ingredients.
- Add ½ cup of diced carrot or parsnip along with the rice.
- Add 1½ cups of chopped spinach or kale along with the artichoke hearts.
- Replace the basmati rice with other rice, or quinoa (see page 219).

Italian Wedding Stew with Vegan Sausage

You may be surprised to learn that Italian Wedding Soup is not a dish that has its origins in some Italian Renaissance wedding ritual. *Au contraire*—the soup has its origins in the US of A, where the marriage is between green vegetables and an animal product that the soup would typically contain. Our version uses vegan sausage, which, when combined with the green veggies, is a match made in heaven. Feel free to replace the endives and escarole with greens of your choosing. Serve with Crostini (page 198) and Tapenade (page 193).

SERVES 6 TO 8

6 cups vegetable stock (see page 25) or water

1 cup thinly sliced yellow onion

5 to 6 garlic cloves, pressed or minced

2 teaspoons dried oregano

¾ cup thinly sliced fennel bulb

1 cup peeled and chopped celery root (optional)

1½ cups sliced parsnip (½-inch slices)

7 ounces vegan sausage, sliced thinly (1½ cups)

½ cup seeded and diced red bell pepper

1 cup chopped endive

1 cup chopped escarole

2 tablespoons finely chopped fresh flat-leaf parsley

2 tablespoons chiffonaded basil

2 tablespoons nutritional yeast (optional)

2½ teaspoons sea salt, or to taste

½ teaspoon ground black pepper

¼ teaspoon crushed red pepper flakes

Grated mozzarella-style vegan cheese or nutritional yeast, for garnish

1. Place the vegetable stock in a 3-quart pot over medium-high heat. Add the onion, garlic, oregano, fennel, celery root, if using, parsnip, and sausage and cook for 15 minutes, stirring occasionally.
2. Add the bell pepper, endive, and escarole and cook for 8 minutes, stirring occasionally.
3. Add the parsley, basil, nutritional yeast, if using, salt, black pepper, and crushed red pepper flakes and stir well.
4. Garnish each serving with a few tablespoons of grated vegan cheese or 1 tablespoon of nutritional yeast before serving.

Variations

- Feel free to sauté the onion, garlic, and fennel in 1 tablespoon of oil over high heat for 3 minutes, stirring constantly and adding small amounts of water or stock, if necessary, to prevent sticking, before adding the remaining ingredients.
- Replace the celery root with carrot or zucchini.
- Add 2 teaspoons of freshly squeezed lemon juice along with the basil.
- Replace the endive and escarole with kale, spinach, collards, and/or chard.
- For a gluten-free version, replace the vegan sausage with Beyond Meat chicken-style strips (see page 7), or cubed and roasted tofu or tempeh (see page 215).

Black Bean Tomato Soup with Polenta Dumplings

This recipe is an innovative twist on the celebrated Tortilla Soup and uses polenta corn-meal dumplings instead of the chips. Old-schoolers can still create the tortilla soup version by following the variation that follows. Top with Vegan Crème Fraîche (page 195) or Chipotle Mayonnaise (see page 195) and serve with Cosmic Corn Bread (page 211).

SERVES 6 TO 8

POLENTA DUMPLINGS

1½ cups water

½ cup uncooked polenta cornmeal

1 tablespoon diced green onion (optional)

1 teaspoon olive oil

½ teaspoon sea salt

⅛ teaspoon ground black pepper

SOUP

1 tablespoon chili powder

1½ teaspoons ground cumin

5 cups vegetable stock (see page 25) or water

1 (14.5-ounce) can diced fire-roasted tomatoes, or ½ cup diced tomato

2 teaspoons seeded and diced jalapeño pepper

1 cup thinly sliced yellow onion

½ cup diced celery

5 to 6 garlic cloves, pressed or minced

¼ teaspoon chipotle chile powder (optional)

1 (15-ounce) can black beans, rinsed and well drained, or 1 ½ cups cooked (see page 220)

2 teaspoons wheat-free tamari or other soy sauce (optional)

1 teaspoon sea salt, or to taste

¼ teaspoon ground black pepper

Pinch of cayenne pepper (optional)

3 tablespoons finely chopped fresh cilantro

continues

Black Bean Tomato Soup with Polenta Dumplings *continued*

1. Prepare the dumplings. Place the water in a small pot over high heat. Bring to a boil. Add the polenta, green onion, if using, olive oil, salt, and pepper, and very carefully whisk well. Lower the heat to medium and cook uncovered for 7 minutes, whisking frequently and being careful not to let it burn. Lower the heat to low if the polenta begins to bubble up. Remove from the heat, cover, and allow to sit for 5 minutes. Stir well.

2. To form your dumplings, use two spoons—one tablespoon and one smaller spoon. Scoop out a rounded spoonful with the tablespoon. Use the smaller spoon to form the pieces into small balls or football-shaped ovals, and place on a plate. If you wish, you can reform the pieces once they have cooled on the plate. Chill in the freezer for 10 minutes.

3. Meanwhile, place a 3-quart pot over medium heat. Add the chili powder and cumin and cook for 1 minute, stirring constantly. Lower the heat to medium-high, add all the remaining soup ingredients, except the cilantro, and cook for 20 minutes, stirring occasionally.

4. When the polenta is done chilling, add to the soup and cook for 3 minutes, stirring occasionally. Add the cilantro and stir well before serving.

Variations

- For **Tortilla Soup,** replace the polenta with tortilla chips. Garnish each bowl of soup with a handful of chips before serving.
- For a quicker version, use store-bought premade polenta (see page 96), chopped into 1-inch pieces.
- Get creative with your dumplings. Add 1 teaspoon of minced fresh cilantro and ½ teaspoon each of chili powder and ground cumin to the polenta after it has cooked and before it is chilled.
- Sauté the onion, celery, and garlic in 1 tablespoon of oil over high heat for 3 minutes, stirring constantly and adding small amounts of water or stock, if necessary, to prevent sticking, before adding the remaining ingredients.
- Replace the black beans with pinto, kidney, or navy.
- You can use **flour dumplings**. To do so, combine ½ cup of all-purpose or white spelt flour in a bowl with 1 teaspoon minced flat-leaf parsley, 1 teaspoon of baking powder, ¼ teaspoon of sea salt and a pinch each of ground black pepper and crushed red pepper flakes. Add ¼ cup of soy, rice, or almond milk and 2 teaspoons of olive or coconut oil and knead into a ball. Add additional soy milk, if necessary, to have a just slightly moist dough. Allow to sit for 10 minutes. Break off rounded half-tablespoon-size pieces in small, football-shaped ovals and add to the soup. Cook for 10 minutes before serving. Feel free to serve these dumplings in any of the lighter soups in this book.

continues

continued

- For an Italian version, replace the chili powder, and cumin with 2 teaspoons of dried oregano, 1 teaspoon of dried thyme, and ½ teaspoon of minced fresh rosemary. Replace the cilantro with 2 tablespoons each of finely chopped fresh basil and flat-leaf parsley. Add 2 teaspoons of balsamic vinegar along with the tamari.
- You can enhance the polenta dumplings by adding the following after it is cooked and before it is chilled: 1 tablespoon each of minced fresh basil and flat-leaf parsley, ½ teaspoon of dried oregano, and ¼ teaspoon of dried thyme.

Veggie Coq au Vin

Popularized by Julia Child and said to grace the tables of Julius Caesar, coq au vin is considered a classic in French cuisine. This vegan version spares the chicken and uses a vegan chicken-style alternative to create a memorable meal. Serve over rice or quinoa and top with Caramelized Onions (page 205) and Crispy Sunchokes (page 202).

SERVES 6 TO 8

4 cups vegetable stock (see page 25) or water

2 cups red wine (try Burgundy)

2 bay leaves

1 teaspoon dried thyme, or 1 tablespoon fresh

10 pearl onions, peeled and halved (1 cup)

½ cup thinly sliced celery

6 garlic cloves, pressed or minced

1 cup thinly sliced carrot

1 cup chopped potato (½-inch pieces)

1 cup quartered cremini mushrooms

10 to 12 ounces Beyond Meat chicken-style strips, or chicken-style seitan, chopped into ½-inch pieces (1 ½ cups)

3 tablespoons tomato paste

1 tablespoon balsamic vinegar

¼ to ½ teaspoon liquid smoke, or 2 teaspoons smoked paprika (optional)

3 tablespoons finely chopped fresh flat-leaf parsley

2 teaspoons sea salt, or to taste

½ teaspoon ground black pepper

Pinch of cayenne pepper

2 teaspoons wheat-free tamari or other soy sauce (optional)

3 tablespoons flour (try gluten-free)

1½ tablespoons olive oil

1. Place the vegetable stock in a 3-quart pot over medium-high heat. Add the wine, bay leaves, thyme, onion, celery, garlic, carrot, and potato and cook for 5 minutes, stirring occasionally.
2. Add the mushrooms, vegan chicken, and tomato paste and cook for 15 minutes, stirring occasionally.
3. Add the balsamic vinegar and liquid smoke, if using, and the parsley, salt, black pepper, cayenne pepper, and tamari and stir well.
4. Create a roux by placing a small sauté pan over high heat. Add the flour and cook for 1 minute, stirring constantly. Add the oil and stir well. Transfer to the pot and mix well. Cook until the soup thickens slightly, about 5 minutes, stirring occasionally. Remove the bay leaves before serving.

Variations

- Sauté the onion, celery, and garlic in 1 tablespoon of oil over high heat for 3 minutes, stirring constantly, before adding the remaining ingredients.
- You can omit the toasting of the flour and just combine the flour and oil in a bowl before adding to the soup. For an oil-free version, omit the flour and oil altogether.
- Replace the cremini mushrooms with morel, porcini, or chanterelle.
- Add 2 tablespoons of chiffonaded fresh basil and 1 tablespoon of chopped fresh marjoram along with the parsley.

 Split Pea Soup

Enjoyed since ancient Greek and Roman times, and even garnering a mention in Aristophanes' *The Birds*, split pea soup is another essential dish to include in any soup book, even if it does go over thirty minutes. The longer you cook this soup, the thicker it will become. For a quicker version, replace the split peas with red lentils and add only 6 cups of water. Top with Vegan Crème Fraîche (page 195) and Herbed Croutons (page 200) or serve with Herbed Bread Sticks (page 209).

SERVES 6 TO 8

8 cups vegetable stock (see page 25)

1¼ cups diced yellow onion

¾ cup thinly sliced celery

¾ cup uncooked yellow or green split peas, rinsed and drained well

2 bay leaves

¾ teaspoon minced fresh rosemary

½ teaspoon dried thyme

Pinch of crushed red pepper flakes

1½ cups diced carrot

1 cup diced potato

½ teaspoon liquid smoke

5 ounces tempeh bacon, store-bought or homemade (see page 208)

1 tablespoon finely chopped fresh marjoram

2¾ teaspoons sea salt, or to taste

½ teaspoon ground black pepper

1 tablespoon plus 2 teaspoons wheat-free tamari or other soy sauce (optional)

1. Place the vegetable stock in a 3-quart pot over medium heat. Add the onion, celery, split peas, bay leaves, rosemary, thyme, and crushed red pepper flakes and cook for 40 minutes, stirring occasionally.

2. Add the carrot, potato, and liquid smoke and cook until the soup thickens, about 15 minutes, stirring occasionally.

3. Meanwhile prepare the tempeh bacon according to the package instructions, or follow the recipe on page 208. Chop into small pieces and set aside.

4. Remove the bay leaves, season the soup with marjoram, salt, black pepper, and tamari, and stir well. Top each serving with the tempeh bacon.

Variations

- Add ½ cup of diced shiitake mushrooms along with the onion.
- Add 3 tablespoons of finely chopped fresh flat-leaf parsley and stir well, just before serving.
- You can sauté the onion in 1 tablespoon of oil over high heat for 3 minutes, stirring constantly and adding small amounts of water or stock, if necessary, to prevent sticking, before adding the remaining ingredients.

Brazilian Black Bean Soup with Baked Plantain

Black beans form the base of this ultimate Latin American soup. The addition of orange juice adds a subtle sweetness and the distinctive Brazilian twist. If no plantains are available, you may use just-ripe bananas. Amazing with Vegan Crème Fraîche (page 195) and Candied Pepitas (page 192) or toasted pepitas (see page 213), and a sprig of cilantro.

SERVES 6 TO 8

BAKED PLANTAINS

1 large ripe plantain (see page 57), sliced diagonally into ¼-inch slices (2 cups)

1 tablespoon pure maple syrup or sweetener of choice

1 tablespoon freshly squeezed orange juice

2 teaspoons oil (try coconut)

Pinch of sea salt

Pinch of chili powder (try chipotle)

Pinch of ground cinnamon

BLACK BEAN SOUP

2 teaspoons ground cumin

1 teaspoon chili powder

1¼ cups diced yellow onion

4 large garlic cloves, pressed or minced

1 teaspoon seeded and diced jalapeño pepper

4 cups vegetable stock (see page 25) or water

2 (15-ounce) cans black beans, rinsed and drained well, or 3 cups cooked (see page 220)

¾ cup diced carrot

½ cup seeded and diced red bell pepper

1 cup fresh or frozen corn

½ teaspoon orange zest

¼ cup freshly squeezed orange juice

2 teaspoons sea salt, or to taste

¼ teaspoon ground black pepper

⅛ teaspoon chipotle chile powder (optional)

⅛ teaspoon ground cloves (optional)

¼ teaspoon liquid smoke (optional)

2 tablespoons finely chopped fresh cilantro

continues

continued

1. Preheat the oven to 375°F. Prepare the plantains: Place the plantain ingredients in a small bowl and mix well. Transfer to a well-oiled baking sheet and bake until golden brown, about 10 minutes, flipping once after 6 minutes. Carefully transfer to a serving plate so the plantains do not stick to the pan as they cool down.
2. Meanwhile, place a 3-quart pot over high heat. Place the cumin and chili powder in the pot and cook for 1 minute, stirring constantly. Add the onion, garlic, and jalapeño, and stir well.
3. Lower the heat to medium-high, add the vegetable stock, black beans, and carrot, and cook for 15 minutes, stirring occasionally. Add the red bell pepper and corn and cook for 5 minutes, stirring occasionally. Add all the remaining ingredients, except the cilantro, and cook for 5 minutes, stirring occasionally. Add the cilantro and mix well.
4. Top each serving with a few pieces of plantain and enjoy.

Variations
- For a thicker soup, you can carefully blend half of the soup before serving. Or you may give it several buzzes with an immersion blender before serving.
- You can sauté the spices in 1 tablespoon of oil before adding the onion.
- Replace the black beans with pinto, kidney, adzuki, or your favorite.
- Replace the carrot, bell pepper, and corn with assorted vegetables, including chopped kale, parsnip, or cauliflower.

Adzuki Bean Soup with Enoki Mushrooms

Adzuki beans, also known as azuki or aduki beans, are an ancient food with origins in East Asia and the Himalayas. Beloved in Japanese, Chinese, and Korean cuisine, the bean is often used as the base of sweet desserts. This savory soup has the addition of enoki mushrooms—the long, slender, and delicately flavored white mushroom that is another popular ingredient in the region. Feel free to substitute shiitakes or other mushrooms, if necessary. Top with Sweet and Spicy Toasted Nori Sheets (page 191).

SERVES 6 TO 8

1½ tablespoons toasted sesame oil

1¼ cups diced yellow onion

1½ tablespoons peeled and minced fresh ginger

2 teaspoons seeded and diced hot chile pepper (see the Scoville scale on page 57)

½ cup diced shiitake mushrooms

4 cups vegetable stock (see page 25) or water

2 (15-ounce) cans adzuki beans, rinsed and drained well, or 3 cups cooked (see page 220)

½ cup thinly sliced carrot

¾ cup thinly sliced burdock root or additional carrot

½ cup seeded and diced red bell pepper

2 tablespoons plus 1 teaspoon wheat-free tamari or other soy sauce

2 to 3 tablespoons arame (optional)

1 teaspoon sea salt, or to taste

5 ounces enoki mushrooms, bottoms trimmed (about 1 cup)

2 tablespoons finely chopped fresh cilantro

1. Place the toasted sesame oil in a 3-quart pot over medium-high heat. Add the onion, ginger, chile pepper, and shiitake mushrooms and cook for 3 minutes, stirring frequently and adding small amounts of water, if necessary, to prevent sticking.
2. Add all the remaining ingredients, except the enoki mushrooms and cilantro, and cook for 15 minutes, stirring occasionally.
3. Add the enoki mushrooms and cook for 8 minutes, stirring occasionally. Add the cilantro and stir well before serving.

Variations

- Add 1½ cups of thinly sliced kale, spinach, dandelion greens, or nettles along with the enoki mushrooms.
- Replace the enoki mushrooms with ¾ cup of diced cremini, oyster, or button mushrooms and add along with the shiitakes.
- Replace the adzuki beans with other beans, such as great northern, black, or kidney.

North African Tagine with Broiled Tofu

Named after the earthenware dish in which it is traditionally prepared, tagine is a stew of North African origins. To transport yourself to Casablanca for the evening, serve over a bed of millet (see page 218), top with a dollop of Vegan Crème Fraîche (page 195), a spoonful of Tapenade (page 193) or diced olives, and a sprinkle of chopped pistachio nuts or toasted slivered almonds (see page 213).

SERVES 6 TO 8

TAGINE

- 1 tablespoon ground cumin
- 2 teaspoons ground coriander
- 5 cups vegetable stock (see page 25) or water
- ¼ teaspoon saffron threads (see page 42)
- 6 ounces tomato paste
- ½ cup freshly squeezed orange juice
- 2 cups cubed eggplant (½-inch pieces)
- 1 cup diced yellow onion
- 5 garlic cloves, pressed or minced
- ½ teaspoon ground cinnamon
- ¼ teaspoon ground cardamom
- ½ cup raisins
- 1 tablespoon plus 1 teaspoon wheat-free tamari or other soy sauce
- 1 teaspoon sea salt, or to taste
- ½ teaspoon ground black pepper
- Pinch of crushed red pepper flakes
- ¾ cup diced carrot
- 1 cup chopped zucchini (½-inch pieces)
- 3 tablespoons finely chopped fresh flat-leaf parsley
- 2 tablespoons chiffonaded fresh mint, for garnish

BROILED TOFU

- 2 tablespoons wheat-free tamari or other soy sauce
- 1½ tablespoons oil (try coconut)
- 14 ounces extra-firm tofu, cut into ¼-inch cubes

1. Prepare the tagine: Place a 3-quart pot over medium-high heat. Add all the remaining Tagine ingredients, except the zucchini, parsley, and mint, and cook for 15 minutes, stirring occasionally.
2. Meanwhile, prepare the tofu. Heat the oven to HIGH BROIL. Place the tamari and the oil on a small baking sheet and stir well. Add the tofu and stir until evenly coated. Broil for 8 minutes, carefully stirring a few times to ensure even cooking. Add to the pot.
3. Add the zucchini to the pot and cook for 8 minutes, stirring occasionally. Add the parsley and stir well. Garnish with mint before serving.

Variations
- Add ½ cup of uncooked millet along with the vegetable stock.
- Add ½ cup of red wine along with the vegetable stock.

continues

117

North African Tagine with Broiled Tofu *continued*

- Add 2 bay leaves along with the vegetable stock. Remove before serving.
- You can sauté the onion and garlic in 1 tablespoon of oil over high heat for 3 minutes, stirring constantly and adding small amounts of water or stock, if necessary, to prevent sticking, before adding the remaining ingredients.
- Replace the zucchini and carrot with parsnip and Brussels sprouts.
- Replace the parsley with fresh cilantro or 1 tablespoon of minced fresh dill.
- Replace the tofu with chickpeas or cannellini beans.
- You can add ½ cup of chopped kalamata olives along with the zucchini.
- Replace the eggplant with peeled and seeded butternut or buttercup squash.

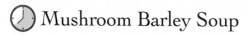 Mushroom Barley Soup

With ten thousand years on the world's culinary scene, barley is one of the oldest culti-vated crops. Another must-have in any soup book, this recipe will go over the thirty minutes, given the cooking time for the barley. You may need to add additional water, depending on temperature of the stove and how much liquid evaporates during the cooking process (you are looking for a soupy consistency). Top with Crispy Kale (page 203) and Tempeh Bacon (page 208).

SERVES 6 TO 8

1 tablespoon oil (try coconut)

1¼ cups diced yellow onion

¾ cup thinly sliced celery

6 garlic cloves, pressed or minced

7 cups vegetable stock (see page 25) or water

1 cup red wine

2 bay leaves

¾ cup diced shiitake mushrooms

½ cup uncooked pearl barley, rinsed and drained well

½ teaspoon ground black pepper

½ teaspoon ground nutmeg

Pinch of crushed red pepper flakes

2 cups diced cremini mushrooms

1 cup diced carrot

¾ cup seeded and diced red bell pepper

1 teaspoon sea salt, or to taste

2½ tablespoons wheat-free tamari or other soy sauce (optional)

3 tablespoons finely chopped fresh flat-leaf parsley

1. Place the oil in a 3-quart pot over high heat. Add the onion, celery, and garlic and cook for 3 minutes, stirring frequently and adding small amounts of water, if necessary, to prevent sticking.
2. Lower the heat to medium-high, add the veg-etable stock, wine, bay leaves, shiitake mush-rooms, barley, pepper, nutmeg, and crushed red pepper flakes, and cook for 30 minutes, stirring occasionally.
3. Add the mushrooms and carrot and cook for 10 minutes, stirring occasionally. Add the bell pepper, salt, and tamari, if using, and cook until the barley is tender, about 10 minutes, stirring occasionally. Remove the bay leaves, add the parsley, and stir well before serving.

Variations

- You can create an oil-free version by omitting the oil and using the water sauté method discussed on page 217.
- Replace the cremini with shiitake, oys-ter, portobello, or button mushrooms.
- Add 1 cup of cubed and roasted tofu or tempeh (see page 215), or seitan.
- Add ¼ to ½ teaspoon of liquid smoke.
- For a thirty-minute version, replace the barley with red lentils and use only 6 cups of vegetable stock. Season to taste with salt and pepper.

Cha-Cha Chili with Tempeh

Looking for a dish to bring to your next chili cook-off? Give this one a try. I guarantee that you will not miss the meat in this scrumptious vegan chili, made with tempeh. Top with Vegan Crème Fraîche (page 195) and Candied Pepitas (page 192) or toasted pepitas (see page 213).

SERVES 6 TO 8

1½ tablespoons chili powder

1 tablespoon ground cumin

2 cups vegetable stock (see page 25) or water

1½ cups diced yellow onion

5 garlic cloves, pressed or minced

2 teaspoons seeded and diced jalapeño pepper

1 (14.5-ounce) can diced fire-roasted tomatoes, or 1½ cups chopped tomato

8 ounces tempeh, diced finely (see page 215)

1 (15-ounce) can pinto beans, rinsed and drained well, or 1½ cups cooked (see page 221)

¾ cup diced carrot

½ cup seeded and diced red bell pepper

1 cup fresh or frozen corn

2 teaspoons sea salt, or to taste

¼ teaspoon ground black pepper

½ teaspoon chipotle chile powder (optional)

1 tablespoon freshly squeezed lime juice

1 tablespoon wheat-free tamari or other soy sauce

Pinch of cayenne pepper (optional)

3 tablespoons finely chopped fresh cilantro

1. Place a 3-quart pot over high heat. Place the chili powder and cumin in the pot and cook for 1 minute, stirring constantly. Lower the heat to medium-high. Add the vegetable stock, onion, garlic, jalapeño pepper, fire-roasted tomatoes, tempeh, pinto beans, carrot, and bell pepper and cook for 10 minutes, stirring occasionally.
2. Add all the remaining ingredients, except the cilantro, and cook for 10 minutes, stirring occasionally. Add the cilantro, and stir well before serving.

Variations

- You can sauté the onion and garlic in 1 tablespoon of oil for 3 minutes over high heat, stirring frequently, before adding the vegetable stock.
- Replace the pinto beans with black beans.
- Replace the tempeh with an equivalent amount of grated extra-firm tofu or chopped seitan.

PART FOUR

CREAMY BLENDED SOUPS

This is the section where vegan soups truly shine. It is pretty much guaranteed that you will receive the "I can't believe it's vegan!" response from your guests as they *ooh* and *aah* with delight with each spoonful.

Here we will explore several of the ways in which we create the creaminess effect without the cream. The first way is by blending the soup with nuts or seeds, either whole or in a nut butter form. The nuts and seeds can be raw or roasted. Nuts can include cashews, as featured in Creamy Grilled Vegetable Soup with Cilantro Cream; Brazil nuts, as in the Garlic Lovers' Roasted Garlic Soup; pine nuts, as in the Grilled Eggplant Soup with Pine Nuts; macadamia nuts, as in the Creamy Broccoli with Shiitake Mushrooms; hazelnuts, as in the Bavarian Asparagus Soup with Hazelnuts; and almonds, as in the Green Bean Amandine Soup. Seeds, such as sesame, may also be used, as when tahini (sesame seed butter) is included in the Mideast Chickpea Soup.

Another technique involves blending the soups with the inclusion of a plant-based milk, such as coconut (Roasted Squash with Coconut Soup), soy milk (Rosemary Potato Soup with Roasted Leek and Garlic), or soy creamer (Curried Pumpkin Soup). You can also use vegan cheese (Cheesy Cauliflower Soup) and even vegan yogurt (Spinach Soup with Vegan Yogurt and Toasted Sesame Seeds).

Experiment with other plant-based milks on the market, such as almond, rice, hemp, and oat, to see how each type creates a new flavor for your soups.

An additional way to create creaminess is to include starchy vegetables, such as potato, carrot, squash, or parsnip, in your soup. Simply blending the ingredients will create a creamy soup. Blending with beans, such as the cannellini beans in the Creamy White Bean Soup with Broiled Artichoke Hearts, will also produce the desired outcome. Finally, our Holy Mole Soup with Veggies is made creamy by blending the soup with dark chocolate chips. Go figure!

Chef's Tips and Tricks

Blending Soups

All the soups in this section involve blending. For best results, I recommend using a strong blender, such as a Vitamix (see page 247). It is strong enough that you will get an amazing texture when blending the nuts with the rest of the ingredients. It is also large enough so that you will not often need to blend in batches. If you are using a smaller blender, carefully blend in small batches, using a large bowl or extra pot to which you can transfer the blended portions before returning them to the original pot. Keep in mind that you are dealing with very hot liquids, so err on the side of caution and blend in smaller batches if you are not sure how much liquid your blender can handle without overflowing. You can also allow the soup to cool before blending. The strength of your blender will determine how creamy your soups will be.

Reaching Desired Consistency

If, after blending, you find that your blended soup is thicker than you prefer, add small amounts of plant-based milk to thin it to your desired consistency. You can also use this technique for soups that you are reheating after refrigerating.

Creamy Fire-Roasted Tomato Soup with Dill

My guess is that you were not aware that the first-known recipe for tomato soup was created by Maria Parloa, one of the first celebrity chefs, way back in 1872. The Campbell's soup version appeared several years later, and the rest is culinary history. Fire roasting adds a smoky depth to this vegan version, creaminess courtesy of soy creamer. Compare this soup to the Raw Cream of Tomato Soup (page 173) to see how cooking can influence the flavor of a dish. Top with Vegan Crème Fraîche (page 195) and Herbed Croutons (page 200).

SERVES 6 TO 8

2 cups vegetable stock (see page 25) or water

2 (14.5-ounce) cans fire-roasted tomatoes, or 3 cups chopped tomato with juices

1¼ cups diced yellow onion

½ cup thinly sliced celery

5 garlic cloves

¼ cup chopped fennel bulb (optional)

½ cup diced shiitake mushrooms

3 tablespoons tomato paste

2½ teaspoons sea salt, or to taste

¼ teaspoon ground black pepper

Pinch of crushed red pepper flakes

1 tablespoon balsamic vinegar

2 cups soy creamer or soy, rice, or almond milk (see page 222)

1½ tablespoons minced fresh dill

1. Place the vegetable stock in a 3-quart pot over medium-high heat. Add all the remaining ingredients, except the soy creamer and dill, and cook for 15 minutes, stirring occasionally. Lower the heat, if necessary, to prevent boiling.

2. Carefully transfer to a strong blender and blend until very creamy. Return the mixture to the pot over medium heat.

3. Add the soy creamer, stir well, and cook for 5 minutes, stirring occasionally. Add the dill and stir well before serving.

Variations

- You can sauté the onion, celery, and garlic in 1 tablespoon of oil for 3 minutes over high heat, stirring frequently, before adding the vegetable stock.
- Add ⅛ cup of red wine along with the onion.
- Replace the dill with 3 tablespoons of chiffonaded basil.
- You can add 1 tablespoon of olive oil along with the dill.

Roasted Red Pepper Soup

Vibrant and velvety, this creamy soup is also a source of the important antioxidant lycopene, found in abundance in red bell peppers. The creaminess comes from silken tofu. Enjoy this soup with a topping of Tofu Feta (page 207) or Vegan Crème Fraîche (page 195), a drizzle of Balsamic Reduction (page 189) and a spoonful of Tapenade (page 193) or diced olives.

SERVES 6 TO 8

4 large red bell peppers (about 3 cups roasted)

Olive oil, for basting

3 cups vegetable stock (see page 25) or water

1½ cups diced yellow onion

5 large garlic cloves

½ cup thinly sliced celery

½ cup thinly sliced shiitake mushrooms

2 teaspoons seeded and diced jalapeño pepper

1½ cups chopped tomato (½-inch pieces), or 1 (14.5-ounce) can fire-roasted diced tomatoes

12.3 ounces soft silken tofu

1½ teaspoons sea salt, or to taste

¼ teaspoon ground black pepper

Pinch of cayenne pepper

2 tablespoons balsamic vinegar

2 tablespoons wheat-free tamari or other soy sauce (optional)

1 tablespoon minced fresh dill

Shredded unsweetened coconut, for garnish (optionally toasted; see page 190)

1. Preheat the oven to 475°F. Slice the peppers in half and remove the seeds. Lightly baste the peppers with oil, place on a baking sheet, and roast for 25 minutes. Remove from the oven. Transfer the peppers to a large blender.
2. Meanwhile, place the vegetable stock in a 3-quart pot over medium-high heat. Add all the ingredients, except the dill and coconut, and cook for 15 minutes, stirring occasionally.
3. Carefully transfer to the blender with the bell peppers and blend until creamy.
4. Return the mixture to the pot, add the dill, and stir well. Garnish with shredded coconut before serving.

Variations
- You can broil the peppers until charred, about 10 minutes, flipping periodically to ensure even cooking.
- Add 2 cups of your favorite veggies after blending. Try with corn, peas, diced carrot, or chopped spinach.
- Replace the dill with 3 tablespoons of finely chopped fresh chives.
- Replace the tofu with an equivalent amount of soy, rice, or almond milk.

Cream of Mushroom Soup

How can something so simple taste so divine? This is a vegan twist on a favorite American soup with French and Italian origins. You can blend all or part of the soup to reach your desired consistency. Experiment with different mushrooms and notice the different flavor profiles created. Over-the-top delicious when topped with Vegan Crème Fraîche (page 195) and Red Pepper Coulis (page 197).

SERVES 6 TO 8

3½ cups vegetable stock (see page 25) or water

1¼ cups diced yellow onion

4 garlic cloves, pressed or minced

4 cups chopped cremini mushrooms (½-inch pieces)

½ cup diced shiitake mushrooms

¼ teaspoon ground nutmeg

2 teaspoons sea salt, or to taste

¼ teaspoon ground black pepper

Pinch of crushed red pepper flakes

1½ cups soy creamer, or soy, rice, or almond milk (see page 222)

1 tablespoon freshly squeezed lemon juice

2 tablespoons minced fresh flat-leaf parsley

1 tablespoon minced fresh chives or additional tablespoon fresh flat-leaf parsley

2 teaspoons nutritional yeast (optional)

2 teaspoons wheat-free soy tamari or other soy sauce to taste (optional)

¼ teaspoon smoked paprika (optional)

3 tablespoons finely chopped green onion, for garnish

1. Place the vegetable stock in a 3-quart pot over medium heat. Add the onion, garlic, mushrooms, nutmeg, salt, black pepper, and crushed red pepper flakes and cook for 15 minutes, stirring occasionally.
2. Carefully transfer to a large blender, add the soy creamer, and blend until very creamy. Return the mixture to the pot.
3. Add the remaining ingredients and cook over medium-high heat for 5 minutes, stirring occasionally. Garnish with green onion before serving. Enjoy!

Variations

- Replace the soy creamer with ¾ cup of cashews or macadamia nuts (optionally toasted; see page 213) blended with ¾ cup of water until very creamy.
- Add 2 cups of well-rinsed and drained chopped spinach after blending.
- Add 1 cup of seeded and diced red bell pepper after blending.
- Replace the cremini mushrooms with an assortment that can include portobello, shiitake, button, oyster, morel, porcini, and chanterelle.
- You can sauté the onion and garlic in 1 tablespoon of oil for 3 minutes over high heat, stirring frequently, before adding the vegetable stock.

Coconut Carrot Soup
with Ginger and Dill

Loaded with nutrients and bursting with flavor, this is your go-to soup when you are looking for a simple healthy meal. Carrots and other starchy vegetables, such as parsnips or potatoes, make a perfect base for creamy soups, especially when combined with a plant-based milk, such as coconut. Top with Vegan Crème Fraîche (page 195), Herbed Croutons (page 200), and toasted pepitas (see page 213).

SERVES 6 TO 8

4 cups vegetable stock (see page 25) or water

1 (15-ounce) can coconut milk

1¼ cups diced yellow onion

¾ cup thinly sliced celery

2 tablespoons peeled and minced fresh ginger

2 teaspoons seeded and diced jalapeño pepper

4 cups chopped carrot (½-inch pieces)

½ cup diced shiitake mushrooms

2 teaspoons sea salt, or to taste

¼ teaspoon ground black pepper

¼ teaspoon ground nutmeg

Pinch of cayenne pepper

1½ tablespoons minced fresh dill

1. Place the vegetable stock in a 3-quart pot over medium-high heat. Add all the remaining ingredients, except the dill, and cook for 15 minutes, stirring occasionally.
2. Carefully transfer to a blender and blend until creamy.
3. Return the mixture to the pot, add the dill, and stir well before serving.

Variations
- Add 1 tablespoon of curry powder and replace the dill with fresh cilantro.
- Add 2 cups of assorted vegetables, chopped small, after the soup is blended. Try with broccoli, corn, asparagus, purple cabbage, or your favorites. Cook over low heat until the veggies are just tender, and stir well before serving.

Corn Chowder

Another bell ringer, this soup delivers a rich, creamy flavor without the cream. Perfect in the height of summer when corn is in abundance. Compare this version with the Raw Corn Chowder (page 179) to experience how cooking the corn adds a new dimension of taste sensations. Top with Red Pepper Coulis (page 197) and Crispy Kale (page 203).

SERVES 6 TO 8

4½ cups vegetable stock (see page 25) or water

4 cups fresh or frozen corn

1¼ cups diced yellow onion

¾ cup thinly sliced celery

¼ cup diced shiitake mushrooms

5 garlic cloves

2 teaspoons sea salt, or to taste

¼ teaspoon ground black pepper

1 teaspoon ground turmeric (optional)

½ teaspoon chipotle chile powder, or 1 teaspoon chili powder (optional)

Pinch of cayenne pepper

¾ cup cashews (optionally toasted; see page 213)

1 tablespoon freshly squeezed lime juice

1½ tablespoons minced fresh dill

1 cup sliced cherry tomatoes or seeded and diced red bell pepper

Black sesame seeds, for garnish

1. Place the vegetable stock in a 3-quart pot over medium heat. Add 3 cups of the corn and all the remaining ingredients, except the cashews, lime juice, dill, cherry tomatoes, and sesame seeds, and cook for 15 minutes, stirring occasionally.
2. Place the cashews in a large blender with 2 cups of the liquid from the pot and blend until very creamy. Carefully place the remaining contents of the pot in the blender and blend until very creamy. Return the mixture to the pot over medium heat.
3. Add the remaining ingredients, including the remaining cup of corn, and except the sesame seeds, and cook for 5 minutes, stirring occasionally. Garnish with sesame seeds before serving.

Variations

- Replace the cashews with macadamia nuts, Brazil nuts, toasted hazelnuts (see page 213), or slivered almonds.
- Replace the cashews with 1½ cups of soy, coconut, or rice milk and omit ½ cup of the vegetable stock.
- Replace the dill with fresh cilantro, basil, or flat-leaf parsley.
- You can sauté the onion, celery, and garlic in 1 tablespoon of oil for 3 minutes over high heat, stirring frequently, before adding the vegetable stock.

Spinach Soup with Vegan Yogurt and Toasted Sesame Seeds

This exquisite soup derives its creamy goodness from blending the ingredients with soy yogurt. You may enjoy it warm, or allow it to cool in the refrigerator and serve chilled on warm summer days, for a revitalizing meal. The addition of corn mentioned in the variations adds another layer of flavor and fun color. Serve with Crostini (page 198) topped with Tapenade (page 193).

SERVES 6 TO 8

4 cups vegetable stock (see page 25) or water

1¼ cups diced yellow onion

½ cup thinly sliced celery

6 garlic cloves

½ cup diced shiitake mushrooms

2 cups, tightly packed, rinsed and well-drained fresh spinach (5 ounces)

2 teaspoons sea salt, or to taste

¼ teaspoon ground black pepper

¼ teaspoon crushed red pepper flakes, or to taste

2 cups unsweetened plain soy yogurt

1 to 1½ tablespoons minced fresh dill

1½ cups chopped tomatoes, for garnish

Toasted sesame seeds, for garnish (see page 213)

Sprigs of fresh dill, for garnish

1. Place the vegetable stock in a 3-quart pot over medium heat. Add the onion, celery, garlic, and mushrooms and cook for 10 minutes, stirring occasionally. Add the spinach, salt, black pepper, and crushed red pepper flakes and cook for 5 minutes, stirring occasionally.
2. Add the soy yogurt and stir well. Carefully transfer the contents of the pot to a strong blender and blend until creamy. Return the mixture to the pot.
4. Add the remaining ingredients except for the dill and stir well. Garnish with tomatoes, sesame seeds, and a sprig of dill before serving.

Variations
- Add 1 cup of fresh or frozen corn after blending.
- Sauté the onion, celery, and garlic in 1½ tablespoons of oil for 3 minutes over medium-high heat, stirring frequently, before adding the remaining ingredients.
- Replace the dill with 2 tablespoons of minced fresh basil or parsley. Add 1 teaspoon each of fresh oregano and thyme.
- Add ¼ cup of diced fennel bulb along with the celery.
- Add an additional cup of chopped fresh spinach after blending. Stir well before serving.

▲ Mayan Tomato and Corn Soup • page 38

▲ Thai Coconut Soup with Lemongrass • page 43

⊿ Ragout of Spring/Summer Vegetables • page 45

⊿ Roasted Root Vegetable Soup • page 63

▲ Un-Chicken Noodle Soup • page 79

▲ Hot Pot with Soba Noodles, Seared Shiitake Mushrooms,
and Baby Bok Choy • page 80

▲ Brazilian Black Bean Soup with Baked Plantain • page 114

▲ Roasted Red Pepper Soup • page 126

▲ Corn Chowder • page 129

▲ Cheesy Cauliflower Soup • page 144

▲ Curried Pumpkin Soup • page 150

▲ Cantaloupe Rose Soup with Blueberry Cream • page 165

▲ Spicy Kale Soup with Pepitas • page 177

▲ Chilled Avacado Soup with
Cherry Tomato Salsa Fresca • page 183

Creamy Parsnip Soup
with Smoked Cherry Tomatoes

Parsnips are one of my favorite veggies. They add a sublime creaminess to dishes that is hard to top. Stove-top smokers are a wonderful addition to your kitchen gear, very simple to use, and will add a distinctive flavor to your creations (if you don't have a smoker, see Variations for a broil method). Top with Crispy Sunchokes (page 202) and a drizzle of Basil Oil (page 188).

SERVES 6 TO 8

1 pint cherry tomatoes

4 cups vegetable stock (see page 25) or water

1¼ cups diced yellow onion

¾ cup diced celery

5 large garlic cloves

4 cups chopped parsnip (½-inch pieces)

3 tablespoons nutritional yeast (optional)

1 teaspoon prepared horseradish (optional, but recommended)

⅛ teaspoon cayenne pepper

1½ cups soy, rice, or almond milk (see page 222)

2½ teaspoons sea salt, or to taste

¼ teaspoon ground black pepper

2 tablespoons finely chopped fresh flat-leaf parsley

Prepared horseradish, for garnish (optional)

Black sesame seeds, for garnish

1. Place wood chips in a smoker. Add the cherry tomatoes and smoke according to the manufacturer's instructions, about 15 minutes. Set aside.

2. Meanwhile, place the vegetable stock in a 3-quart pot over medium-high heat. Add the onion, celery, garlic, and parsnip and cook for 10 minutes, stirring occasionally.

3. Carefully transfer to a blender along with the nutritional yeast, horseradish, if using, and cayenne, and blend until creamy.

4. Return the mixture to the pot over medium heat, add the soy milk, salt, black pepper, and parsley, and stir well. Garnish each serving with a large spoonful of cherry tomatoes, a small dollop of horseradish, if using, and black sesame seeds before serving.

Variations

- Once the soup is blended, you can add 2 cups of chopped vegetables, such as sunchoke, zucchini, carrot, or your favorites.

- Replace the parsnip with 3 cups of chopped potato and 1 cup of chopped cauliflower.

continues

131

Creamy Parsnip Soup with Smoked Cherry Tomatoes *continued*

- Replace the cherry tomatoes with a combination of seeded and chopped red bell pepper and sliced shiitake mushrooms.
- Replace the parsley with fresh cilantro or basil, or 1 tablespoon of minced fresh dill.
- No smoker? No problem—you can broil the cherry tomatoes. Preheat the oven to HIGH BROIL. Place the cherry tomatoes on a baking sheet with 2 teaspoons of olive oil, a pinch each of sea salt and ground black pepper, and ¼ teaspoon of liquid smoke. Broil for 8 minutes. Add to the blended soup.

Garlic Lovers' Roasted Garlic Soup

A culinary as well as medicinal plant, garlic has its origins in Central Asia and has been enjoyed by humans for over seven thousand years. The creaminess of the soup comes from blending it with Brazil nuts. Hard-core garlic lovers can add an extra ½ cup of whole roasted cloves to the soup after blending. Super hard-core garlic lovers can add a few cloves of pressed or minced raw cloves just before serving. Drizzle with Basil Oil (page 188) and Red Oil (page 187), and top with Red Pepper Coulis (page 197) and Herbed Croutons (page 200).

SERVES 6 TO 8

4 to 5 large garlic heads (for 1 cup cloves)

Olive oil, for basting

2 teaspoons sea salt, or to taste

¼ teaspoon ground black pepper

¾ cup Brazil nuts

5 cups vegetable stock (see page 25) or water

1¼ cups diced yellow onion

½ cup thinly sliced celery

1 cup diced carrot

1 cup diced shiitake mushrooms

Pinch of cayenne pepper

1½ cups chopped zucchini or gold bar squash (½-inch pieces)

2 tablespoons finely chopped fresh flat-leaf parsley

2 tablespoons chiffonaded fresh basil

1 tablespoon freshly squeezed lemon juice

2 to 3 raw garlic cloves, pressed or minced (optional)

1. Preheat the oven to 450°F. Slice off the very top portion of the garlic heads. Lightly baste with olive oil and add a pinch of salt and pepper. Place on a small casserole dish with a small amount of water, and cover. Roast for 25 minutes, or until soft and golden brown. Remove the garlic from the skins and measure out 1 cup of cloves. Place in a strong blender.

2. Meanwhile, place the Brazil nuts on a dry baking sheet and roast until golden brown, about 7 minutes. Transfer to the blender.

3. While the garlic and nuts roast, place the vegetable stock in a 3-quart pot over medium-high heat. Add all the remaining ingredients, except the zucchini, parsley, basil, lemon juice, and raw garlic, and cook for 10 minutes, stirring occasionally. Add the zucchini and cook for 5 minutes, stirring occasionally.

4. Once the garlic and Brazil nuts are in the blender, add 2 cups of the liquid from the pot to the blender and blend until very creamy. Return the mixture to the pot and stir well. Add the parsley, basil, lemon juice, and raw garlic, if using, and stir well before serving.

continues

Garlic Lovers' Roasted Garlic Soup *continued*

Variations

- You can sauté the onion and celery in 1 tablespoon of oil for 3 minutes over high heat, stirring frequently, before adding the vegetable stock.
- Add 1 cup of seeded and diced red bell pepper after blending.
- Replace the Brazil nuts with cashews or macadamia nuts.
- Replace the Brazil nuts with 1 cup of soy or coconut creamer, or soy or almond milk (see page 222).

Mideast Chickpea Soup

Believe it or not, peace in the Middle East can start in your own kitchen, with this recipe. Try it and I think you will understand why. The creaminess comes from blending the chickpeas with tahini, a ground sesame seed paste that is the Middle Eastern equivalent of our Western peanut butter. Top with Tofu Feta (page 207) and Basil Oil (page 188) and serve with Pita Chips (page 199).

SERVES 6 TO 8

2 teaspoons ground cumin

5 cups vegetable stock (see page 25) or water

1¼ cups diced onion

½ cup diced celery

6 garlic cloves, 5 left whole and 1 pressed

2 (15-ounce) cans chickpeas, rinsed and drained well

¾ cup creamy tahini

3 tablespoons freshly squeezed lemon juice

2 tablespoons nutritional yeast (optional)

Pinch of cayenne pepper

2 teaspoons sea salt, or to taste

¼ teaspoon ground black pepper

3 tablespoons finely chopped fresh flat-leaf parsley

1 tablespoon olive oil (optional)

¼ cup diced kalamata olives or Tapenade, for garnish (see page 193)

Fresh parsley or fresh oregano leaves, for garnish

1. Place the cumin in a 3-quart pot over high heat. Toast until golden brown and aromatic, about 2 minutes, stirring constantly.
2. Add the vegetable stock, onion, celery, the five whole cloves of the garlic, and one can of the chickpeas and cook for 10 minutes, stirring occasionally.
3. Carefully transfer to a blender and blend until creamy.
4. Return the mixture to the pot, add the remaining ingredients, except the pressed garlic, parsley, olive oil, if using, and olives, and cook for 10 minutes over medium-high heat, stirring occasionally. Add the pressed garlic, parsley, and olive oil, if using, and stir well. The whole chickpeas will sink to the bottom of the pot, so be sure to stir well before serving.
5. Garnish each serving with about 2 teaspoons of olives and a leaf of parsley.

Variations
- Replace the salt with 1½ tablespoons wheat-free tamari or other soy sauce.
- Add 1 cup of corn and 1 cup of seeded and diced red bell pepper after blending.
- Replace the chickpeas with cannellini beans or your favorite.
- Add 1 tablespoon of curry powder along with the cumin, and replace the parsley with cilantro for an Indian flair.

Roasted Squash with Coconut Soup

Combine coconut milk with freshly roasted squash and you will experience culinary magic unfold. Experiment with different types of squash such as acorn, buttercup, or kabocha and notice the amazing variety of flavor possible. For a thicker soup, leave out one cup of the vegetable stock. Top with Krispy Kale (page 203) or Crispy Sunchokes (page 202) and Toasted Coconut (see page 202).

SERVES 6 TO 8

6 cups seeded and cubed, unpeeled butternut squash (¾-inch cubes; 1 medium squash)

1 tablespoon oil (try coconut)

½ cup water

2 teaspoons sea salt, or to taste

Pinch of ground black pepper

2 cups vegetable stock (see page 25) or water

1¼ cups chopped onion

½ cup diced celery

5 garlic cloves

2 (15-ounce) cans coconut milk

¼ teaspoon ground cinnamon

⅛ teaspoon ground nutmeg

⅛ teaspoon crushed red pepper flakes

2 tablespoons toasted unsweetened shredded coconut (page 213) (optional)

2 teaspoons wheat-free tamari or other soy sauce (optional)

¼ teaspoon ground white pepper

2 tablespoons finely chopped fresh cilantro

1. Preheat the oven to 475°F. Place the squash, oil, water, and a pinch each of salt and black pepper on a small baking sheet or in a casserole dish and mix well. Bake for 20 minutes, stirring occasionally to ensure even cooking. Carefully transfer to a large blender.

2. Meanwhile, place the vegetable stock in a 3-quart pot over medium heat. Add all the remaining ingredients, except the remaining salt, white pepper, and cilantro, and cook for 15 minutes, stirring occasionally. Add the salt and white pepper and mix well.

3. Carefully transfer half of the contents of the pot to the blender. Blend until creamy. Transfer to a large serving bowl. Place the remaining mixture in the blender and carefully blend until creamy. Add to the serving bowl, along with the cilantro, and mix well before serving.

Variations

- Replace the squash with other winter varieties, or sweet potatoes or yams.
- Replace the coconut milk with coconut creamer, soy milk or creamer, or rice or almond milk (see page 222).
- For a lighter soup, replace one can of coconut milk with an equivalent amount of vegetable stock or water.
- Replace the cilantro with fresh basil or flat-leaf parsley.
- Feel free to peel the squash before chopping.

Creamy Broccoli Soup
with Shiitake Mushrooms

The beloved broccoli has been cultivated for thousands of years and is a nutritional powerhouse with lots of vitamin C and other valuable nutrients. This is the quintessential Template Recipe, with hundreds of possible variations. See how many you can come up with! Top with Vegan Crème Fraîche (page 195) and Caramelized Onions (page 205).

SERVES 6 TO 8

6 cups vegetable stock (see page 25) or water

1¼ cups chopped onion

¾ cup thinly sliced celery

6 garlic cloves

4 cups small broccoli florets

2½ teaspoons sea salt, or to taste

¼ teaspoon ground black pepper

Pinch of crushed red pepper flakes

1½ tablespoons oil (try coconut)

1½ cups diced shiitake mushrooms

¾ cup chopped macadamia nuts (optionally toasted; see page 213)

1 cup fresh or frozen corn

2 tablespoons finely chopped fresh cilantro

1. Place the vegetable stock in a 3-quart pot over medium-high heat. Add the onion, celery, garlic, and broccoli and cook for 15 minutes, stirring occasionally. Add the salt, pepper, and red pepper flakes, and stir well.

2. Meanwhile, place the oil in a sauté pan over high heat. Add the mushrooms and a pinch of salt and cook until the mushrooms are just soft, about 5 minutes, stirring frequently and adding small amounts of vegetable stock or water, if necessary, to prevent sticking. Set aside.

3. Place the macadamia nuts in a strong blender. Carefully transfer 4 cups of the soup to the blender and blend until very creamy. Add the remaining soup to the blender and blend well.

4. Return the mixture to the pot over medium-high heat, add the shiitake mushrooms and corn, and cook for 5 minutes, stirring occasionally. Add the cilantro, and stir well before serving.

Variations

- You can sauté the onion, celery, and garlic with 1 tablespoon of oil for 3 minutes over high heat, stirring frequently, before adding the vegetable stock.

continues

Creamy Broccoli Soup with Shiitake Mushrooms *continued*

- Replace the broccoli with romenesco, cauliflower, or mixed vegetables, such as zucchini, carrot, and parsnip.
- Replace the macadamia nuts with cashews, Brazil nuts, or blanched almonds.
- Replace the macadamia nuts with 1½ cups of nondairy milk, such as coconut, soy, rice, or almond (see page 222), and reduce the vegetable stock by ½ cup.
- Replace the shiitake mushrooms with cremini, portobello, button, or a combination.
- Replace the shiitake mushrooms and corn with chopped broccoli, cauliflower, peas, and diced carrot.
- Replace the cilantro with parsley, lovage, sorrel, marjoram, or 1 tablespoon of fresh dill
- Add 2 tablespoons of arame (see page 9) after the soup has been blended.

Bavarian Asparagus Soup with Hazelnuts

Considered the king of the veggies in Germany, asparagus reigns supreme in this soup. Toasted hazelnuts, another abundant food in the region, gives this soup its creaminess and solidifies its place in the zeitgeist of vegan cuisine. Top with Red Pepper Coulis (page 197) and Vegetable Chips (page 201).

SERVES 6 TO 8

¾ cup hazelnuts

4 cups vegetable stock (see page 25) or water

1¼ cups diced yellow onion

½ cup thinly sliced celery

5 garlic cloves

¼ cup diced shiitake mushrooms

5 cups chopped green or white asparagus, ends trimmed (½-inch pieces)

2 teaspoons sea salt, or to taste

¼ teaspoon ground black pepper

Pinch of crushed red pepper flakes

1 cup soy or coconut creamer, or soy, rice, or almond milk (see page 222)

1 tablespoon wheat-free tamari or other soy sauce, or to taste (optional)

2 tablespoons freshly squeezed lemon juice

1 tablespoon minced fresh dill

1. Preheat the oven to 375°F. Place the hazelnuts on a baking sheet and roast until golden brown and aromatic, about 15 minutes. Remove from the oven and allow to cool. Place between two clean dish towels and rub vigorously to remove the skins. Remove as much of the skin as possible. Place in a strong blender.
2. Meanwhile, place the vegetable stock in a 3-quart pot over medium-high heat. Add all the remaining ingredients, except the soy creamer, tamari, if using, lemon juice, and dill, and cook for 10 minutes, stirring occasionally.
3. Carefully transfer the contents of the pot to the blender and blend until very creamy. Return the mixture to the pot over low heat.
4. Add the remaining ingredients, except the dill, and cook for 10 minutes, stirring occasionally. Add the dill and stir well before serving.

Variations
- Live on the edge and use a hazelnut-flavored soy or coconut creamer.
- Replace the dill with 2 tablespoons of minced fresh cilantro, flat-leaf parsley, or basil.
- Add 2 cups of chopped asparagus, broccoli, cauliflower, or romenesco broccoli after the soup is blended.
- You can sauté the onion, celery, and garlic in 1 tablespoon of oil for 3 minutes over high heat, stirring frequently, before adding the vegetable stock.

Creamy Grilled Vegetable Soup
with Cilantro Cream

This is a creative way to enjoy the abundance of summer vegetables available during grilling season. Each assortment of veggies you use in the recipe will create a new and uniquely flavored soup. Be sure to grill extra vegetables to add back into the soup once it's blended. Top with Crispy Kale (page 203) or Vegetable Chips (page 201).

SERVES 6 TO 8

SOUP

5 cups vegetable stock (see page 25) or water

½ cup diced celery

6 garlic cloves

½ cup diced shiitake mushrooms

1 medium-size yellow onion, sliced into ½-inch rounds

1 large portobello mushroom

1 large red bell pepper, quartered and seeded

1 large zucchini, cut lengthwise into ½-inch strips

1½ tablespoons olive oil

2½ teaspoons sea salt, or to taste

½ teaspoon ground black pepper

¾ cup unsalted, roasted cashews

1 tablespoon freshly squeezed lime juice

½ teaspoon chili powder

¼ teaspoon chipotle chile powder (optional)

1 tablespoon wheat-free tamari or other soy sauce (optional)

2 teaspoons balsamic vinegar

Pinch of crushed red pepper flakes

2 tablespoons finely chopped fresh cilantro

Cilantro sprigs, for garnish

CILANTRO CREAM

Makes 1 cup cilantro cream

1 cup vegan mayonnaise (Vegenaise or homemade; see page 226)

¼ cup finely chopped fresh cilantro

2 tablespoons freshly squeezed lime juice

Pinch of sea salt

Pinch of ground black pepper

Pinch of chipotle chile powder (optional)

1. Prepare the soup: Preheat a grill. Place the vegetable stock in a 3-quart pot over medium heat. Add the celery, shiitake mushrooms, and garlic and cook for 15 minutes, stirring occasionally.
2. Place the onion, portobello mushroom, bell pepper, and zucchini on a baking sheet. Drizzle with the olive oil and add ¼ teaspoon each of salt and pepper. Transfer the vegetables to the grill and grill until just tender and char marks appear on both sides, about 8 minutes, flipping a few times to ensure even cooking.

continues

continued

3. Chop the grilled vegetables into ½-inch pieces and measure out 4 cups. Place in the pot with all the remaining soup ingredients, including the remaining salt and pepper, and except the chopped cilantro, and cook for 5 minutes, stirring occasionally.

4. Meanwhile, prepare the cilantro cream: Place all its ingredients in a blender and blend until creamy. Transfer to a small bowl.

5. Carefully transfer the contents of the pot to a strong blender and blend until very creamy. Return the mixture to the pot, add the chopped cilantro (but not the sprigs), and stir well. Garnish each serving with a dollop of cilantro cream and a fresh sprig of cilantro before serving.

Variations

- Change up the vegetables you are grilling to include eggplant, bok choy, broccoli rabe, corn, tomato, and your favorites.
- If no grill is available, you can roast the vegetables. To do so, preheat the oven to 400°F. Chop the veggies and place them on a large baking sheet. Drizzle with olive oil and add ¼ teaspoon each of the salt and pepper. Roast for 20 minutes before adding to the soup.
- Replace the cilantro with fresh dill, basil, or flat-leaf parsley.

Grilled Eggplant Soup with Pine Nuts

Turn to this hearty and deeply satisfying recipe on those summer grilling nights. In addition to preparing with the common black-skinned eggplant, experiment with the purple, white or even the long, thin Japanese eggplants as well. Grill some extras to make sure you have enough eggplant for the 2 cups that the recipe calls for. Serve with Vegan Crème Fraîche (page 195) and garnish with additional pine nuts.

SERVES 6 TO 8

2 tablespoons olive oil

2¾ teaspoons sea salt

½ teaspoon ground black pepper

2 medium or 1 large eggplant, sliced lengthwise into ½-inch slices

5½ cups vegetable stock (see page 25) or water

1¼ cups diced yellow onion

½ cup thinly sliced celery

6 garlic cloves

1 (14.5-ounce) can diced fire-roasted tomatoes, or 1½ cups diced tomato

½ teaspoon dried oregano

¼ teaspoon dried thyme

¼ teaspoon crushed red pepper flakes

2 teaspoons balsamic vinegar

¾ cup pine nuts (optionally toasted; see page 213)

2 tablespoons finely chopped fresh flat-leaf parsley

2 tablespoons chiffonaded fresh basil

1 tablespoon chiffonaded fresh sage (optional)

1. Preheat the grill. Place the olive oil in a small bowl. Add ¼ teaspoon each of the sea salt and black pepper and stir well. Place the eggplant on the grill and cook, flipping a few times during the cooking process and basting each side with the olive oil, salt, and pepper, until char marks appear on both sides and the eggplant is just tender, about 10 minutes, depending upon the temperature of the grill. Transfer the eggplant to a measuring cup and measure out 2 cups, tightly packed, for use in this recipe. Transfer to a strong blender.

2. Meanwhile, place the vegetable stock in a 3-quart pot over medium heat. Add the onion, celery, garlic, tomatoes, oregano, thyme, and crushed red pepper flakes and cook for 15 minutes, stirring occasionally. Add the balsamic vinegar, pine nuts, remaining 2½ teaspoons of sea salt and ¼ teaspoon of black pepper, and stir well.

3. Carefully transfer to the blender, and blend until creamy. Return the mixture to the pot. Add the parsley, basil, and sage, if using, and stir well before serving.

continues

continued

Variations

- You can add 1½ cups of grilled and chopped broccoli rabe or portobello mushroom after the soup is blended.
- You can add 1 teaspoon each of dried oregano, thyme, and basil to the olive oil before basting.
- Replace the pine nuts with cashews, macadamia nuts, or Brazil nuts.
- If no grill is available, you can broil the eggplant. Preheat the oven to HIGH BROIL. Place the eggplant slices on a lightly oiled baking sheet. Brush with olive oil, and top with about ¼ teaspoon each of salt and pepper. Broil until the eggplant is just soft, about 10 minutes, flipping after 8 minutes. Remove from the oven and transfer to a measuring cup. Measure out 2 cups, tightly packed, for use in this recipe, and transfer to a strong blender.

Cheesy Cauliflower Soup

This is vegan comfort food at its finest, with a real creaminess coming from the cashews. Toast them for optimal flavor. The grated vegan cheese adds a richness that is glorious to experience. This is a perfect soup for a cold autumn day. Top with Red Pepper Coulis (page 197) and Krispy Kale (page 203).

SERVES 6 TO 8

5 cups vegetable stock (see page 25) or water

1¼ cups chopped onion

½ cup diced celery

4 large garlic cloves, pressed or minced

4 cups small cauliflower florets (1 small cauliflower)

¾ cup chopped raw cashews (optionally toasted; see page 213)

2 teaspoons sea salt, or to taste

¼ teaspoon ground black pepper

Pinch of crushed red pepper flakes

3 tablespoons nutritional yeast (optional)

1 tablespoon minced fresh dill

¾ cup seeded and diced red bell pepper

¾ cup grated Cheddar-style vegan cheese

Black sesame seeds, for garnish

Sprigs of fresh dill, for garnish

1. Place the vegetable stock in a 3-quart pot over high heat. Add the onion, celery, garlic, and cauliflower and cook until the cauliflower is just tender, about 7 minutes, stirring occasionally.

2. Carefully transfer to a blender with the remaining ingredients, except the dill, bell pepper, vegan cheese, and black sesame seeds, and dill sprigs, and blend until creamy.

3. Return the mixture to the pot, add the minced dill, bell pepper, and vegan cheese, and cook for 10 minutes over medium-low heat, stirring occasionally. Garnish with sesame seeds and sprigs of dill before serving.

Variations

- Replace the cauliflower with broccoli, romenesco broccoli, or a mixture of vegetables, such as carrot, zucchini, and parsnip.
- Replace the minced dill with 2 tablespoons of finely chopped flat-leaf parsley, basil, or cilantro.
- Replace the cashews with macadamia nuts, Brazil nuts, or 1½ cups of soy or coconut creamer, or soy or coconut milk.
- Replace the red bell pepper with 1 cup of roasted small cauliflower florets. To do so, preheat the oven to 400°F. Toss the florets with 2 teaspoons of olive or coconut oil, a pinch of salt, and ground black pepper. Place on a well-oiled baking sheet and roast until golden brown, about 20 minutes.

Holy Mole Soup with Veggies

Virtually synonymous with Mexican cuisine, mole sauce, traditionally made with poblano chile peppers, has countless variations. It is served at weddings, bar mitzvahs, and other celebratory occasions throughout the country. Top with Vegan Crème Fraîche (page 195) and serve with Pita Chips (page 199).

SERVES 6 TO 8

1 tablespoon oil (try coconut)

1 cup diced yellow onion

3 poblano chiles, seeded and chopped small (1 cup)

5 garlic cloves

2 teaspoons chili powder

1 tablespoon ground cumin

1 teaspoon ground cinnamon

½ teaspoon chipotle chile powder

4 cups vegetable stock (see page 25) or water

1½ cups chopped tomato (½-inch pieces), or 1 (14.5-ounce) can diced fire-roasted tomatoes

¾ cup dark vegan chocolate chips

2 cups small cauliflower florets

1½ cups sliced zucchini (sliced into half-moons)

1½ cups sliced carrot (sliced into half-moons)

1 cup fresh or frozen corn

2½ teaspoons sea salt, or to taste

¼ teaspoon ground black pepper

2 tablespoons freshly squeezed lime juice

1½ tablespoons wheat-free tamari or other soy sauce

3 tablespoons finely chopped fresh cilantro

1. Place the oil in a 3-quart pot over high heat. Add the onion, chiles, and garlic and cook for 3 minutes, stirring constantly and adding small amounts of water, if necessary, to prevent sticking. Add the chili powder, cumin, cinnamon, and chipotle chile powder and cook for 1 minute, stirring constantly.
2. Lower the heat to medium-high, add 1 cup of the vegetable stock, tomatoes, and chocolate chips and cook for 8 minutes, stirring occasionally.
3. Carefully transfer to a strong blender and blend until very creamy.
4. Add the remaining 3 cups of vegetable stock to the pot. Add the cauliflower, zucchini, and carrot and cook for 5 minutes, stirring occasionally. Add the remaining ingredients, except the cilantro, and cook for 5 minutes, stirring occasionally. Add the cilantro, and stir well before serving.

Variations

- Replace 1½ cups of the vegetables with cubed and roasted tofu or tempeh (see page 215).
- For an oil-free version, use the water sauté method discussed on page 217.
- Replace the cauliflower with broccoli, romenesco broccoli, or potatoes.
- Replace the chocolate chips with vegan carob chips.

Italian Pesto Soup with Gnocchi

This innovative soup combines two of the most iconic foods of Italy. Pesto, with origins in Genoa, is traditionally made with a mortar and pestle. Fortunately, the modern chef can use a strong blender to create the creaminess of this dish. Gnocchi, made from potatoes and flour, are the official dumpling of Italy. The results are astounding. Top with toasted pine nuts (see page 213) before serving. *Buon appetito!*

SERVES 6 TO 8

GNOCCHI

1 cup chopped russet potato
   (½-inch pieces)
3 tablespoons flour (try white spelt
   or gluten-free)
¼ teaspoon sea salt
Pinch of ground black pepper
Pinch of ground nutmeg

PESTO SOUP

2 tablespoons olive oil
1¼ cups diced yellow onion
6 large garlic cloves
¾ cup thinly sliced leek, rinsed and
   drained well
½ to ¾ cup pine nuts, chopped
   cashews or macadamia nuts, or
   a combination
Pinch of crushed red pepper flakes
1½ cups tightly packed fresh basil
5 cups vegetable stock (see page 25)
   or water
3 tablespoons freshly squeezed
   lemon juice
2 teaspoons wheat-free tamari or
   other soy sauce (optional)
1 teaspoon sea salt, or to taste
½ teaspoon ground black pepper
3 tablespoons nutritional yeast
   (optional)
1½ cups chopped tomato (½-inch
   pieces)
2 tablespoons finely chopped fresh
   flat-leaf parsley

continues

continued

1. Prepare the gnocchi dough: Place a steamer basket in a pot with 1 inch of water over high heat. Add the potato, cover, and cook until the potato is just soft, about 10 minutes. Transfer the potato to a small bowl and mash well, making sure there are no big pieces. Add the remaining ingredients and form into a ball. The dough should be soft and moist, but with enough flour to not crumble or break when molded. Set aside until after the soup is blended.
2. Meanwhile, prepare the soup: Place the oil in a 3-quart pot over high heat. Add the onion, garlic, leek, pine nuts, and crushed red pepper flakes and cook for 5 minutes, stirring frequently and adding small amounts of water or vegetable stock, if necessary, to prevent sticking. Lower the heat to medium-high, add the basil, vegetable stock, lemon juice, tamari, salt, pepper, and nutritional yeast, if using, and cook for 5 minutes, stirring occasionally.
3. Carefully transfer to a blender and blend until creamy. Return the mixture to the pot over medium heat. Add the tomato and parsley and cook until the gnocchi are completed (see step 4), being careful not to boil the soup.
4. To complete the gnocchi, place water in another 3-quart or larger pot over high heat. (It could be the same pot used to steam the potatoes.) Cover and bring to a boil. Meanwhile, place the kneaded dough on a clean, dry, and flour-dusted cutting board and roll into two 8-inch logs. Slice into ¾-inch pieces and flatten slightly with a fork. Drop into the pot of boiling water and cook until the gnocchi float to the top, about 5 minutes. Place on a well-oiled plate until ready to serve.
5. To serve, pour the soup into individual bowls and add the gnocchi.

Variations

- Add ¼ cup of chopped fennel along with leek.
- Add 2 teaspoons each of finely chopped fresh oregano and sage, ½ teaspoon of fresh thyme, and ¼ teaspoon of minced fresh rosemary along with crushed red pepper flakes.
- Replace all or some of the basil with finely chopped spinach.
- Replace the potatoes in the gnocchi with sweet potato.

Chef's Tips and Tricks

True gnocchi aficionados will want to purchase a gnocchi board, to create the perfect markings that are on the traditional dish. A ricer is also a worthy investment, to grate the potatoes in the perfect fashion. See Appendix D for info on where to purchase.

Creamy White Bean Soup with Broiled Artichoke Hearts

Take a visit to central and southern Italy and you are likely to come across many dishes using the white cannellini bean. Blending this delicate bean is what gives the soup its creaminess. Combine this with another Mediterranean favorite, broiled artichoke hearts, and you will know the meaning of *amore!* Serve with Crostini (page 198) and Tapenade (page 193) or Cherry Tomato Salsa Fresca (page 183).

SERVES 6 TO 8

5 cups vegetable stock (see page 25) or water

1 cup diced yellow onion

¼ thinly sliced fennel bulb

½ cup thinly sliced celery

5 garlic cloves, pressed or minced

1 teaspoon minced fresh rosemary

¼ teaspoon dried thyme

2 (15-ounce) cans cannellini beans, rinsed and well drained, or 3 cups cooked (see page 220)

1 cup chopped artichoke hearts, rinsed well

1 cup seeded and diced red bell pepper

1½ tablespoons olive oil

2½ teaspoons sea salt, or to taste

½ teaspoon ground black pepper

2 teaspoons balsamic vinegar

1 tablespoon nutritional yeast (optional)

2 tablespoons chiffonaded fresh basil

2 teaspoons finely chopped fresh marjoram

1. Place the vegetable stock in a 3-quart pot over medium heat. Add the onion, fennel, celery, garlic, rosemary, thyme, and cannellini beans and cook for 15 minutes, stirring occasionally.

2. Meanwhile, preheat the oven to HIGH BROIL. Place the artichoke hearts and bell pepper on a small baking sheet. Add the olive oil and add ¼ teaspoon each of the salt and black pepper, and toss well. Broil for 10 minutes, checking periodically to avoid burning. Remove from the oven.

3. Carefully transfer about 4 cups of the contents of the pot to a blender and blend until creamy. (The more beans you add, the creamier the soup will be.) Return the mixture to the pot.

4. Add all the remaining ingredients, including the broiled artichoke hearts and bell pepper, and the remaining salt and black pepper. Cook for 5 minutes, stirring occasionally. Enjoy!

Variations

- You can sauté the onion, fennel, celery, and garlic in 1½ tablespoons of oil for 3 minutes over medium-high heat, stirring frequently, before adding the remaining ingredients.

continues

148

continued

- Replace the cannellini beans with pinto, navy, great northern, or gigante beans.
- Replace the marjoram with fresh oregano or 1 tablespoon of minced fresh sage or tarragon.
- Add 1 tablespoon of chili powder and 2 teaspoons of ground cumin along with the onion. Replace the basil with fresh cilantro.

Curried Pumpkin Soup

Halloween is around the corner and you are wondering what to serve after the apple bobbing? Try this creamy, fall-themed soup, served in ornamental pumpkins and topped with a drizzle of Balsamic Reduction (page 189) and Candied Pepitas (page 192).

SERVES 6 TO 8

4 cups vegetable stock (see page 25) or water

1¼ cups diced yellow onion

¾ cup diced celery

½ teaspoon seeded and diced hot chile pepper (see the Scoville scale on page 57)

4 large garlic cloves

4 cups peeled, seeded, and chopped pumpkin (½-inch pieces)

2 to 3 teaspoons curry powder

½ teaspoon ground cumin (try toasting; see page 213)

2½ teaspoons sea salt, or to taste

¼ teaspoon ground black pepper

1 teaspoon coconut nectar (see page 227), agave nectar, or maple syrup

1½ cups soy creamer or nondairy milk, such as coconut, soy, rice, or almond (see page 222)

2 teaspoons freshly squeezed lime juice

2 tablespoons finely chopped fresh cilantro

1. Place the vegetable stock in a 3-quart pot over high heat. Add all the remaining ingredients, except the soy creamer, lime juice, and cilantro, and cook until the pumpkin is just soft, about 15 minutes, stirring occasionally.
2. Add the soy creamer, carefully transfer to a blender, and blend until creamy.
3. Return the mixture to the pot, add the lime juice and cilantro, and cook for 5 minutes over medium-low heat, stirring occasionally.

Variations
- Replace the pumpkin with any winter squash, such as butternut, acorn, or buttercup. You can also use an equivalent amount of canned pureed pumpkin.
- Replace the curry powder with 2 teaspoons of chili powder and ½ teaspoon of chipotle chile powder, for a Mexican theme.

Green Bean Amandine Soup

America's favorite holiday side dish can now be served as America's favorite holiday soup. Be sure to use the slivered almonds, for the creamiest soup. Top with Red Pepper Coulis (page 197) and diced Tempeh Bacon (page 208).

SERVES 6 TO 8

1½ cups slivered almonds

5 cups vegetable stock (see page 25) or water

1¼ cups diced yellow onion

¾ cup diced celery

4 large garlic cloves

¼ cup diced shiitake mushrooms

¾ pound green beans, ends trimmed, cut on the diagonal into ½-inch slices (about 2½ cups)

½ cup diced carrot

½ cup fresh or frozen corn

3 tablespoons finely chopped fresh flat-leaf parsley

2 teaspoons wheat-free tamari or other soy sauce, or to taste (optional)

1½ tablespoons nutritional yeast (optional)

2 teaspoons sea salt, or to taste

¼ teaspoon ground black pepper

½ teaspoon minced fresh rosemary

¼ cup seeded and diced red bell pepper, for garnish

1. Preheat the oven to 375°F. Place the almonds on a baking sheet and bake until golden brown, 8 to 10 minutes. Remove from the oven and place 1 cup in a large blender, reserving ½ cup for garnish.

2. Meanwhile, place the vegetable stock in a 3-quart pot over medium-high heat. Add the onion, celery, garlic, and shiitake mushrooms and cook for 10 minutes, stirring occasionally.

3. Carefully transfer a few cups of the mixture to the blender and blend until very creamy. Add the rest of the contents of the pot to the blender and blend again until creamy. Return the mixture to the pot.

4. Add the green beans and all the remaining ingredients, except the bell pepper and reserved almonds, and cook over medium heat for 10 minutes, stirring occasionally. Garnish with toasted almonds and bell pepper before serving.

Variations

- It wouldn't quite be amandine, but you can replace the almonds with toasted cashews, macadamia nuts, or Brazil nuts.
- Replace the green beans with your favorite vegetables, such as broccoli, cauliflower, or yellow summer squash (try gold bar).
- Roast some extra almonds and use as a garnish.

Rosemary Potato Soup
with Roasted Leek and Garlic

Another irresistible comfort soup for the colder months, this dish combines potatoes with its favorite accompaniments—fresh rosemary, and roasted leeks and garlic. Can you say, "Pass me another serving?" Serve with Vegan Crème Fraîche (page 195) and Tapenade (page 193).

SERVES 6 TO 8

3 cups sliced leek, rinsed and drained well

6 large garlic cloves

1½ tablespoons olive oil

2 teaspoons sea salt, or to taste

¼ teaspoon ground black pepper

4 cups vegetable stock (see page 25) or water

1 cup diced yellow onion

3 cups cubed potato (½-inch cubes) (try Yukon Gold or Yellow Finn)

1½ teaspoons minced fresh rosemary

Pinch of crushed red pepper flakes

1 cup soy milk or creamer, or rice or almond milk (see page 222)

2 tablespoons finely chopped fresh flat-leaf parsley

2 tablespoons finely chopped chives, for garnish (optional)

1. Preheat the oven to 400°F. Place the leek, garlic, oil, and a pinch each of salt and black pepper on a baking sheet and toss well. Roast for 15 minutes. Carefully stir once or twice to ensure even cooking. Transfer to a large blender.
2. Meanwhile, place the vegetable stock in a 3-quart pot over high heat. Add the onion, potato, and rosemary and cook until the potato is just soft, about 10 minutes, stirring occasionally. Add the salt, black pepper, and crushed red pepper flakes, and mix well.
3. Carefully transfer to the blender and blend until just creamy. Be careful not to overblend the potatoes, as they can turn gummy. Return the mixture to the pot over medium-high heat, add the soy milk and parsley, and cook for 5 minutes, stirring occasionally. Garnish with Vegan Crème Fraîche (page 195) and chives, if using.

Variations
- Garlic lovers, increase the garlic to 10 cloves.
- Experiment with different potatoes, or live on the edge and replace with butternut squash, yam, or sweet potato.

continues

152

continued

- Omit the rosemary and add 1 tablespoon of curry powder, 1 teaspoon of ground cumin, and 2 tablespoons of minced fresh cilantro, for a Mexican version.
- Instead of roasting, you can sauté the leeks, onion, and garlic in the oil for 5 minutes over medium-high heat, stirring frequently, before adding the remaining ingredients.
- For **Vichyssoise** (chilled potato soup), allow the soup to cool to room temperature, or chill in the refrigerator until cooled. Add soy milk, if necessary, before serving to reach your desired consistency.

New England Chowder

This vegan makeover of a staple in the Northeast gets its creaminess from blending the potato and from the addition of soy milk. The sea vegetable arame imparts the flavor of the sea that many are accustomed to. For even more creaminess, top with Vegan Crème Fraîche (page 195) and serve with Herbed Bread Sticks (page 209) or Pita Chips (page 199).

SERVES 6 TO 8

3 cups vegetable stock (see page 25) or water

1 cup diced yellow onion

½ cup thinly sliced celery

5 large garlic cloves, pressed or minced

3½ cups chopped potato (½-inch pieces) (try Yukon Gold or Yellow Finn)

½ cup diced shiitake mushrooms

1 teaspoon minced fresh rosemary

2 cups unsweetened soy milk or creamer, or rice or almond milk (see page 222)

1 cup diced carrot

1 cup fresh or frozen peas

¾ cup fresh or frozen corn

1 tablespoon wheat-free tamari or other soy sauce (optional)

3 tablespoons arame

2 teaspoons sea salt, or to taste

¼ teaspoon ground black pepper

Pinch of crushed red pepper flakes

3 tablespoons finely chopped fresh flat-leaf parsley

1. Place the vegetable stock in a 3-quart pot over medium-high heat. Add the onion, celery, garlic, potato, mushrooms, and rosemary and cook for 15 minutes, stirring occasionally.
2. Carefully transfer 1½ cups of the mixture to a strong blender and blend until just creamy. Be careful not to overblend the potatoes, as they can get gummy. Return the mixture to the pot.
3. Add all the remaining ingredients, except the parsley, and cook for 8 minutes, stirring occasionally. Add the parsley, and stir well before serving.

Variations

- Sauté the onion, celery, and garlic in 1½ tablespoons oil for 3 minutes over medium-high heat, stirring frequently, before adding the remaining ingredients.
- Replace the peas, carrots, and corn with assorted diced vegetables of your choosing, such as broccoli, cauliflower, cabbage, or zucchini.

PART FIVE

RAW SOUPS AND DESSERT SOUPS

Vibrant and full of nutrients, raw soups are on the cutting edge of soup cuisine. Enjoy the savory soups as a starter course, and the sweet soups as a refreshing dessert and even for a light breakfast. You will probably find yourself craving these recipes in the warmer spring and summer months, especially when an abundance of fresh fruit becomes available. In this section we will explore several of the main techniques involved in raw soup creation. Once you grasp these basic techniques, there is no end to the number of innovative and life-giving soups you will create.

One main technique involves blending vegetables to create a flavorful base and then adding additional chopped veggies for texture, as in the Golden Gazpacho with Saffron, and the Raw Cucumber Mint Soup. Vegetable juice may also form the base, as with the Raw Mediterranean Onion Soup and Raw Chopped Vegetable Soup with Shaved Fennel.

Fruits, either on their own or with the addition of water or juice, may also be blended to create the base for our sweet and dessert soups. This is demonstrated in the Pineapple Ginger Soup with Apricot Puree, Lavender-Infused Watermelon Soup, or Spicy Strawberry Soup. Added texture can be created by freezing the soup slightly, as in the Slushy Summer Fruit Soup.

As far as techniques for creating creamy raw soups, just as with the cooked soups, we can create creaminess by blending ingredients with nuts or seeds. This is illustrated in the Raw Creamy Greens Soup and Raw Corn Chowder, where soaked and blended cashews impart the creaminess. Pepitas are used in the Spicy Kale Soup with Pepitas. Blending avocado is another way to create creaminess. To experience this, check out the Chilled Avocado Soup with Cherry Tomato Salsa Fresca.

Another technique involves using a raw plant–based milk as the base for a creamy soup. This is accomplished with Brazil nuts, in both a sweet (Creamy Brazil Nut Fig Soup with Kiwi Compote) and savory (Savory Brazil Nut Soup with Jicama) version. Almond milk is used as the base for the Raw Chocolate Mint Soup with Raspberries, and blended coconut meat creates the creaminess in the Raw Thai Coconut Soup.

This section also explores the art of the raw vegan cream sauces. Soaked cashews or macadamia nuts blended with water are perfect to form the base. This base can then have a savory twist, as when blended with bell pepper in the Raw Papaya Soup with Red Pepper Cream or Raw Crème Fraîche. It can also go in the sweet direction, as when it is sweetened with coconut nectar in the Raw Peaches and Cream Soup, or with other fruit, such as blueberries in the Cantaloupe Rose Soup with Blueberry Cream.

For your culinary pleasure and exploration, I have included raw variations of three soups in the cooked soup section, so you can compare the different flavors. These soups include the Raw Corn Chowder, Raw Cream of Tomato Soup, and the Raw Thai Coconut Soup. And now for the recipes . . . to life!

Chef's Tips and Tricks

Garnishing Raw Soups

It is easy and fun to create vibrant garnishes for your raw soups. Fruit soups may be decorated with berries and other colorful fruits. Vegetable-based soups can be decorated with julienned strips of colorful vegetables. If you have never experienced the joys of a spiralizer, I encourage you to pick one up. You can create veggie "noodles" from carrot, beet, daikon radish, jicama, and zucchini, which will add amazing texture and color to your soups. Spiralizers are available at kitchen supply stores or online at various raw food websites or Amazon.com.

♥ Lavender-Infused Watermelon Soup

With origins in ancient Africa, and a rumored favorite of Egyptian pharaohs, watermelons are a favorite of picnics worldwide. Now you can enjoy a picnic in a bowl with this sublime summertime dessert soup. The infused lavender adds a chicness that is not to be missed. Be sure to purchase culinary-grade flowers, as opposed to a potpourri blend (see Chef's Tips and Tricks). Serve chilled.

SERVES 4

2 tablespoons culinary-grade lavender flowers

¼ cup boiling water

6 cups seeded and chopped watermelon (1-inch pieces)

¼ cup loosely packed fresh mint leaves

1 cup ice

¼ cup freshly squeezed lime juice

Pinch of sea salt

Pinch of cayenne pepper (optional)

Raw coconut nectar (see page 227), agave nectar, or sweetener of choice

½ cup blueberries, for garnish

1. Place the lavender flowers and boiling water in a small bowl and allow to sit for 20 minutes.
2. Meanwhile place all the remaining ingredients, except the coconut nectar and blueberries, in a large blender or food processor and blend until just smooth. Be careful not to overblend, or it will get too frothy. Transfer to a bowl and refrigerate to chill while the lavender flowers are soaking.
3. Remove the bowl from the refrigerator, strain out the lavender flowers, adding the liquid to the fruit bowl and discarding the flowers. Mix well, add the coconut nectar to taste, if necessary, and garnish with blueberries before serving.

Variations
- For Watermelon Rose Soup, replace the lavender with 1 to 2 teaspoons of culinary-grade rose water (see Chef's Tips and Tricks).
- Replace the watermelon with other melons, such as honeydew or crenshaw.
- Replace the watermelon with other fruit, such as nectarines, plums, peaches, or mangoes.

continues

Lavender-Infused Watermelon Soup *continued*

If You Have More Time

Pour 1 cup of soup into small ice cube trays and freeze (see page 186). Add to the soup before serving.

Chefs Tips and Tricks

Culinary Grade Lavender and Rose Water

Lavender flowers and rose water make wonderful fragrant additions to your culinary creations. Be sure you are purchasing a food-grade variety, as some brands of lavender contain higher amounts of camphor oil or are sprayed with chemicals and are best used for potpourri. Likewise some brands of rose water are higher in rose oil and are more suited for use as perfume. The package should indicate whether it is for culinary uses. Lavender flowers purchased in the bulk spice section of a natural food store are generally culinary grade, though it does not hurt to ask! Purchase the freshest ones possible so the maximum flavor will be imparted to your dishes.

♥ Spicy Strawberry Soup

Nothing quite heralds the beginning of spring quite like the first strawberry harvest. These sumptuous delights form the base of this sweet and spicy soup. Be sure to purchase only organic strawberries, to avoid unwanted pesticides as ingredients in your dish. Serve chilled with Sweet Cashew Cream (page 166).

SERVES 4

2 pounds strawberries, hulled and chopped (5 cups)

½ teaspoon orange zest

½ cup freshly squeezed orange juice

½ cup water

3 tablespoons coconut nectar (see page 227), pure maple syrup, or raw agave nectar, or to taste

2 teaspoons peeled and minced fresh ginger

½ teaspoon seeded and diced hot chile pepper (see the Scoville scale on page 57)

½ teaspoon vanilla extract

¼ teaspoon ground cinnamon

⅛ teaspoon ground cardamom

Pinch of cayenne pepper

Pinch of sea salt

Pinch of ground black pepper

2 tablespoons chiffonaded fresh mint

1. Place all the ingredients, except the mint, in a blender and blend until smooth.
2. Transfer to a bowl, add the mint, and stir well.
3. Allow to chill for 10 minutes or longer before serving.

If You Have More Time

Pour 1 cup of soup into small ice cube trays and freeze (see page 186). Add to the soup before serving.

♥ Pineapple Ginger Soup with Apricot Puree

This sweet and exotic dessert soup features the tropical superstar, pineapple, which is loaded with vitamins and nutrients, such as manganese, vital for bone health. Apricots have been cultivated for thousands of years and add an additional burst of yumminess. Try adding a dollop of Sweet Cashew Cream (page 166) and garnishing with fresh blueberries, raspberries, or blackberries.

SERVES 4 TO 6

APRICOT PUREE

½ cup dried unsulfured apricots (about 16)

3 pitted dates

¾ cup water

¼ cup freshly squeezed orange juice

⅛ teaspoon orange zest

Pinch of ground cinnamon

Pinch of ground nutmeg

PINEAPPLE GINGER SOUP

1 large ripe pineapple, cored and chopped into ½-inch pieces (5 cups)

½ cup freshly squeezed orange juice

1½ tablespoons peeled and minced fresh ginger

1 teaspoon seeded and diced hot chile pepper (see the Scoville scale on page 57)

1 tablespoon minced fresh cilantro

Pinch of crushed red pepper flakes

6 dried unsulfured apricots, diced, for garnish

1 tablespoon chiffonaded fresh mint, for garnish

1. Prepare the apricot puree: Place the apricots and dates in the water and allow to soak for 20 minutes.
2. Meanwhile, place all the soup ingredients, except the diced apricots and mint, in a strong blender and blend well. Transfer to a bowl and place in the refrigerator.

continues

continued

3. Place all the Apricot Puree ingredients, including the soak water, in the blender and blend until smooth.
4. Remove the soup from the refrigerator, stir well, and pour into individual bowls. Place a dollop of the Apricot Puree in the center of each bowl. Garnish with diced apricots and mint before serving.

Variations
- Replace the orange juice with other fruit juice, such as mango, apple, or peach.
- Replace the apricots with other dried fruit, such as figs, mango, or raisins.

♥ Raw Papaya Soup with Red Pepper Cream

Experience tropical bliss in a bowl with this papaya-based fruit soup. The spiciness of the chili powder, as well as the tang of the lime, accentuates the sweetness of the papaya and has your taste buds singing with joy. It's a winning combination in this soup, as well as on whole raw papayas. The Red Pepper Cream gets its creaminess from soaked and blended cashews. The natural sweetness of the pepper complements the tropical tones of the papaya.

SERVES 4

RED PEPPER CREAM

Makes ¾ cup red pepper cream

½ cup chopped raw cashews or macadamia nuts

¾ cup seeded and diced red bell pepper

2 tablespoons water

3 tablespoons unsweetened shredded coconut

1 tablespoon coconut oil (optional)

⅛ teaspoon sea salt

PAPAYA SOUP

4 cups peeled, seeded, and chopped papaya (½-inch pieces) (3 sunrise variety or 1 large Mexican variety)

1 cup coconut water or plain water

¼ cup freshly squeezed lime juice

Pinch of chili powder (try chipotle)

¼ cup coconut nectar (see page 227), raw agave nectar, coconut crystals, or pure maple syrup (see page 228), or to taste

2 tablespoons unsweetened shredded coconut, for garnish

Fresh mint leaves, for garnish

1. Place the cashews in a bowl with ample water to cover and soak for 20 minutes.
2. Meanwhile, place all the Papaya Soup ingredients in a large blender and blend until creamy. Transfer to a bowl.
3. Prepare the cream: Drain and rinse the cashews well. Transfer to the blender with the remaining Red Pepper Cream ingredients and blend until creamy. Transfer to a small bowl.
4. To serve, pour the soup into a bowl, add a dollop of the cream, and top with coconut and a mint leaf.

Variations
- Replace the papayas with mangoes, pineapple, peaches, or nectarines.

♥ Cantaloupe Rose Soup with Blueberry Cream

Rose water adds a distinctive floral flavor to this melon-based dessert soup. Enjoy at the height of summer, when melons abound, and experiment with the different varieties available. The amount of additional sweetener you add will depend upon the sweetness of the melon. If you really want to impress your guests, serve with frozen melon balls immersed in the soup (see page 186.)

SERVES 4

BLUEBERRY CREAM

Makes 1 cup blueberry cream

½ cup chopped raw cashews

½ cup blueberries

½ cup coconut water or water

½ teaspoon vanilla extract

Pinch of ground cinnamon

Pinch of ground cardamom

CANTALOUPE SOUP

6 cups seeded and chopped
    cantaloupe (½-inch pieces)

2 teaspoons vanilla extract

¼ cup coconut water or water

¼ cup freshly squeezed lime juice

1 teaspoon culinary-grade rose
    water (see page 160)

1 tablespoon coconut nectar (see
    page 227), pure maple syrup, or
    other sweetener, to taste

Pinch of sea salt

Pinch of ground cinnamon

Pinch of ground cardamom

1 cup blueberries

1. Place the cashews in a bowl with ample water to cover and soak for 20 minutes.
2. Meanwhile, place all the Cantaloupe Soup ingredients, except the blueberries, in a large blender and blend until creamy. Transfer to a bowl.
3. Prepare the cream: Drain and rinse the cashews well. Transfer to the blender with the remaining Blueberry Cream ingredients and blend until creamy. Transfer to a small bowl.
4. Stir the soup very well just before serving. To serve, pour the soup into a bowl, add a dollop of the sauce, and top with the blueberries.

Variations
- Replace the cantaloupe with honeydew, crenshaw, or other sweet melon.
- Replace the blueberries with strawberries, papaya, or mango.
- Feel free to omit the rose water.

♥ Raw Peaches and Cream Soup

This heavenly dessert soup is incredibly simple to prepare. The sweet cashew cream serves as a substitute for heavy cream and is an important and versatile technique in vegan and raw food preparation. When blended with different fruits, it creates countless flavorful and colorful creams for your culinary delight.

SERVES 4

SWEET CASHEW CREAM

¾ cup chopped raw cashews

¾ cup water

1½ tablespoons raw coconut or agave nectar, or sweetener of choice, or to taste

RAW PEACH SOUP

7 ripe peaches, pitted and chopped (5 cups)

1½ cups fruit juice (try apple)

2 tablespoons raw coconut nectar (see page 227), agave nectar, or pure maple syrup, or to taste

1 tablespoon freshly squeezed lemon juice

¼ teaspoon ground allspice

⅛ teaspoon ground cinnamon

Pinch of sea salt

2 teaspoons mirin (optional, but recommended)

2 tablespoons chiffonaded fresh mint, for garnish

1. Place the cashews in a small bowl with ample water to cover. Allow them to sit for 20 minutes. Drain and rinse well.
2. Meanwhile, place all the Peach Soup ingredients, except the mint, in a strong blender, and blend until creamy. Transfer to a bowl.
3. Place the cashews in the blender with the water and the coconut nectar and blend until very creamy. Transfer to a small bowl.
4. Garnish each bowl of soup with a drizzle of cashew cream and top with fresh mint before serving.

Variations

- It would be a raw foodist's call to 911, but you can grill the peaches until char marks appear, about 5 minutes, lightly basting with melted coconut oil before blending.
- Replace the peaches with nectarines, mangoes, blueberries, or papayas.
- Replace the apple juice with orange, pineapple, or mango juice, or a combination of your favorites.
- Create differently flavored Sweet Cashew Creams by adding ½ cup of fruit, such as blueberries, strawberries, or mango.

♥ Raw Chocolate Mint Soup with Raspberries

Aptly translated from the Nahuatl as "food of the gods," cacao is the raw unprocessed form of chocolate. It is a true superfood, loaded with nutrients, and forms the base of this divine dessert soup. It is thickened and sweetened by the bananas and dates. For the full download, enjoy after chilling in the refrigerator for 20 minutes or longer. Top with Sweet Cashew Cream (see page 166) and chopped almonds before serving.

SERVES 4 TO 6

1 cup raw almonds

4 cups water

½ cup tightly packed pitted dates

½ cup mashed ripe banana

3 tablespoons raw cacao powder

⅛ teaspoon ground cinnamon

⅛ teaspoon ground cardamom

Pinch of sea salt

1 tablespoon coconut nectar (see page 227), pure maple syrup, or agave nectar, or to taste

½ teaspoon vanilla extract (optional)

2 tablespoons chiffonaded fresh mint

1 pint raspberries or sliced strawberries

½ cup raw cacao nibs, for garnish (optional)

1. Place the almonds in a bowl with ample water to cover. Allow them to sit for 20 minutes. Drain and rinse well. Place in a strong blender with the 4 cups of water and blend until very creamy.
2. Strain through a sprouting bag or very fine mesh strainer. Discard the pulp or save for other uses. Return the liquid (congratulations, you have just made almond milk) to the blender with the remaining ingredients, except the mint, raspberries, and cacao nibs, if using, and blend until very creamy.
3. Transfer to a bowl, add the mint and raspberries, and mix well. Top each serving with cacao nibs.

Variations
- You can add ½ teaspoon of mint extract instead of, or in addition to, the vanilla extract.
- Replace the almonds with Brazil or macadamia nuts.
- Replace the vanilla extract with one vanilla bean. Add to the blender with the whole almonds.

♥ Creamy Brazil Nut Fig Soup with Kiwi Compote

Coming to you straight from the Amazonian rain forest, raw Brazil nuts, blended into a milk, create the base of this wonderful fruit-sweetened dessert or breakfast soup. Remember to use the soak water from the dried figs, but not from the Brazil nuts, when following the recipe. Best when serve chilled and with a small dollop of Sweet Cashew Cream (page 166).

SERVES 6

BRAZIL NUT FIG SOUP

¾ cup chopped dried figs

5 cups water

1 cup Brazil nuts

¼ teaspoon sea salt

⅛ teaspoon ground nutmeg

¼ teaspoon ground cinnamon

⅛ teaspoon ground cardamom

2 tablespoons coconut nectar (see page 227), agave nectar, or other sweetener, or to taste

KIWI FIG COMPOTE

1 cup diced kiwi

1 cup diced fresh figs

½ cup chopped, pitted cherries

2 teaspoons coconut oil (optional)

1 teaspoon mirin (see page 8) (optional)

1 tablespoon coconut nectar (see page 227), raw agave nectar, or sweetener to taste (optional)

1½ tablespoons chiffonaded fresh mint

2 tablespoons sunflower seeds

2 tablespoons diced crystallized ginger (optional)

1. Soak the dried figs in a bowl with the 5 cups of water. Allow them to soak for 15 minutes. Place the Brazil nuts in a separate bowl with ample water to cover. Allow them to soak for 15 minutes. Drain and rinse well.

2. Meanwhile, place the Kiwi Fig Compote ingredients in a bowl and mix well. Place in the refrigerator or freezer to chill.

3. Prepare the soup: Place the soaked figs and their soak water, salt, cinnamon, cardamom, nutmeg, and Brazil nuts in a strong blender and blend until creamy. Add the coconut nectar and blend until creamy. Transfer to a bowl.

4. To serve, garnish each serving of soup with a generous portion of the chilled compote.

Variations

- Replace the dried figs with other dried fruit, such as apricots, prunes, mango, or papaya.
- Replace the Brazil nuts with cashews.
- You can replace the Brazil nuts with almonds. Blend separately and strain (see page 222) before using in the recipe.
- While not raw, some Balsamic Reduction (page 189) can also be drizzled on top of the kiwi compote.

♥ 🕐 Slushy Summer Fruit Soup

Turn to this recipe when you are looking to cool down and liven up. Freezing the soup gives it that oh-so-slushy texture we love from a granita or Italian ices. Be sure not to overfreeze. Of course, if time is an issue, simply blend the soup and enjoy immediately. Top with Sweet Cashew Cream (page 166).

SERVES 6

8 ripe nectarines, pitted and chopped (6 cups)

1 cup coconut water or water

Raw coconut nectar (see page 227), raw agave nectar, or pure maple syrup

2 teaspoons peeled and minced fresh ginger

2 tablespoons freshly squeezed lime juice

¼ teaspoon lime zest

⅛ teaspoon ground cinnamon

Pinch of ground cardamom

Pinch of sea salt

Pinch of cayenne pepper (optional)

2 cups assorted berries

Fresh mint leaves

1. Place all the ingredients, including sweetener to taste, and except the berries and mint leaves, in a blender and blend until smooth. Transfer to a large shallow pan, add the berries, and mix well.
2. Place in the freezer until just starting to get slushy, about 1 hour.
3. Mix well and garnish with mint leaves before serving.

Variations
- Replace the nectarines with peaches, honeydew melons, cantaloupe, pineapple, or a combination.
- Replace the berries with chopped fruit, such as pear, apple, or apricots.
- Replace the lime juice and zest with orange or tangerine.

♥ Danish Fruit Soup

Danish fruit soup is traditionally a cooked fruit soup with various dried fruits and thickened with tapioca flour. This raw version is thickened with pureed dates and banana. Enjoy it as a dessert soup or on its own as a flavorful breakfast dish. Top with Sweet Cashew Cream (page 166). Souperb!

SERVES 4 TO 6

1½ cups water

½ cup pitted dates

2½ cups apple juice

¾ cup raisins or currants

¾ cup chopped dried apricots

¾ cup chopped pitted prunes

½ cup chopped apple

½ cup mashed banana

1 tablespoon peeled and minced
   fresh ginger

1 tablespoon freshly squeezed lime
   juice

¼ teaspoon ground cinnamon

⅛ teaspoon ground nutmeg

Pinch of ground allspice

Pinch of cayenne pepper (optional)

1 tablespoon chiffonaded fresh mint

1. Place the water in a small bowl with the dates. Allow to soak for 15 minutes.
2. Meanwhile, place 1½ cups of the apple juice in a bowl with the raisins, apricots, and prunes.
3. Place ½ cup of apple juice, the apple, banana, ginger, lime juice, cinnamon, nutmeg, allspice, and cayenne, if using, in a blender. Add the dates, and water, and blend until very creamy. Transfer to the bowl with the apple juice and dried fruit, and stir well.
4. Add the mint, and stir well before serving.

Variations

- Replace the apple juice with a juice of your choosing. Try mango, pineapple, peach, or pear.
- Get creative with the fruits you add once the soup is blended. Add fresh berries, or chopped peaches, pears, nectarines, or apricots.

♥ Golden Gazpacho with Saffron

A vastly popular tomato-based soup with origins in the Andalucia region of Spain, gazpacho has many faces. This one is golden due to the yellow tomatoes and the hint of saffron (see page 42). For best results, chill before serving and top with Raw Crème Fraîche (page 196).

SERVES 4 TO 6

½ teaspoon saffron threads

2 tablespoons hot water

5 cups chopped gold tomatoes (½-inch pieces)

1½ cups diced cucumber

½ cup diced red onion

1¼ teaspoons seeded and diced jalapeño pepper

1 garlic clove

1½ teaspoons sea salt, or to taste

⅛ teaspoon ground black pepper

2 tablespoons freshly squeezed lime juice, or to taste

1 teaspoon ground cumin

¼ teaspoon chipotle chile powder, or ½ teaspoon chili powder

Pinch of cayenne

½ cup fresh or frozen corn

¼ cup seeded and diced red bell pepper

1½ tablespoons minced fresh cilantro

1. Place the saffron strands in a small dish with the hot water.
2. Place the tomatoes, 1 cup of cucumber, ¼ cup red onion, the jalapeño, garlic, salt, black pepper, lime juice, cumin, chipotle chile powder, and cayenne in a blender and blend until creamy. Transfer to a serving bowl.
3. Add all the remaining ingredients, including the remaining cucumber and red onion, and mix well. Add the saffron and hot water and mix well before serving.

Variations

- You can use red tomatoes if golden ones are not available. Although most people think of gazpacho as a savory soup, experiment with some sweet versions:
- For **Mango Gazpacho,** replace 2 cups of the tomato with mango. For **Pineapple Gazpacho,** replace all of the tomato with pineapple, and omit the garlic, corn, and bell pepper. For **Watermelon Gazpacho,** replace all of the tomato with watermelon, and omit the garlic, corn, and bell pepper.

♥ Raw Cucumber Mint Soup

Cultivated for over three thousand years, cucumbers form the base of this refreshing and cooling soup and crunchy garnish. Mint, basil, and oregano add that Mediterranean touch that is perfect on hot summer days. If you don't tell the raw food police, you can top with a drizzle of Balsamic Reduction (page 189).

SERVES 4 TO 6

1 cup water

4 large cucumbers, peeled and chopped into ½-inch pieces (6½ cups)

¼ cup freshly squeezed lemon juice

½ teaspoon seeded and diced hot chile pepper (see the Scoville scale on page 57

1 garlic clove

1 tablespoon minced fresh basil

1 tablespoon dried mint (optional)

1½ teaspoons sea salt, or to taste

⅛ teaspoon ground black pepper

½ teaspoon dried oregano

¼ teaspoon dried thyme

Pinch of chipotle chile powder (optional)

¼ cup chiffonaded fresh mint

Sunflower seeds or pepitas, for garnish (optional)

CUCUMBER GARNISH

1 cup peeled, seeded, and diced cucumber

½ teaspoon raw apple cider vinegar

2 teaspoons chiffonaded fresh mint

Pinch of sea salt

Pinch of ground black pepper

1. Place all the soup ingredients, except 2 tablespoons of the mint and the sunflower seeds, in a blender and blend until creamy. Transfer to a bowl, add the remaining mint, and stir well.
2. Prepare the Cucumber Garnish: Combine all of its ingredients in a small bowl and mix well.
3. Give the soup a stir just before garnishing and serving, as it has a tendency to separate. To serve, place the soup in a bowl and top with the Cucumber Garnish and a few pepitas, if using.

Variations
- Replace the Cucumber Garnish with Cherry Tomato Salsa Fresca (page 183).
- Omit the thyme, replace the basil with fresh cilantro, and add 2 teaspoons of chili powder for a Mexican-themed soup.

♥ Raw Cream of Tomato Soup

An invigorating way to start your meal, the sun-dried tomatoes add a nice depth, and the creaminess comes from the soaked cashews. Compare this to the Creamy Fire-Roasted Tomato Soup with Dill (page 125) to experience two versions of an American favorite. For optimal results, chill for 20 minutes before serving. Top with Raw Crème Fraîche (page 196) and sunflower sprouts.

SERVES 4 TO 6

6 to 8 sun-dried tomatoes (about ¼ cup)

½ cup hot water

½ cup raw cashew pieces

2 cups chopped tomato (½-inch pieces)

2 cups water

¼ cup diced red onion

1 tablespoon freshly squeezed lemon juice

1 garlic clove

1 teaspoon sea salt, or to taste

⅛ teaspoon ground black pepper

Pinch of cayenne pepper or crushed red pepper flakes

2 tablespoons olive oil (optional)

1 teaspoon balsamic vinegar (optional)

1 tablespoon minced fresh basil

1 tablespoon minced fresh flat-leaf parsley

1. Place the sun-dried tomatoes in a small bowl with the hot water. Allow them to sit for 20 minutes.
2. Place the cashews in a bowl with sufficient water to cover. Allow them to sit for 20 minutes. Drain and rinse well. Discard the cashew soak water.
3. Meanwhile place the chopped tomato, the 2 cups of water, and the onion, lemon juice, garlic, salt, black pepper, cayenne, oil, and vinegar, if using, in a strong blender.
4. Add the sun-dried tomatoes and their soak water, and the drained and rinsed cashews and blend until very creamy. Transfer to a bowl with the basil and parsley, and mix well before serving.

Variations

- Replace the cashews with macadamia nuts, Brazil nuts, or blanched almonds.
- Add 1 teaspoon of fresh oregano and ½ teaspoon of fresh thyme.
- Replace the basil and parsley with fresh cilantro, and add 1 teaspoon of chili powder and 1 teaspoon of ground cumin.
- Replace the basil and parsley with fresh cilantro and add 2 teaspoons of curry powder and ½ teaspoon each of ground cumin and ground coriander.

♥ Raw Chopped Vegetable Soup with Shaved Fennel

This is another amazing Template Recipe where hundreds of variations are possible. Each vegetable juice you use as a base, and each selection of chopped vegetables added to it, will create a new soup, each with its own nutritional profile. Top with Raw Crème Fraîche (page 196) and pepitas or sunflower seeds.

SERVES 4 TO 6

4 cups mixed vegetable juice

¾ cup mashed avocado

2 tablespoons diced shallot

1 tablespoon freshly squeezed lemon juice

2 teaspoons peeled and minced fresh ginger

½ teaspoon seeded and diced hot chile pepper (see the Scoville scale on page 57)

1 teaspoon sea salt, or to taste

⅛ teaspoon ground black pepper

Pinch of crushed red pepper flakes

1½ cups shredded napa cabbage (cut into ½-inch pieces)

¼ cup fresh or frozen corn

¼ cup seeded and diced red bell pepper

¼ cup thinly sliced celery

¼ cup thinly sliced carrot

1 tablespoon chiffonaded fresh basil

1 tablespoon finely chopped fresh flat-leaf parsley

2 tablespoons shaved fennel (see Chef's Tips and Tricks)

1. Place 2 cups of the juice in a blender with the avocado, shallot, lemon juice, ginger, chile pepper, salt, black pepper, and crushed red pepper flakes, and blend until creamy.
2. Transfer to a bowl with the remaining ingredients and mix well.
3. Chill for 10 minutes or longer in the refrigerator before serving.

Variations

- Experiment with different vegetable juice blends, such as carrot, celery, cucumber, and kale.
- For a creamier soup, add an additional ¼ cup of mashed avocado.
- Add 1 garlic clove instead of or along with the ginger.
- Add 2 teaspoons each of chopped fresh oregano and marjoram, and ½ teaspoon of fresh thyme; or ¾ teaspoon each of dried oregano and marjoram, and ¼ teaspoon dried thyme.

continues

continued

Chef's Tips and Tricks

Shaving Fennel

The inclusion of shaved fennel adds a delicate anise-flavored crunch to your dishes. To shave fennel, first remove the outer layer of the fennel bulb if it is brown or soft. Then cut the bulb into quarters. Cut out the core of each quarter and discard. Using a vegetable peeler, shave off small pieces of the remaining bulb until you have the measured amount.

♥ Raw Mediterranean Onion Soup

This is a raw twist on the classic French Onion Soup (page 40). Here, sweet red onion is added to a base created with blended tomatoes and Mediterranean herbs. If you wish, you can heat this soup until just warm to the touch and still have it be considered raw. Top with Raw Crème Fraîche (page 196) and a spoonful of Tapenade (page 193) or diced olives.

SERVES 4 TO 6

2½ cups water

2½ cups chopped tomato (½-inch pieces)

¼ cup diced shallot

1 tablespoon dried marjoram

½ teaspoon dried oregano

¼ teaspoon dried thyme

1 teaspoon sea salt, or to taste

⅛ teaspoon ground black pepper

1 tablespoon balsamic or red wine vinegar (optional)

1 tablespoon olive oil (optional)

¾ cup very thinly sliced red onion (sliced into ⅛-inch-thick half-moons)

2 tablespoons chiffonaded fresh basil

1 tablespoon finely chopped fresh flat-leaf parsley

8 to 12 teaspoons nutritional yeast, for garnish

4 to 6 teaspoons pine nuts, for garnish

2 to 3 teaspoons minced fresh chives, for garnish (optional)

1. Place all the ingredients, except the red onion, basil, parsley, nutritional yeast, and pine nuts, in a blender and blend until creamy.
2. Transfer to a bowl. Add the red onion, basil, and parsley, and stir well. Allow the soup to sit for 15 minutes.
3. Stir well, and garnish each bowl with 2 teaspoons of nutritional yeast, 1 teaspoon of pine nuts, and ½ teaspoon of chives, if using, before serving.

Variations
- Add 1 cup of additional chopped raw veggies, such as cucumber, red bell pepper, and napa cabbage, along with the red onion.
- Replace the water with a vegetable juice of your choosing.
- Add 1 cup of peeled and grated carrot or jicama, along with the red onion.

♥ Spicy Kale Soup with Pepitas

Here is where amazing flavor and high nutrition come together. Loaded with nutrients, kale is the supreme leader of the green superfoods kingdom. Virtually all of us benefit from the inclusion of more kale in our diet. Pepitas, a.k.a. pumpkin seeds, are also tasty nutritional powerhouses and are a source of protein and zinc. Top with Raw Crème Fraîche (page 196), a touch of Tapenade (page 193), and a few additional pepitas.

SERVES 4 TO 6

½ cup raw pepitas

3 cups fairly tightly packed chopped kale

2½ cups water

3 tablespoons freshly squeezed lemon juice

¼ cup apple juice

½ cup mashed avocado

1 tablespoon peeled and minced fresh ginger

1 teaspoon seeded and diced hot pepper

1½ teaspoons sea salt, or to taste

⅛ teaspoon ground black pepper

Pinch of cayenne pepper

¼ teaspoon chipotle chile powder, or ½ teaspoon chili powder (optional)

1 tablespoon coconut oil or olive oil (optional)

2 teaspoons wheat-free tamari or other soy sauce, or to taste (optional)

1 tablespoon minced fresh cilantro

¼ cup seeded and minced red bell pepper, for garnish

1. Place the pepitas in a small bowl with ample water to cover. Allow them to sit for 15 minutes. Drain and rinse well.
2. Place in a strong blender with all the remaining ingredients, except the cilantro and red bell pepper, and blend until very creamy.
3. Transfer to a bowl, add the cilantro, and stir well. Top with the red bell pepper before serving.

Variations

- Add 2 teaspoons of peeled and minced fresh turmeric.
- Replace the pepitas with pecans, macadamia nuts, or cashews.
- Replace all or some of the kale with other greens, such as spinach, chard, or arugula.
- Replace the cilantro with fresh basil or 2 teaspoons of minced fresh dill.
- Add 1 teaspoon of curry powder or ground cumin.

❤ Savory Brazil Nut Soup with Jicama

I wanted to include both a sweet and savory version of a soup using Brazil nut milk as the base. Here is the savory version. The avocado adds to the creaminess, while nutritional yeast imparts a cheesy flavor. Top with sunflower sprouts and sunflower seeds.

SERVES 6

1 cup Brazil nuts

3 ½ cups water

½ cup mashed avocado

3 tablespoons nutritional yeast

1 garlic clove

2 tablespoons diced celery

¼ cup diced red onion

1½ teaspoons sea salt, or to taste

¼ teaspoon ground black pepper

Pinch of crushed red pepper flakes

1½ cups cubed jicama (½-inch cubes)

1 cup halved cherry tomatoes

¾ cup shredded spinach, rinsed and well drained

1 tablespoon finely chopped fresh basil

1 tablespoon finely chopped fresh flat-leaf parsley

2 tablespoons thinly sliced green onion

1. Place the Brazil nuts in a bowl with ample water to cover. Allow them to sit for 20 minutes.
2. Meanwhile, place the 3½ cups of water, the avocado, nutritional yeast, garlic, celery, 2 tablespoons of the red onion, the salt and black pepper, and the crushed red pepper flakes in a strong blender.
3. Drain and rinse the Brazil nuts well. Transfer to the blender and blend until creamy.
4. Transfer to a bowl with the remaining ingredients, and stir well before serving.

Variations
- Replace the spinach with mustard greens, chard, or kale.
- Replace the jicama with thinly sliced carrot, cabbage, or snow peas.
- Replace the cherry tomatoes with seeded and chopped red bell pepper or corn.
- Replace the Brazil nuts with cashews.
- You can replace the Brazil nuts with almonds. Blend separately and strain (see page 222) before using in the recipe.

♥ Raw Corn Chowder

If you have not experienced raw corn off the cob, get ready for a good time. It lends an unforgettable creaminess to this soup, especially when blended with the soaked macadamia nuts. Corn, or maize, was first grown in the Americas in prehistoric times. Since then it's been growing, and growing, and is now the largest cultivated crop in the Americas. Check out the Corn Chowder (page 129) to compare cooked and raw versions. Serve with Raw Crème Fraîche (page 196) or Red Pepper Cream (page 164).

SERVES 4

½ cup chopped raw macadamia nuts or cashews

3 cups corn, fresh off the cob

1¼ cups water

½ cup diced red onion

1 small garlic clove

¼ cup diced celery

2 tablespoons freshly squeezed lime juice

½ teaspoon seeded and diced hot chile pepper (see the Scoville scale on page 57)

1 teaspoon sea salt, or to taste

½ teaspoon ground turmeric (optional)

⅛ teaspoon ground black pepper

¼ teaspoon chili powder (try chipotle)

2 tablespoons flaxseed or hempseed oil (optional)

2 teaspoons minced fresh dill

½ cup seeded and diced red bell pepper, for garnish

Black sesame seeds, for garnish

1. Place the macadamia nuts in a bowl with ample water to cover and soak for 20 minutes.
2. Meanwhile, place 2 cups of the corn and all the remaining ingredients, except the dill, red bell pepper, and black sesame seeds, in a large blender.
3. Drain and rinse the macadamia nuts well. Transfer to the blender and blend until creamy. Transfer to a bowl. Add the remaining cup of corn and the dill, and mix well. Garnish with red bell pepper and black sesame seeds before serving.

Variations

- For **Indian Corn Chowder,** replace the dill with fresh cilantro, and add 2 teaspoons of curry powder and 1 teaspoon of ground cumin.
- For **Italian Corn Chowder,** replace the dill with 2 tablespoons of chiffonaded fresh basil, 1 tablespoon of finely chopped flat-leaf parsley, 1 teaspoon of minced fresh oregano, and ½ teaspoon of fresh thyme.

♥ Raw Creamy Greens Soup

The plant kingdom provides all the nutrients we need to thrive. Green vegetables, such as spinach, top the list of nutritional powerhouses. The creaminess comes from soaked and blended raw cashews. Top with Raw Crème Fraîche (page 196), Cherry Tomato Salsa Fresca (page 183), and a sprinkle of sunflower seeds.

SERVES 4

¾ cup chopped raw cashews or
   macadamia nuts

2 cups water

2 cups chopped zucchini (½-inch
   pieces)

2 cups stemmed and packed fairly
   tight spinach, rinsed well

¾ cup chopped celery

¼ cup freshly squeezed lemon juice

1 tablespoon miso paste
   (see page 34)

1 garlic clove

¾ teaspoon sea salt, or to taste

¼ teaspoon ground black pepper

Pinch of cayenne pepper

1 tablespoon minced fresh dill

1 tablespoon hemp or flax oil
   (optional)

1 cup fresh or frozen corn

1. Place the cashews in a bowl with ample water to cover and soak for 20 minutes.
2. Meanwhile, place all the remaining ingredients, except the corn, in a large blender.
3. Drain and rinse the cashews well. Transfer to the blender and blend until creamy.
4. Pour into a bowl, add the corn, and mix well.

Variations

- Replace the spinach with other greens, such as kale or chard.
- Replace the corn with peeled and grated carrot and/or beet.
- Replace the corn with seeded and diced red bell pepper.
- Replace the dill with fresh cilantro, basil, or flat-leaf parsley.
- Replace the garlic with fresh ginger.
- For an Indian flair, add 2 teaspoons of curry powder and 1 teaspoon of ground cumin before blending. Replace the dill with fresh cilantro.
- For a Mexican version, add 2 teaspoons of chili powder and 1 teaspoon of ground cumin before blending. Replace the dill with fresh cilantro.

♥ Raw Thai Coconut Soup

Tropical goodness abounds in this raw adaptation of everyone's favorite Thai coconut soup. Energizing and enchantingly delectable, the blended coconut meat and water creates a creamy base for your soup. See Chef's Tips and Tricks to learn how to work with the fresh coconuts. Depending upon how many coconuts you need to open, and your coconut opening skills, this recipe may take longer than 30 minutes. Compare this raw soup with its cooked counterpart, Thai Coconut with Lemongrass (page 43).

SERVES 4 TO 6

2 to 4 Thai coconuts, yielding 4 cups coconut water and ¾ cup coconut meat (see Chef's Tips and Tricks)

1 cup water

3 Kaffir lime leaves, or 2 tablespoons freshly squeezed lime juice plus ½ teaspoon lime zest

1 lemongrass stalk, white part only, very bottom portion removed (about 4 inches)

1 tablespoon peeled and minced fresh ginger

2 teaspoons seeded and diced hot chile pepper, or to taste (see the Scoville scale on page 57)

2 teaspoons wheat-free tamari or other soy sauce (optional)

1 teaspoon sea salt, or to taste

Pinch of crushed red pepper flakes

¾ cup shredded napa cabbage or julienned snow peas

½ cup seeded and diced red bell pepper

¼ cup thinly sliced green onion

1 tablespoon finely chopped fresh cilantro

2 tablespoons unsweetened shredded coconut, for garnish

1 to 2 ounces microgreens, for garnish (see Chef's Tips and Tricks)

1. Place all the ingredients except the cabbage, bell pepper, green onion, cilantro, and garnishes, in a strong blender and blend until creamy. Transfer to a bowl.
2. Add the remaining ingredients, except the garnishes, and stir well. Place in the refrigerator or freezer until just chilled.
3. Garnish with coconut and microgreens before serving.

Variations

- Add 1 cup of coconut noodles after blending. To make, simply slice the coconut meat into thin strips.
- Add ½ cup of fresh corn and ½ cup of fresh peas after blending.
- Add 1 tablespoon of chiffonaded fresh Thai basil after blending.

continues

Chef's Tips and Tricks

Microgreens are tiny, young edible greens from herbs and vegeables. Varieties include red cabbage, cilantro, radish, beets, peas, and more.

Raw Thai Coconut Soup *continued*

Chef's Tips and Tricks

Working with Coconuts

Cutting a coconut isn't difficult, but you should be very careful. Here is a method for opening the Thai coconuts that are commonly available in the States. Place the coconut on its side on a sturdy cutting board and hold the bottom of the coconut. Using a heavy cleaver or machete, carefully give the coconut a whack about 1½ inches below the pointed end. This should cut into the hard shell. If not, you can give it another light whack, being careful not to spill the water. Place the coconut over a bowl or a quart-size mason jar and drain out the liquid. If pieces of the shell got into the water, strain them out. Once the liquid is removed, you can use the knife to carefully pry the remainder of the top off.

If this seems intimidating, feel free to ask someone in the produce department to crack open the coconut for you. They are usually more than happy to oblige.

♥ Chilled Avocado Soup with Cherry Tomato Salsa Fresca

Avocados are an ancient food (a twelve-thousand-year-old seed was found in a cave in Mexico—that's pretty ancient), with over five hundred varieties available. They are a good source of healthy fat, which adds a welcoming creaminess to this soup. The salsa contributes lots of flavor and texture, for a totally awesome soup experience.

SERVES 4 TO 6

AVOCADO SOUP

2 cups mashed avocado (Hass variety recommended)

2 cups carrot juice

1 cup water

¼ cup diced red onion

2 tablespoons freshly squeezed lime juice

½ teaspoon seeded and diced jalapeño pepper

1 garlic clove

2 teaspoons sea salt, or to taste

½ teaspoon ground cumin

¼ teaspoon ground black pepper

⅛ teaspoon chili powder (try chipotle)

Pinch of crushed red pepper flakes

2 tablespoons finely chopped green onion

1½ tablespoons finely chopped fresh cilantro

CHERRY TOMATO SALSA FRESCA

1 cup diced cherry tomatoes

1 tablespoon diced red onion

1 tablespoon diced green onion

2 teaspoons minced fresh cilantro

2 teaspoons freshly squeezed lime juice

Pinch of ground cumin

Pinch of cayenne pepper (optional)

Pinch of sea salt

Pinch of ground black pepper

1. Prepare the soup: Place all the soup ingredients, except the green onion and cilantro, in a blender and blend until creamy. Transfer to a bowl, add the green onion and cilantro, and mix well. Place in the refrigerator or freezer to chill while you prepare the salsa.
2. Prepare the salsa: Combine all the salsa ingredients in a small bowl and mix well.
3. To serve, garnish each bowl of soup with a small scoop of the salsa.

Variations
- Add ½ cup of corn to the salsa.
- Replace the carrot juice with a mixed vegetable juice, such as carrot, beet, and celery, or your favorite.

PART SIX

GARNISHES
AND
SIDES

In this final section we will explore many of the ways you can enhance your soup experience. All of them will add a new dimension of flavor to your dish. Some recipes will add more substance to the soup, turning it from a starter course to more of a light meal, especially when you add a nice big organic salad to the experience. Recipes such as Cosmic Corn Bread, Herbed Bread Sticks, Tofu Feta, and Tapenade will accomplish this.

Other recipes, such as Crispy Sunchokes, Vegetable Chips, Krispy Kale, Sweet and Spicy Toasted Nori Sheets, and Herbed Croutons will add additional texture to your soup. For added color, try the Basil Oil, Red Oil, Vegan or Raw Crème Fraîche, and Balsamic Reduction. Those garnishes with additional flavor as their main role include Caramelized Onions, Tempeh Bacon, Roasted Garlic, and the Vegan or Raw Crème Fraîche.

As with the other sections in *Soup's On!* the recipes are listed roughly in order of the heaviness of the dishes, beginning with the lightest ones.

Flavored Ice Cubes
and Frozen Melon Balls

Pour fruit juice or blended raw soups into small or custom-shaped (try small hearts or stars) ice cube trays. Add berries to fruit-based cubes. Add small leaves of herbs such as mint to fruit-based cubes; parsley, basil, oregano, or marjoram to savory cubes. Place in the freezer until frozen, about two hours. You can also use water as the base, or teas such as green tea, Earl Grey, yerba mate, or your favorite. Get creative with this fun way to spice up your raw soups!

You can also use a melon ball spoon to spoon out melon such as cantaloupe, watermelon, or honeydew. Place on parchment paper on a small tray and place in the freezer until frozen. Add to raw fruit soups. Store in the ice cube trays in the freezer and use within a week.

Red Oil

Sometimes all you need is a little splash of red to transform your soups into a work of art. Simple to prepare, drizzle this red oil on soups as well as your salads and main dishes for that extra visual oomph. Store in a squeeze bottle in the refrigerator and use within a week.

MAKES ½ CUP OIL

½ cup olive, safflower, or
    sunflower oil
1 tablespoon paprika
Pinch of crushed red pepper flakes
    (optional)

1. Place the oil, paprika, and crushed red pepper in a blender and blend for 10 to 15 seconds.
2. Pour through a paper coffee filter and allow to slowly strain into a bowl, about 15 minutes.
3. Transfer to a squeeze bottle and use as a garnish on soups.

Basil Oil

Going green has never been easier. This colored oil, especially when served with its Red Oil stepsister (page 187), will turn your soup bowl and even the plate underneath the bowl, into a blank canvas for you to express your artistic creativity with swirls, drops, and lines of color. Store in a squeeze bottle in the refrigerator and use within a week.

MAKES ABOUT ½ CUP OIL

½ teaspoon sea salt

1 cup packed fairly tight fresh basil, thick stems removed

½ cup olive oil

1. Bring water to a boil in a small pot over high heat. Add the salt.
2. Meanwhile, prepare an ice bath by placing several ice cubes in a small bowl with water to cover.
3. When the water boils, place the basil in the pot for 5 seconds, making sure all the leaves are immersed and turn a dark green. Using a small strainer, remove the basil and immediately transfer it to the ice bath.
4. As soon as the basil is cooled, strain it well and squeeze out any excess liquid. You can use a clean, dry towel for this purpose. Transfer to a strong blender with the olive oil and blend very well.
5. Pour through a coffee filter, or double layer of cheesecloth placed in a fine strainer, to strain out as much of the solid matter as possible.
6. Transfer to a squeeze bottle. Store in the refrigerator and use within a few days.

Balsamic Reduction

Use this sweet and tangy syrup to provide an intense burst of flavor to your soups. Transfer to a squeeze bottle and have fun creating unique and artistic garnishes. This nectar will last for a week or longer when stored in the refrigerator. You can add a tiny amount of water, if necessary, and stir well to reconstitute the reduction to a pourable consistency once it is cooled.

MAKES ¾ CUP REDUCTION

1½ cups balsamic vinegar

1. Place the vinegar in a small saucepan over high heat. Cook for 5 minutes, whisking constantly and being careful not to let it burn.
2. Lower the heat to low and cook until the liquid is reduced by half, about 10 minutes, whisking frequently.
3. Pour into a glass container and let it cool. It will take on a syrupy consistency as it cools. Transfer to a squeeze bottle and use it to garnish soups.

Variations

- Try adding a few sprigs of fresh herbs, such as rosemary or thyme, several whole peppercorns, or one garlic clove. Strain before using.
- You can also make a reduction using one part red wine and one part balsamic vinegar.

Toasted Coconut

Preheat an oven or toaster oven to 375°F. Place unsweetened shredded coconut or coconut flakes on a dry baking sheet and bake until just golden brown and aromatic, about 3 minutes. Be careful not to let them burn! If you are in a rush for time, you can also toast the coconut in a dry sauté pan, though sometimes it's tricky to get a uniform browning with this method. To do so, place the pan over high heat. Add the coconut and cook until golden brown and aromatic, about 3 minutes, stirring constantly. Store in a glass container in a cool, dry place or the refrigerator, and use within three or four days. Adds an amazing flavor and texture on top of any of the coconut-based soups.

Sweet and Spicy Toasted Nori Sheets

Nori is paper-thin sheets of edible seaweed that is most commonly used as a wrapper for veggie sushi and maki rolls. Here we are creating a sweet and spicy sauce containing wasabi powder and Japanese horseradish, and brushing it on the sheets with a pastry brush. These crispy treats will add a touch of nirvana to your Asian-themed soups and also serve as an amazing snack on their own. Store in a glass container in a cool, dry place or the refrigerator, and use within three or four days.

MAKES 5 SHEETS NORI

2 teaspoons wasabi powder

1 tablespoon water

1 tablespoon sesame oil

1 teaspoon toasted sesame oil

⅛ teaspoon sea salt

1 tablespoon coconut nectar (see page 227), agave nectar, or pure maple syrup

Pinch of crushed red pepper flakes

5 nori sheets

3 tablespoons sesame seeds

1. Preheat the oven to 250°F. Place the wasabi powder in a small bowl. Add the water and whisk well. Add all the remaining ingredients, except the nori sheets and sesame seeds, and whisk well.
2. Lay out the nori sheets, smooth side down, on a couple of large, dry baking sheets.
3. Using a pastry brush, coat the nori sheets with the mixture in the bowl and sprinkle with the sesame seeds. Do this step, and place in the oven, as fast as possible, as the nori will begin to wilt once it is in contact with the mixture.
4. Bake for 20 minutes. Remove from the oven, carefully transfer to a clean, dry cutting board, and slice into 1 by 3-inch strips.

Variations
- Replace the sesame seeds with hemp seeds.
- Replace the sesame oil with coconut oil.

Candied Pepitas

Pepitas, or pumpkin seeds, are a highly nutritious and tasty addition to your soups, adding a pleasant crunch, especially on the creamy soups, or bean soups. They make the perfect snack as well. They can be stored in a glass container at room temperature for several days.

MAKES 1 CUP PEPITAS

1 cup pumpkin seeds

1 tablespoon plus 1 teaspoon pure maple syrup or sweetener of choice

1½ teaspoons wheat-free tamari or other soy sauce

2 teaspoons freshly squeezed lime juice

Pinch of sea salt

Pinch of chili powder (try chipotle)

1. Preheat the oven to 375°F. Place all the ingredients in a small bowl and mix well.
2. Transfer to a lightly oiled baking sheet and bake for 10 minutes, stirring a few times to ensure even cooking.
3. Remove from the oven and allow to cool, stirring a few times to prevent sticking.

Variations

- Replace the pumpkin seeds with any seed or nut, or combination. Try with sunflower seeds or chopped cashews, macadamia nuts, or almonds.
- Try adding a few drops of truffle oil.
- Add 2 teaspoons of fennel seeds.
- Add 1 teaspoon of a spice blend (see page 223).
- For **Toasted Pepitas,** you can dry-toast the seeds according the method on page 213. You can also combine 1 cup of pepitas with 1 to 1½ tablespoons of melted coconut oil in a small bowl. Mix to coat well. Place on a baking sheet and bake in a preheated 375°F oven until the seeds begin to pop and turn golden brown, about 5 minutes. Remove from the oven, place in a bowl, and sprinkle with salt to taste, if desired. Store in a glass jar.

♥ Tapenade

Use this flavorful olive paste as a garnish for soups (especially those with a Mediterranean theme) or on top of Crostini (page 198) as a side dish. Store in a glass container in the refrigerator and enjoy within three or four days.

MAKES ¾ CUP TAPENADE

1 cup diced olives

1 tablespoon olive oil (optional)

1 garlic clove, pressed or minced

1 tablespoon freshly squeezed lemon juice

¼ teaspoon ground black pepper

¼ teaspoon dried thyme

1 teaspoon minced fresh rosemary (optional)

1 tablespoon chiffonaded fresh basil

1 teaspoon capers

1 tablespoon nutritional yeast (optional)

Place all the ingredients in a food processor and pulse until smooth. Be careful not to over-process.

Variations

- Add a few cloves of roasted garlic, mashed well.
- Add ¼ cup sautéed and diced shiitake mushrooms.

193

Roasted Garlic Spread

Garlic lovers are well aware of the culinary ecstasy they experience when a schmear of roasted garlic is added to their dishes. Join in on the fun and spread on Crostini (page 198) along with Tapenade (page 193) for a radically flavorful accompaniment to some of the lighter recipes in the book. Look for heads of garlic with large cloves. Store in a glass container in the refrigerator and enjoy within three or four days.

2 to 3 heads garlic
Olive oil
Sea salt and ground black pepper
Crushed red pepper flakes
    (optional)

1. Preheat the oven to 450°F. Slice off the very top portion of the garlic heads, about ½ inch, so that almost all the cloves are exposed. Drizzle with olive oil and make sure all the cloves are coated. Sprinkle with salt and black pepper.
2. Place in a small, covered casserole dish with about ¼ inch of water. If you do not have a cover for the dish, you can cover with aluminum foil, or leave uncovered.
3. Roast until the cloves are just soft and golden brown, about 25 minutes. Allow to cool sufficiently to handle.
4. Squeeze the garlic out of the skins into a small bowl. Mash well with a fork. (You can also puree the garlic in a small food processor.) Add about 1 teaspoon of olive oil for every 3 tablespoons of garlic. Add salt, black pepper, and crushed red pepper flakes, if using, to taste and mix well.

Vegan Crème Fraîche

Typically made with a soured cream with high butterfat content, these vegan versions of crème fraîche have all the richness you could want and will take pretty much all of your soups to the next level of culinary excellence. (You will notice that Crème Fraîche is the most frequently recommended garnish!) A cooked and a raw version are provided so you can compare the different flavor profiles. Store in a glass container in the refrigerator and enjoy within three or four days.

COOKED

Makes ½ cup

½ cup vegan mayonnaise (Vegenaise recommended) or homemade (see page 226)

1½ teaspoons freshly squeezed lemon juice

Pinch of sea salt

Combine all the ingredients in a large bowl and mix well.

Variation

- For **Chipotle Mayonnaise,** add ½ teaspoon of chipotle chile powder.

♥ Raw Crème Fraîche

MAKES ½ CUP

½ cup chopped raw cashews

½ cup plus 2 tablespoons water

1½ tablespoons freshly squeezed
    lemon juice

¼ teaspoon sea salt, or to taste

1. Soak the cashews in ample water to cover. Allow to soak for 25 minutes.
2. Rinse and drain well.
3. Place in a strong blender with the measured amount of water, lemon juice, and salt and blend until very creamy.

Variations
- Try adding 1 tablespoon of olive oil when blending.
- Replace all or some of the cashews with macadamia nuts, Brazil nuts, or blanched almonds.

Red Pepper Coulis

Looking to add a deep, rich accented flavor to your soups? This is your sauce. Coulis is a French sauce made from blended and strained vegetables or fruits. This one requires no straining. Adding the toasted coconut listed in the variations puts it over the top. This coulis goes particularly well (both in terms of flavor and in color contrast) with any of the recipes that recommend the Vegan or Raw Crème Fraîche. Store in a glass container in the refrigerator and enjoy within three or four days.

MAKES ½ CUP COULIS

1 tablespoon olive oil, plus more for basting

2 red bell peppers (1 cup after roasting)

4 garlic cloves

½ teaspoon balsamic vinegar

⅛ teaspoon sea salt, or to taste

Pinch of ground white pepper

Pinch of cayenne pepper

1. Preheat the oven to HIGH BROIL. Lightly oil the peppers and place on a baking sheet. Place them in the oven. Place the garlic in a small ramekin with the olive oil and place on a low rack in the oven. Cook the garlic until just golden brown, about 5 minutes. Remove and set aside. Cook the peppers until the skin is charred, about 20 minutes, flipping a few times to ensure even cooking.
2. Place the peppers in a small bowl and cover with a plate to allow them to steam. Once cool enough to handle, about 10 minutes, carefully remove the skin and seeds. (Do not rinse under cold water or you will lose some of that distinctive roasted red pepper flavor.)
3. Place the peppers in the blender or a food processor with the garlic and remaining ingredients and blend well.

Variations
- Add 1 tablespoon of shredded coconut (optionally toasted; see page 213) before blending.
- Sauté 2 tablespoons of diced shallots in a small amount of oil for 2 minutes over high heat, stirring constantly while the peppers are roasting. Add to the blender with the remaining ingredients and blend well.

Crostini

Translated as "little toasts" in Italian, serve these as a side for any of your soups, with or without toppings such as Tapenade (page 193), Cherry Tomato Salsa Fresca (page 183), Guacamole (page 204), or Tofu Feta (page 207). Store in a glass container in a cool, dry place and enjoy within two or three days.

MAKES 1 BAGUETTE'S WORTH OF TOAST

About 3 tablespoons olive oil

¼ teaspoon sea salt, or to taste

¼ teaspoon ground black pepper, or to taste

Pinch of crushed red pepper flakes (optional)

2 tablespoons Italian Spice Mix (see page 223) (optional)

1 baguette, ½-inch slices

1. Preheat the oven to 375°F. Place the oil in a small bowl, add the salt, black pepper, crushed red pepper flakes, if using, and Italian Spice mix, if using, and mix well.
2. Place the baguette slices on a baking sheet. Using a pastry brush, lightly brush each slice with the oil mixture.
3. Bake until crisp, about 10 minutes.

Pita Chips

Why purchase pita chips when it's so easy to make your own? Serve along with any of the soups, especially the Mideast Chickpea Soup (page 135). Store in a glass container in a cool, dry place and enjoy within three days.

MAKES 40 CHIPS

3 tablespoons olive oil

¼ teaspoon sea salt

⅛ teaspoon ground black pepper

½ teaspoon dried oregano

¼ teaspoon dried thyme

Pinch of cayenne pepper (optional)

5 pieces pita bread (one 10-ounce package)

1. Preheat the oven to 400°F. Place all the ingredients, except the pita bread, in a small bowl and mix well. Baste both sides of each piece of pita, using a pastry brush.
2. Slice each pita in half, then cut each half into four triangles.
3. Place the triangles on a large baking sheet and bake until golden brown, about 10 minutes, depending upon the type of bread used.

Herbed Croutons

Croutons top the list of favorite soup garnishes, especially on the creamy soups. There is no end to the flavorful varieties you can create. Try with different types of bread (see the Cosmic Corn Bread on page 211), oils, and herb combinations. The moisture of the bread will determine how long the croutons need to cook. You want them to be crispy, so check periodically. Croutons may be stored in a glass container in a cool, dry place for up to three days.

MAKES 3 CUPS CROUTONS

1½ tablespoons oil (try coconut or olive)
1 teaspoon dried oregano
1 teaspoon dried basil
¼ teaspoon dried thyme
¼ teaspoon sea salt
⅛ teaspoon ground black pepper
⅛ teaspoon garlic powder
½ teaspoon onion flakes
Pinch of crushed red pepper flakes
3 cups cubed bread (½-inch cubes) (try gluten free)

1. Preheat the oven to 350°F. Place all the ingredients, except the bread, in a large bowl and mix well. Add the bread and toss well to evenly coat.
2. Transfer to a baking sheet.
3. Bake until crispy, about 25 minutes, depending upon the type of bread used. Allow to cool before storing.

Variations
- Replace the oregano, basil, thyme, garlic powder, and onion flakes with 1 tablespoon of Mexican Spice Mix (page 224) or Indian Spice Mix (page 223).

Vegetable Chips

Adding color and crunch to your soups, especially the creamy blended ones, these veggie chips are exquisitely simple to prepare. The secret is to get a uniform and thin slice. For best results, use a mandoline (see Chef's Tips and Tricks), or a large vegetable peeler to create the slices. Store in a glass container in a cool, dry place and enjoy within two or three days.

SERVING SIZE VARIES

½ sweet potato
½ large beet
Coconut, olive, or sesame oil
Sea salt
Ground black pepper
Dehydrated onion flakes (optional)
Garlic powder (optional)
Crushed red pepper flakes
    (optional)

1. Preheat the oven to 400°F. Thinly slice the vegetables (about ⅟₁₆-inch slices) and place on a large baking sheet.
2. Lightly brush with oil and top with a sprinkle of salt, black pepper, and a pinch of any or all of the optional spices.
3. Bake until just crispy, about 15 minutes, depending upon the thickness of the vegetables. Be careful not to let them burn.

Variations
- You can toss the vegetables in oil in a large bowl and then place on a baking sheet instead of basting them once on the baking sheet.
- For Mexican, sprinkle with chili powder and ground cumin.
- For Indian, sprinkle with curry powder and ground cumin.
- For Italian, sprinkle with dried oregano, thyme, and rosemary.

Chef's Tips and Tricks

Working with a Mandoline

Pronounced very similarly to the musical instrument *mandolin*, a mandoline is a handy kitchen gadget that allows you to create superthin slices or to julienne strips of vegetables and fruits. Follow the manufacturer's guidelines carefully as the blades are super sharp. I speak from experience on this one.

Crispy Sunchokes

If you have yet to experience the glory of roasted sunchokes (a.k.a. Jerusalem artichokes), you are in for a real treat. With origins in North America, and an earthly flavor and a delightful crunch, these tubers make an amazing addition to your creamy soups as well as to salads. The thickness and size of the chips will determine how long they need to cook. Check frequently and carefully remove the thinner and smaller chips with a spatula as they crisp. Store in a glass container in a cool, dry place and enjoy within two or three days.

MAKES ½ CUP SUNCHOKES

2 cups very thinly sliced Jerusalem artichokes, well cleaned (about ¹⁄₁₆-inch slices)

2 tablespoons olive oil

1 tablespoon freshly squeezed lemon juice

Pinch of ground black pepper

Pinch of crushed red pepper flakes (optional)

⅛ to ¾ teaspoon sea salt

1. Preheat the oven to 400°F. Place all the ingredients, except the salt, in a large bowl and toss well. Add ⅛ teaspoon of the salt and toss well.

2. Transfer to a baking sheet and bake for 20 minutes, or until crispy. Be careful not to let them burn.

3. Transfer to the bowl, add the remaining salt, if desired, and toss well before serving.

Krispy Kale

Kale chips are the potato chip of the future, equally as flavorful and far superior in nutrition. Experiment to create a variety of flavors to complement the type of soup you are preparing. Go Mexican with the Mexican-themed soups, Indian for Indian . . . I think you see where this is going! Store in a glass container in a cool, dry place and enjoy within two or three days.

MAKES 4 CUPS KALE

4 cups curly kale, thick stems removed, chopped into bite-size pieces, fairly tightly packed

2 tablespoons coconut or olive oil

1 tablepoon freshly squeezed lemon juice

3 tablespoons nutritional yeast

¼ to ½ teaspoon sea salt

¼ teaspoon ground black pepper

Pinch of red pepper flakes

1. Preheat the oven to 350°F. Place all the ingredients in a large bowl and toss well.
2. Transfer to one large or two small baking sheets. Spread to a single layer.
3. Bake until crispy, about 15 minutes, gently stirring after 10 minutes. Serve immediately, or store in an airtight container at room temperature for a few days.

Variations

- For **Mexican Kale Chips,** add 2 tablespoons of fresh cilantro, 1 teaspoon of ground cumin, 1 teaspoon of chili powder, and ¼ teaspoon of chipotle chile powder.
- For **Italian Kale Chips,** add 2 tablespoons of fresh basil, 2 tablespoons of fresh flat-leaf parsley, and 1 teaspoon each of dried oregano and thyme.
- For **Indian Kale Chips,** add 2 tablespoons of fresh cilantro, 2 tablespoons of curry powder, and 1 teaspoon of ground cumin.

♥ Guacamole

Serve this popular Mexican condiment as a garnish on any Mexican or tomato-based soups. Served on top of Crostini (page 198), it will transform your soup into a filling meal. Store in a glass container in the refrigerator for up to twenty-four hours.

MAKES 1½ CUPS GUACAMOLE

3 small avocados, peeled, pitted, and chopped (1½ cups)

3 tablespoons diced red onion

2 tablespoons minced fresh cilantro

1½ to 2 tablespoons freshly squeezed lime juice

1½ teaspoons seeded and diced jalapeño pepper

1 small garlic clove, pressed or minced

¾ teaspoon ground cumin (optionally toasted) (see page 213)

¼ teaspoon chili powder

Pinch of cayenne pepper

Pinch of chipotle chile powder (optional)

Sea salt and ground black pepper

1. Place the avocado in a small bowl and mash it with a fork.
2. Add the remaining ingredients, seasoning to taste with salt and black pepper, and mix well.

Caramelized Onions

Onions are naturally sweet. When you cook them for an extended period of time the sugars are released and a deep, rich flavor is created. At the end of the process, you can add a small amount of balsamic vinegar or red wine to deglaze the bottom of the pan for added flavor (see Chef's Tips and Tricks). Adding a spoonful of these onions on top of your soups, especially those featuring beans and grains, will contribute a new dimension of flavor. Store in a glass container in the refrigerator for up to three days.

MAKES 1 CUP ONIONS

1 tablespoon oil

1 large onion, sliced into ⅛- to ¼-inch-thick half-moons

1. Place the oil in a heavy-bottomed sauté pan over high heat.
2. Add the onion and cook for 5 minutes, stirring frequently and adding small amounts of water if necessary, to prevent sticking.
3. Lower the heat to medium and cook for 20 minutes, stirring occasionally, and adding small amounts of water if necessary, to prevent sticking. Be careful not to let it burn!

Variations
- Add 2 tablespoons of red wine or balsamic vinegar after cooking, and scrape the bottom of the pan well.

Chef's Tips and Tricks

Deglazing

Deglazing is the process of removing the juices and oils that have stuck to the bottom of the pan during the cooking process. It is accomplished by adding a small amount of liquid, such as wine, balsamic vinegar, or water, and scraping the bottom of the pan. This adds more flavor to the dish.

♥ Pesto Magnifico

Recipe courtesy of *The 30-Minute Vegan's Taste of Europe*

This pesto is perfecto when served on top of Crostini (page 198). You can also try a dollop on Ragout of Fall Vegetables (page 60), or Mediterranean-themed soups such as Creamy White Bean Soup (page 148) and Raw Mediterranean Onion Soup (page 176). Store in a glass container in the refrigerator for three or four days.

MAKES ¾ CUP PESTO

1 cup tightly packed fresh basil

¼ cup pine nuts

1 garlic clove

3 to 4 tablespoons olive oil

1 tablespoon freshly squeezed lemon juice

½ teaspoon sea salt, or to taste

⅛ teaspoon ground black pepper

2 teaspoons nutritional yeast (optional)

1 tablespoon minced green onion or red onion (optional)

¼ teaspoon crushed red pepper flakes, or ½ teaspoon seeded and diced hot chile pepper (see the Scoville scale on page 57)

Combine all the ingredients in a small food processor and process until smooth.

Variations

- Replace the pine nuts with cashews, macadamia nuts, walnuts, pistachios, or pecans, either raw or toasted (see page 213).
- Add more or less oil to create different textures of pesto.

Tofu Feta

This recipe proves that you do not need to use animal products to create a "cheese" that is bursting with flavor. This version uses a firm tofu as the base. The miso paste and lemon juice give the dish its distinctive tang. Serve as a garnish on soups, especially those with a Mediterranean theme, when you are looking to add a little more substance and an extra layer of flavor. Store in a glass container in the refrigerator and enjoy within three days.

MAKES 2 CUPS TOFU FETA

14 ounces firm tofu

3 tablespoons light miso paste (see page 34)

3 tablespoons freshly squeezed lemon juice

¼ teaspoon sea salt

½ teaspoon minced fresh rosemary

1 teaspoon dried oregano

¼ teaspoon dried thyme

¼ teaspoon ground black pepper

1 tablespoon nutritional yeast (optional, but recommended)

1. Bring water in a small pot to a boil over high heat. Slice the tofu into ½-inch cubes and place in the boiling water. Cook for 5 minutes.
2. Meanwhile, place the remaining ingredients in a bowl and mix well.
3. Remove the tofu, drain well, and transfer to the bowl with the remaining ingredients. Mix well with a fork, mashing about one-quarter of the tofu.
4. Allow to cool in the refrigerator for 15 minutes or longer. The longer it sits, the more the flavors will mature.

Tempeh Bacon

Recipe courtesy *The 30-Minute Vegan*

Certified Miss Piggy approved, use this recipe as a bacon alternative to add a hearty flavor to your dishes. Dice well and serve on top of soups. Will add substance and flavor to the vegetable- and grain-based stews. Store in a glass container in the refrigerator and use within two or three days.

SERVES 4

2 tablespoons wheat-free tamari or other soy sauce

3 tablespoons water

1 tablespoon pure maple syrup or agave nectar

¼ teaspoon liquid smoke

½ teaspoon garlic powder

½ teaspoon onion powder

8 ounces tempeh, sliced into ⅛-inch or thinner strips

1. Place all the ingredients, except the tempeh, in a shallow dish and whisk well. Add the tempeh and marinate for 10 minutes, flipping frequently.
2. You have two options for cooking. A healthier version is to preheat the oven or toaster oven to 375°F and place the tempeh on a well-oiled baking sheet. Bake for 8 minutes, flip, and bake for another 7 minutes.
3. For the full, crispy, almost-like-bacon effect, place 2 tablespoons of coconut oil or your favorite oil in a medium-size sauté pan. Sauté over medium-high heat until crispy, flipping occasionally to cook both sides evenly.

Variations

- You can replace the tempeh with 8 ounces of thinly sliced extra-firm tofu. To create the slices, cut the block of tofu in half and then slice thinly.
- Replace the liquid smoke with 1 teaspoon of smoked paprika.

Herbed Bread Sticks

This is a versatile recipe that allows countless variations, depending upon the herbs and spices added. Be sure to allow time for the yeast to bubble before adding the flour. I am sure that you realize these bread sticks will enhance any of your soup experiences. Store in a glass container in a cool, dry place and use within two or three days for optimal flavor.

MAKES 12 BREADSTICKS

⅓ cup olive oil

1½ teaspoons minced garlic

1½ teaspoons minced fresh basil

1½ teaspoons minced fresh
    flat-leaf parsley

1 teaspoon minced fresh sage
    (optional)

1 teaspoon dried oregano

½ teaspoon dried thyme

¾ teaspoon sea salt

⅛ teaspoon ground black pepper

Pinch of crushed red pepper flakes

½ teaspoon organic sugar
    (see page 227)

½ cup plus 2 tablespoons water,
    warm to the touch (about
    105°F)

½ tablespoon dry active yeast

1⅔ cups white spelt flour, sifted
    well

⅛ cup cornmeal

1. Preheat the oven to 375°F. Place the olive oil in a small bowl with the garlic, herbs, spices, salt, black pepper, and crushed red pepper, mix well, and allow it to sit for 10 minutes or longer.
2. Meanwhile, place the sugar and warm water in a large bowl and whisk until the sugar dissolves. Add the yeast.
3. When the yeast starts to bubble, add the oil mixture and whisk well. Slowly add the flour and cornmeal and knead into a ball. Cover the bowl with a towel and put it in a warm place. After 10 minutes, thump the dough down, gently knead it into a ball, re-cover the bowl with the towel, and let it rise again for 10 additional minutes.
4. Divide the dough into twelve equal portions and roll on a cornmeal-dusted surface to form pencil-shaped rods. Baste with additional olive oil. Bake until golden brown, about 20 minutes. Bake longer for crisper sticks. Serve warm or cooled.

Variations

- For a gluten-free version, use Bob's Red Mill gluten-free flour mix or the flour mix on page 223, and add 1 teaspoon of xanthan gum.

continues

Herbed Bread Sticks *continued*

- Create **Mexican Bread Sticks** by adding 1 tablespoon of chili powder, 1 teaspoon of ground cumin, and ¼ teaspoon of chipotle chile powder, and by replacing the basil, parsley, and sage with an equal amount of fresh cilantro.
- Create **Indian Bread Sticks** by replacing the oregano and thyme with 1 tablespoon of curry powder and 1 teaspoon of ground cumin. Replace the basil, parsley, and sage with an equal amount of fresh cilantro.

 Cosmic Corn Bread

This savory bread is the perfect companion for many of the soups in this book, especially the Cha-Cha Chili (page 120), Black Bean Tomato Soup (page 109), and the Brazilian Black Bean Soup with Baked Plantain (page 114). The adventurous can use this corn bread as the base for Herbed Croutons (page 200). Store in a glass container in a cool, dry place and use within three or four days. Enjoy it reheated!

MAKES ONE 9 X 13-INCH CORN BREAD

DRY

2 cups white spelt flour, sifted well

1 cup cornmeal

¾ cup millet, optionally lightly toasted in a dry sauté pan until golden brown and aromatic

2½ tablespoons baking powder, sifted to remove any lumps

¾ teaspoon sea salt

WET

12.3 ounces silken firm tofu

1¾ cups water

¾ cup pure maple syrup

½ cup safflower, sunflower, or coconut oil

1. Preheat the oven to 350°F. Combine the dry ingredients in a large bowl and whisk well. Place the wet ingredients in a blender and blend until creamy. Add the wet to the dry and mix well.

2. Pour into a parchment paper-lined 9 x 13-inch baking pan and bake until a toothpick comes out clean, about 45 minutes, or until the top browns and cracks appear.

Variations

- For **Southwestern Corn Bread**, add the following to the dry mixture: ¼ cup of ancho chiles, soaked in hot water, seeded and diced; ½ cup of seeded and diced red bell pepper, ¼ cup of finely chopped cilantro, and ½ cup of fresh or frozen corn.

- For **Double Corn Bread**, add 1½ cups of fresh or frozen corn after all the other ingredients have been mixed together.

- For a gluten-free version, use Bob's Red Mill gluten-free flour mix or the flour mix on page 223, and add 1¼ teaspoons of xanthan gum.

CONVERSION CHART

- The recipes in this book have not been tested with metric measurements, so some variations might occur.
- Remember that the weight of dry ingredients varies according to the volume or density factor: 1 cup of flour weighs far less than 1 cup of sugar, and 1 tablespoon doesn't necessarily hold 3 teaspoons.

General Formulas for Metric Conversion

Ounces to grams	❯ ounces × 28.35 = grams
Grams to ounces	❯ grams × 0.035 = ounces
Pounds to grams	❯ pounds × 453.5 = grams
Pounds to kilograms	❯ pounds × 0.45 = kilograms
Cups to liters	❯ cups × 0.24 = liters
Fahrenheit to Celsius	❯ (°F − 32) × 5 ÷ 9 = °C
Celsius to Fahrenheit	❯ (°C × 9) ÷ 5 + 32 = °F

Linear Measurements

½ inch	=	1½ cm
1 inch	=	2½ cm
6 inches	=	15 cm
8 inches	=	20 cm
10 inches	=	25 cm
12 inches	=	30 cm
20 inches	=	50 cm

Volume (Dry) Measurements

¼ teaspoon = 1 milliliter
½ teaspoon = 2 milliliters
¾ teaspoon = 4 milliliters
1 teaspoon = 5 milliliters
1 tablespoon = 15 milliliters
¼ cup = 59 milliliters
⅓ cup = 79 milliliters
½ cup = 118 milliliters
⅔ cup = 158 milliliters
¾ cup = 177 milliliters
1 cup = 225 milliliters
4 cups or 1 quart = 1 liter
½ gallon = 2 liters
1 gallon = 4 liters

Volume (Liquid) Measurements

1 teaspoon = ⅙ fluid ounce = 5 milliliters
1 tablespoon = ½ fluid ounce = 15 milliliters
2 tablespoons = 1 fluid ounce = 30 milliliters
¼ cup = 2 fluid ounces = 60 milliliters
⅓ cup = 2⅔ fluid ounces = 79 milliliters
½ cup = 4 fluid ounces = 118 milliliters
1 cup or ½ pint = 8 fluid ounces = 250 milliliters
2 cups or 1 pint = 16 fluid ounces = 500 milliliters
4 cups or 1 quart = 32 fluid ounces = 1,000 milliliters
1 gallon = 4 liters

Weight (Mass) Measurements

1 ounce = 30 grams
2 ounces = 55 grams
3 ounces = 85 grams
4 ounces = ¼ pound = 125 grams
8 ounces = ½ pound = 240 grams
12 ounces = ¾ pound = 375 grams
16 ounces = 1 pound = 454 grams

Oven Temperature Equivalents, Fahrenheit (F) and Celsius (C)

100°F = 38°C	350°F = 180°C
200°F = 95°C	400°F = 205°C
250°F = 120°C	450°F = 230°C
300°F = 150°C	

APPENDIX A

Preparation Basics

Here are some basic principles of vegan natural food preparation used in the recipes in *Soup's On!*

Techniques

Toasting Spices, Nuts, and Seeds

Toasting is a method to bring out a deeper flavor of ingredients. There are two methods I commonly use.

1. Dry sauté pan. For this method, place the food in a pan, turn the heat to high, and cook until the item turns golden brown, stirring constantly. This method is good for spices, grains, and small quantities of nuts or seeds. If you wish, you can use an oil sauté for seeds or nuts by placing a small amount of high-heat oil, such as coconut, in the pan before adding the seeds or nuts.

2. Oven. Preheat your oven to 350°F. Place the food on a dry baking sheet and leave in the oven until golden brown, stirring occasionally and being mindful to avoid burning. This method is best for nuts, seeds, and shredded coconut. Nuts become crunchier after cooling down. As mentioned earlier, if you have more time, you can enhance the flavor even more by roasting at lower temperatures for longer periods of time. For instance, nuts roasted at 200°F for 45 minutes, have a richer, toastier flavor than those roasted at a high temperature for shorter periods of time.

Working with Tofu

Tofu is sold in a number of different forms, including extra-firm, firm, soft, and silken. There is even a superfirm variety available, as well as sprouted tofu, which is said to be easier to digest.

Each different form, described below, lends itself to a particular type of food preparation. The recipes will describe which form of tofu is required for the dish.

> *Silken style:* May be blended and used to replace dairy products in puddings, frostings, dressings, creamy soups, and sauces.
> *Soft:* May be used cubed in soups or pureed in sauces, spreads, or dips.
> *Medium and firm styles:* May be scrambled, grated in casseroles, or cubed in stir-fries.
> *Superfirm and extra-firm styles:* May be grilled or baked as cutlets, or cubed and roasted. It may also be steamed and used in steamed veggie dishes.

Leftover tofu should be rinsed and covered with water in a glass container in the refrigerator. Changing water daily is recommended. Use within 4 days. Firm and extra-firm tofu may be frozen for up to 3 months. Frozen tofu, once defrosted, has a spongy texture that absorbs marinades more than does tofu that has not been frozen.

How to press tofu: Some recommend pressing tofu to remove excess water, to create a firmer tofu, and to help the tofu absorb marinades more effectively. Pressing is generally not needed for the superfirm and many extra-firm varieties. If you would like to press your tofu, place the block of tofu on a clean surface, such as a plate, baking sheet, or casserole dish. Place a clean plate on top of the tofu and weigh down with a jar or other weight. Allow it to press for 15 to 45 minutes, draining the liquid periodically.

To make tofu cutlets: Slice a block of extra firm tofu into thirds or fourths. If you wish, you can then cut these cutlets in half to yield six or eight cutlets per pound. You can also cut the tofu diagonally to create triangular cutlets. Cutlets can be marinated and then roasted or grilled.

To make tofu cubes: To make medium-size cubes, slice the tofu as you would for three or four cutlets. Then make four cuts along the length and three cuts along the width of the tofu. You can make the cubes larger or smaller by altering the number of cuts.

Working with Tempeh

Tempeh is a cultured soy product that originates in Indonesia and tastes best when thoroughly cooked before consuming. There are many brands on the market. I prefer Turtle Island. It is typically available in an 8-ounce package. Several varieties come in a thick, square block; others, as a thinner rectangle. Some recommend steaming the tempeh before using in dishes, to remove the bitterness and help it absorb marinades more effectively. To do so, place a steamer basket in a large pot with about 1 inch of water over high heat. Cover, bring to a boil, and add the tempeh. Lower the heat to medium and cook covered for 10 minutes. Store leftover tempeh in a sealed glass container in the refrigerator for up to 3 days.

To make tempeh cutlets: You can slice the square block in half to create a thinner block and then cut it in half or into triangles. The longer block may also be sliced into thinner cutlets. These cutlets may then be cut into cubes.

Roasting Tofu and Tempeh

Tofu and tempeh cubes can be marinated, roasted, and then stored for a couple of days in a glass container in the refrigerator, to be used in salads, stir-fries, or on their own as a snack. With tofu, it is best to use extra-firm or superfirm varieties, for optimal texture.

To roast tofu and tempeh cutlets, and cubes, follow these three simple steps:

1. Preheat the oven or toaster oven to 375°F to 400°F. Cut the tofu or tempeh into cutlets or cubes as mentioned earlier.

2. Place them in a marinade of your choosing. Allow them to sit for at least 5 minutes and up to overnight. If marinating overnight, store in an airtight container in the refrigerator.

3. Place on a well-oiled baking sheet or casserole dish. Roast until golden brown, about 15 to 20 minutes, stirring the cubes occasionally to ensure even cooking. Because brands and oven temperatures differ, check periodically to attain your desired level of doneness. If making cutlets, you can flip after 10 minutes. Try a convection oven or use a BROIL setting, for a crispier crust.

Working with Seitan

Originating in ancient China, seitan is sometimes referred to as "meat of wheat." It is wheat gluten dough that has been cooked in a broth with different types of seasonings. Seitan can be used as an animal product replacement in virtually any dish. Several brands are available on the market. Experiment with them all to find your favorite. If you are ambitious and wish to make your own, go to www.about.com and enter "making seitan," which gives step-by-step instructions. Note: Seitan is pure wheat gluten—it's definitely not the dish for the gluten intolerant!

Seitan comes in different shapes and sizes (cubes, strips, or pieces) and has a chewy texture. For the best flavor, you can sauté the seitan, with a small amount of diced onion and minced garlic, in a little coconut oil over medium-high heat for 3 minutes, stirring frequently. Add a splash of wheat-free tamari or other soy sauce, and mix well before adding to the recipes.

Another tip for enhancing the flavor of seitan in these recipes is to allow it to sit in the soup for longer than the recipe calls for, so that it can better absorb the flavors of the soup. To do so, when the soup is done cooking, remove from the heat. Allow to sit for 30 minutes, stirring occasionally. Reheat the soup and enjoy!

Grilling

Consider grilling tempeh and tofu cutlets, as well as many vegetables, such as portobello mushrooms, corn, onions, baby bok choy, carrots, bell peppers, asparagus, zucchini, coconut meat, or eggplant. You can even grill fruit, such as pineapple slices, peaches, apples, or pears. If you wish for added flavor, place the food in a marinade from a few minutes to overnight before grilling. Baste or brush lightly with oil, brushing occasionally and grilling until char marks appear and the food is heated thoroughly, flipping periodically. If using a gas grill, avoid placing produce items over a direct flame.

Another grilling option is to use a stove-top grill. Kitchen supply stores sell cast-iron pans that are flat, straddle two burners, and have a griddle on one side and a grooved side for grilling. The flavor is similar and you get the fancy char marks without having to fuss with (or own) a grill.

Steam or Water Sautéing

Steam or water sautéing may be used if you wish to eliminate the use of heated oils in your diet. Water or stock is used instead of oil in the initial cooking stages for dishes that are sautéed. Place a small amount of water or stock in a heated pan, add vegetables, and follow the recipes as you would if using oil. Add small amounts of water at a time, if necessary, to prevent sticking. Lemon juice or wheat-free tamari may also be mixed in with the water, for added flavor.

Cooking Grains

Simply follow these instructions and you will always have perfectly cooked grains.

1. Rinse the grain thoroughly and drain the excess water.

2. Bring the measured amount of grain and liquid (either vegetable stock or filtered water) to a boil. You may wish to add a pinch of sea salt.

3. Cover with a tight-fitting lid, lower the heat to low, and simmer for the recommended time. As the grain is being steamed, do not lift the lid until the grain is finished cooking.

Cooking times may vary, depending upon altitude and stove cooking temperatures. The grain is generally finished cooking when it is chewy and all the liquid is absorbed.

Enhance the flavor of your grain dishes by adding such ingredients as minced garlic or ginger, diced onion, a couple of bay leaves, or crushed lemongrass while cooking. If you wish to use a rice cooker, Miracle puts out a stainless-steel version. Steer clear of aluminum or nonstick rice cookers.

Grain Cooking Chart				
Grain	Liquid per cup of grain (cups)	Approx. cooking time (minutes)	Approx. yield (cups)	Comments
Amaranth	2½	25	2½	Ancient grain of Aztecs, higher in protein and nutrients than most grains.
Barley, pearled	3	45	3½	Good in soups and stews.
Buckwheat	2	15	2½	Hearty, nutty flavor. When toasted, it's called kasha and takes less time to cook. Also used as a breakfast cereal.
Cornmeal	3	20	3½	From ground corn—a staple of Native Americans; use in corn bread or grits.
Couscous	1½	15	1½	A North African staple made from ground semolina.
Kamut	3	60	3	An ancient variety of wheat that many with wheat allergies are able to tolerate.
Millet	2½	20	3	A highly nutritious grain that is used in casseroles, stews, and cereals. Especially tasty with flax oil.
Oats				A versatile grain that is popular as a cereal, for baking, and for milks.
Steel cut	3	30 to 40	3	
Groats	3	60	3	
Rolled	3	10	3	
Quick	2	5	2	
Polenta	3	15	3	A type of cornmeal—used in Italian cooking. To cook, bring liquid to a boil. Lower the heat to a simmer and whisk in the polenta, stirring until done.

continues

Grain Cooking Chart *continued*

Grain	Liquid per cup of grain (cups)	Approx. cooking time (minutes)	Approx. yield (cups)	Comments
Quinoa	2	20	2½	Ancient grain of the Inca. High in protein and nutrients. Has a delicate, nutty flavor. One of my favorites!
Rice				Rice has a high nutrient content and is a staple in many of the world's cultures, to say the least. Basmati rice has a nutty flavor and is used in Indian cooking. I prefer brown short-grain rice for its taste and nutritional value.
Brown basmati	2	35 to 40	2¼	
White basmati	1½	20	2	
Brown long grain	2	45	3	
Brown short grain	2	45	3	
Wild	3	60	4	
Jasmine	1¾	20	3½	
Sushi	1¼	20	3	
Rye				A staple grain throughout Europe. Used as a cereal or ground to make breads, including pumpernickel. Spelt is the most pure and ancient form of wheat. It contains much more protein and nutrition than wheat does and is infinitely more digestible.
Berries	4	60	3	
Flakes	3	20	3	
Spelt	3½	90	3	
Teff	3	20	1½	From Ethiopia, the smallest grain in the world, and the main ingredient for *injera* flatbread.
Wheat				A primary bread grain. Bulgur is used in Middle Eastern dishes, such as tabbouleh. Cracked may be used as a cereal.
Whole	3	120	2¾	
Bulgur	2	15	2½	
Cracked	2	25	2½	

Cooking Legumes

Before you cook legumes, it is recommended to pick over them thoroughly (remove any stones or debris). This improves digestibility and reduces gas. Other methods for improving digestibility include adding some fennel seeds, a handful of brown rice, or a few strips of the sea vegetable kombu to the legumes while cooking. If you forget to soak beans overnight, a quick method is to bring beans and four times the amount of water to boil, remove from the heat, cover, and allow to sit for a few hours.

After soaking the legumes or boiling them in this fashion, discard the soak water, add the measured amount of vegetable stock or filtered water to a heavy-bottomed pot, bring to a boil, cover, lower the heat to a simmer, and cook until tender. Please see the following legume cooking chart. The times in the chart are for cooking dry legumes. Please reduce the cooking time by 25 percent when legumes are soaked.

Do not add salt to the cooking liquid; it can make the legumes tough. Legumes are done cooking when they are tender but not mushy. They should retain their original shape.

Legume Cooking Chart				
Legume	Liquid per cup of legume (cups)	Approx. cook time (hours)	Approx. yield (cups)	Comments
Aduki beans	3¼	45 min.	3	Tender red bean used in Japanese and macrobiotic cooking.
Anasazi beans	3	2	2	Means "the ancient ones" in Navajo language; sweeter and meatier than most beans.
Black beans (turtle beans)	4	1¼	2½	Good in Spanish, South American, and Caribbean dishes.
Black-eyed peas	3	1	3	Popular bean in Asia and in the southern United States.
Cannellini beans	4	1 to 1½	2½	Creamy white bean popular in Tuscan and other Italian cuisine. Also called white Italian kidney bean.

continues

Legume Cooking Chart *continued*				
Legume	Liquid per cup of legume (cups)	Approx. cook time (hours)	Approx. yield (cups)	Comments
Chickpeas (garbanzo beans)	4	3 to 4	2	Used in Middle Eastern and Indian dishes. Pureed cooked chickpeas form the base of hummus.
Great northern beans	4	1½	2	Beautiful, large white beans.
Kidney beans	4	1½	2	Medium-size red beans. The most popular bean in the United States; also used in Mexican cooking.
Lentils	3	45 min.	2¼	Come in green, red, and French varieties. A member of the pea family used in Indian dal dishes and soups.
Lima beans Baby limas	3 3	1½ 1½	1¼ 1¾	White beans with a distinctive flavor; high in nutrients.
Mung beans	3	45 min.	2¼	Grown in India and Asia. Used in Indian dal dishes. May be soaked and sprouted and used fresh in soups and salads.
Navy beans (white beans)	4	2½	2	Hearty beans used in soups, stews, and cold salads.
Pinto beans	4	2½	2	Used in Mexican and South-western cooking. Used in soups and as refried beans in burritos.
Split peas	3	45 min	2¼	Come in yellow and green varieties. Used in soups and Indian dals.
Soybeans	4	3+	2	Versatile, high-protein beans widely used in Asia. May be processed into tofu, tempeh, miso, soy milk, soy sauce, and soy cheese.

Basic Recipes

♥ Basic Nut or Seed Milk

Recipe courtesy of *The 30-Minute Vegan*

Use this base recipe to create countless varieties of nut and seed milks. Each combination will provide its own unique flavor. Partake of this milk in all recipes that call for milk, or on its own as a refreshing beverage. If you have more time and for best results, see the chart at the end of the recipe for recommended soak times.

MAKES 1 QUART MILK

---

1 cup nuts or seeds	Pinch of sea salt
4 cups water	Coconut nectar (see page 227), or sweetener to taste (optional)

▶ Rinse the nuts or seeds well and drain. Place them in a blender with the water and blend on high speed for 30 seconds, or until creamy. Strain the milk through a fine-mesh strainer, cheesecloth, or mesh bag. If using a fine-mesh strainer, use a spoon or rubber spatula to swirl the nut or seed meal around, which allows the milk to drain faster.

Note: This recipe also works for rice milk. Just follow the ratios, using uncooked brown rice and water. It's a convenient way to save on packaging; it's fresh and tastes better!

Nut, seed, and rice milks will last for 3 to 4 days when stored in a glass jar in the refrigerator.

If You Have More Time

Soaking Chart

Rinse nuts or seeds well and place them in a bowl or jar with water in a ratio of 1 part nut or seed to 3 or 4 parts water. Allow them to sit for the recommended time before draining, rinsing, and using in recipes.

Nut/Seed	Soak time (hours)	Nut/Seed	Soak time (hours)
Almonds	4 to 6	Pecans	4 to 6
Macadamia nuts	1 to 2	Pine nuts	1 to 2
Hazelnuts	4 to 6	Sesame seeds	1 to 4
Cashews	1 to 2	Pumpkin seeds	1 to 4
Brazil nuts	4 to 6	Sunflower seeds	1 to 4
Walnuts	4 to 6		

Gluten-Free Flour Mix

▶ Use this to replace the flour called for in the recipes.
▶ Combine equal parts of sorghum flour, brown rice flour, and tapioca flour. Use ¼ teaspoon of xanthan gum for each cup of flour.

Spice Blends

Spice blends allow you to create ethnic variations to your soups with the toss of your hand. Start by adding a small amount of the blend and increase the quantity to taste. Remember that it will take some time for the flavors to absorb, so use sparingly at first.

Italian Spice Mix

MAKES ½ CUP SPICE MIX

3 tablespoons dried basil
2 tablespoons dried marjoram
1 tablespoon dried oregano
1 tablespoon dried sage
2 teaspoons dried thyme
1 teaspoon garlic powder

▶ Place all the ingredients in a medium-size bowl and mix well. Store in a glass jar.

Indian Spice Mix

MAKES ABOUT ½ CUP SPICE MIX

3 tablespoons curry powder
2 tablespoons ground cumin (optionally toasted; see page 213)
1 tablespoon ground coriander
1 tablespoon brown mustard or fennel seeds
1 teaspoon ginger powder
½ teaspoon ground cardamom
¼ teaspoon ground cloves

▶ Place all the ingredients in a medium-size bowl and mix well. Store in a glass jar.

Mexican Spice Mix

MAKES ABOUT ½ CUP SPICE MIX

¼ cup chili powder
2 tablespoons ground cumin (optionally toasted; see page 213)
1 tablespoon dried oregano
½ teaspoon ground cinnamon
½ teaspoon chipotle chile powder

▶ Place all the ingredients in a medium-size bowl and mix well. Store in a glass jar.

Moroccan Spice Mix

MAKES ABOUT ½ CUP SPICE MIX

2 tablespoons ground cumin
2 tablespoons ground coriander
1½ tablespoons paprika
1 tablespoon ground turmeric
1 teaspoon ground ginger
1 teaspoon ground cinnamon
1 teaspoon ground allspice
½ teaspoon cayenne pepper

▶ Place all the ingredients in a medium-size bowl and mix well. Store in a glass jar.

Marinades

Marinade ingredients greatly determine the flavors of a dish. Simply by placing something like tofu or a portobello mushroom in different marinades creates dramatically different flavor profiles.

Creating marinades is a key technique in vegan food preparation, especially when working with tofu, which will take on the flavor of the marinade. Following are two versatile recipes. Place the items in the marinade for a minimum of 10 minutes. The longer they sit in the marinade, the more of its flavors they will acquire. I like to marinate our tofu (as well as vegetables) overnight, if possible. These are simple marinades that make enough for 1 pound of tofu or tempeh or two servings of veggies.

Be bold in your exploration of different marinades. Please use the following marinades as a starting point on your own voyage of discovery. Some of my favorite marinade ingredients include toasted sesame oil, mirin, mustard, brown rice vinegar, horseradish, minced garlic or ginger, maple syrup, balsamic vinegar, red or white wine, and a variety of spices and herbs.

Lemon Dijon Marinade

MAKES ABOUT ¾ CUP MARINADE

½ cup freshly squeezed lemon juice
¼ cup filtered water
2 tablespoons minced fresh herbs (try thyme, oregano, and parsley)
1½ teaspoons Dijon or stone-ground mustard
½ teaspoon sea salt
¼ teaspoon ground black pepper
1 tablespoon olive oil (optional)
⅛ teaspoon cayenne pepper (optional)

▶ Place all the ingredients in a medium-size bowl and whisk well.

Maple Balsamic Marinade

MAKES ABOUT ¾ CUP MARINADE

½ cup filtered water
3 tablespoons wheat-free tamari or other soy sauce
2 tablespoons olive or coconut oil
1 tablespoon pure maple syrup or agave nectar
2 teaspoons balsamic or red wine vinegar
1 teaspoon minced garlic or peeled and minced fresh ginger
1 tablespoon minced fresh herbs (optional)
Pinch of cayenne pepper

▶ Place all the ingredients in a medium-size bowl and whisk well.

Vegan Mayonnaise

▶ Use this egg-free mayonnaise in any recipe in this book that calls for mayo.

MAKES 2 ¼ CUPS MAYO

1½ cups safflower oil
¾ cup soy milk
½ teaspoon Dijon mustard
1 teaspoon agave nectar (optional)
¾ teaspoon sea salt, to taste
1½ teaspoons freshly squeezed lemon juice

1. Combine all the ingredients, except the lemon juice, in a blender and blend until smooth.
2. Slowly add the lemon juice through the top while blending until the mixture thickens.

Natural Sweeteners

Many people believe that eating foods with refined white sugar can lead to certain health problems, including emotional disorders, obesity, diabetes, and tooth decay. It is believed that because refined sugars are missing the nutrients that are contained in naturally sweet whole foods, the body is drained of its own store of minerals and nutrients in its efforts to metabolize the sugar.

Vegan Fusion natural food preparation makes use of various naturally occurring and minimally processed sweeteners. You can replace traditional white sugar with raw cane sugar or organic sugar at a one-to-one ratio without making any changes to your recipes. You can also replace the white sugar with any of the sweeteners that follow. These sweeteners are superior to white sugar, but it is still believed that most of them need to be used in moderation.

The following chart indicates how much of a sweetener is needed to replace 1 cup of white, refined sugar. The chart indicates how much liquid to delete from the recipe to maintain its consistency if the sweetener is a liquid.

Natural Sweeteners Chart

Sweetener	Replace 1 cup of refined sugar with	Reduce liquids by	Comments
Agave nectar	¾ cup	⅓	A natural extract from a famous Mexican cactus, with a low glycemic index. There is some controversy surrounding agave and its similarity to high-fructose corn syrup.
Barley malt syrup	¾ cup	¼	Roughly half as sweet as honey or sugar. Made from sprouted barley; has a nutty, caramel flavor.
Blackstrap molasses	½ cup	¼	This syrup is a liquid by-product of the sugar refining process. It contains many of the nutrients of the sugar cane plant. Has a strong, distinctive flavor.
Brown rice syrup	1 cup	¼	A relatively neutral-flavored sweetener that is roughly half as sweet as sugar or honey. It's made from fermented brown rice.
Coconut crystals	1 cup	0	Air-dried coconut nectar creates a nutrient-rich granulated sugar that is our recommended sugar for the recipes in this book. It has a dark, rich flavor with a lower glycemic index than cane sugar. Manufactured by Coconut Secret.
Coconut nectar	¾ cup	⅓	A mildly flavored sweetener manufactured by Coconut Secret, which is a wonderful replacement for agave nectar. It has a low glycemic index and is loaded with vitamins, minerals, amino acids, and other nutrients.
Date sugar	⅔ cup	0	A granulated sugar produced from drying fresh dates.
Fruit syrup	1 cup	¼	The preferred method of sweetening involves soaking, then blending, raisins and dates with filtered water, to create a sweet syrup. Try ½ cup of raisins with 1 cup of water and experiment to find your desired sweetness.
Lucuma powder	1 cup	0	A raw, low-glycemic sweetener with a slight maple flavor. Comes from the *lucuma* fruit, grown in the Peruvian Andes and referred to as the "gold of the Inca."

Natural Sweeteners Chart *continued*			
Sweetener	Replace 1 cup of refined sugar with	Reduce liquids by	Comments
Maple syrup	¾ cup	¼	Forty gallons of sap from the maple tree are needed to create 1 gallon of maple syrup. It is mineral rich and graded according to color and flavor. Grade A is the mildest and lightest, Grade C is the darkest and richest. Good for baking.
Sucanat	1 cup	0	Abbreviation for "sugar cane natural." It is a granular sweetener that consists of evaporated sugar cane juice. It has about the same sweetness as sugar. It retains most of the vitamins and minerals of the sugar cane.
Stevia (powdered)	1 teaspoon	0	Stevia is a plant that originates in the Brazilian rainforest. The powdered form is between 200 and 400 percent sweeter than white sugar. It is noncaloric, does not promote tooth decay, and is said to be an acceptable form of sugar for diabetics and those with blood sugar imbalances. For baking conversions, please visit www.ehow.com/how_2268348_substitute-stevia-sugar-baking.html.
Yacón	¾ cup	⅓	This tuber is a distant relative of the sunflower. From the Andean region of South America, mineral-rich yacón syrup has a dark brown color and is used as a low-calorie sweetener.

Chef's Tips and Tricks

 Date Syrup

This is probably the most healthful, least processed sweetener you can use. Use it to replace maple syrup, agave nectar, or other concentrated sweeteners.

MAKES ABOUT 1 CUP SYRUP

¼ cup pitted dates
1 cup water

▶ Combine the dates and water in a strong blender and blend until smooth. Store in a glass jar in the refrigerator for up to 4 days.

APPENDIX B

Seasonal Growing Charts

Looking for the most incredible flavor and optimal nutrition for your soups? It's a secret of well-respected chefs everywhere to use the freshest possible produce—and that means going with what is in season. Even though we can get almost any produce at any time of the year, I prefer to choose my veggies and fruits with the seasons as much as I'm able. The following charts are easy seasonal guides for selecting your produce.

Seasonal Grow Chart: Spring/Summer

Apricots: End of warmer season of spring

Artichokes: Main harvest spring; also grows in fall

Arugula: Cool-weather crop; late spring

Asparagus: March to June, depending on location

Beets: Temperate climates needed; spring growth all season

Broccoli: Late April to May

Brussels sprouts: Late fall to winter

Cabbage: Spring, usually late April to early May

Carrots: Year-round in certain climates; baby carrots spring to early summer

Chard and cooking greens: Harvested in late summer or early fall; bitter when weather is too warm

continues

Seasonal Growing Chart: Spring/Summer continued _____

Cherries: Sweet cherries grow from May to August; sour cherries, mid-June for 2 weeks

Cucumbers: Late spring to early summer

Fava beans: Very early spring through midsummer

Fennel: Can grow from fall to spring in warmer climates

Garlic: Spring to early summer

Green onions: Year-round in temperate climates; full harvest in spring

Kiwis: Winter to spring in warmer climates

Kumquats: Late winter to spring

Leeks: Fall to early spring

Lemons: Winter to early summer

Lettuce: Cooler climates; spring harvest

Mint: Year-round

Okra: 2 weeks after first frost

Peas: Spring to summer

Potatoes: Early spring

Radishes: Early spring

Rhubarb: Early spring

Spinach: Depends on climate; year-round in temperate areas, summer to fall in cooler regions

Spring onions: Early spring to late summer

Strawberries: Generally grown in California and Florida; peak season April to June

Sweet onions: Midspring to summer

Tomatoes: Midspring, generally in May

Turnips: Early spring to summer

Watermelons: May to June

Seasonal Grow Chart: Fall/Winter

Apples: Late summer to late fall

Arugula: Year-round but best in spring and fall

Belgian endive: Fall to winter

Broccoli rabe: Early fall through early spring

Brussels sprouts: Fall to winter

Cabbage: Late fall though early winter

Cantaloupes: Late summer through early fall

Cardoons: Winter and early spring

Cauliflower: Early fall through winter; available year-round but best crops in fall to winter

Celery: Year-round but best crops in fall to winter

Celery root: Fall to winter

Chard: Early fall

Cherries: Late summer to early fall

Chicory: Early fall through winter

Clementines: Late fall to winter

Collard greens: Year-round

Edamame: Fall

Eggplant: Late summer to early fall

Escarole: Starts early fall to winter

Grapefruit: Winter as well as spring

Grapes: Late summer to early fall

Green beans: Late summer to early fall

Green onions: Summer through fall

Horseradish: Midfall through winter

Huckleberries: Late summer through early fall

continues

Seasonal Growing Chart: Fall/Winter continued_____

Jerusalem artichokes/sunchokes: Fall through winter

Kale: Year-round but best fall to winter

Kiwis: Midwinter to spring

Kumquats: Late winter to spring

Leeks: Fall through early spring

Lemongrass: Winter to spring

Mandarins: Winter

Melons: Late summer to fall

Mushrooms: Spring through early fall

Okra: Late summer to fall

Oregano: Year-round

Parsley: Year-round

Parsnips: Fall through spring

Peppers (sweet): Summer to fall

Pomegranates: Fall

Pomelos: Winter

Potatoes: Late summer

Pumpkins: Fall

Radicchio: Late spring to fall

Rosemary: Year-round

Sage: Year-round

Shelling beans: Summer and early fall

Spinach: Year-round

Squash (winter): Early fall through winter

Sweet potatoes: Fall through winter

Tangerines: Winter

Thyme: Year-round

Watercress: Year-round

APPENDIX C

Supplemental Information

Why Vegan?

*Nothing will benefit human health and increase
the chances for survival of life on Earth
as much as the evolution to a vegetarian diet.*

—ALBERT EINSTEIN

A vegetarian diet is one that does not include meat, fish, or poultry. There are three types of vegetarian diets. A "lacto-ovo vegetarian" diet includes eggs and dairy products. A "lacto-vegetarian" diet includes dairy products, but not eggs. "Vegan" is used to describe a diet and lifestyle that does not include the use or consumption of any animal-based products, including dairy or eggs. This also means vegans avoid wearing fur, leather, and silk, and products tested on animals. The phrase *plant-based* is often used instead of the word *vegan*.

In the years since the first *30-Minute Vegan* book was published in 2009, there has been an explosion of interest in vegan foods. A slew of celebrities, high-performance athletes, powerful entrepreneurs, and folks from every walk of life are experimenting with this transformational lifestyle.

The reasons people choose to enjoy vegan foods are many. First and foremost, these foods taste incredible! People also turn to vegan foods for weight loss and disease prevention. It seems that every week there are new studies and testimonials published of people who have regained their health by dropping their cholesterol levels, losing weight, and coming off heart and diabetes medications by including more plant-based foods in their diet. There are now numerous studies demonstrating that many serious illnesses, such as heart disease, obesity, and diabetes, can be prevented and reversed by enjoying more vegan foods. Please check out the movie *Forks Over Knives* if you are interested in learning more about the many health benefits of a vegan diet.

Want to be Earth friendly? In addition to providing an out-of-this-world culinary experience, eating vegan foods also happens to be one of the most effective steps we can take to protect the environment. The UN's Food and Agriculture Organization estimates that meat production accounts for nearly a fifth of global greenhouse gas emissions—more than the entire world's transportation industry combined. We do more for the environment by switching meals to vegan than by trading in our gas-guzzlers for an electric car or jogging to work.

Optimal Health

Training is important, but when you get to be my age,
you're not going to able to train at all unless your body holds
up. I simply cannot overemphasize the importance of
the plant-based diet to my performance.
—Mike Fremont, 91,
Finishes Knoxville Half Marathon

There is a true revolution occurring in the medical world, regarding the benefits of vegan foods. Renowned doctors, such as Dr. Caldwell Esselstyn Jr. and Dr. Dean Ornish, have successfully reversed instances of heart disease with programs that incorporate vegan foods. Dr. John McDougall, Dr. Gabriel Cousens, and Joel Fuhrman have likewise had success reversing certain forms of diabetes.

The evidence continues to mount that overconsumption of the saturated fat and cholesterol in animal products leads to serious health problems, such as obesity, heart disease, diabetes, hypertension, gout, kidney stones, and certain forms of cancer.

In addition, animals raised on factory farms are routinely given hormones to accelerate their rate of growth for maximum profit. Antibiotics are used to protect their health as they are housed and transported in less than sanitary conditions. These drugs inevitably make their way into the body of the humans that consume them.

In a 1995 report, the US Department of Agriculture and the US Department of Health and Human Services affirmed that all the body's nutritional needs can be met through a well-planned plant-based diet.

In 2009, the American Dietetic Association restated their position that "well-planned vegan and other types of vegetarian diets are appropriate for all stages of the life cycle, including during pregnancy, lactation, infancy, childhood, and adolescence." It is their official opinion as well as of the Dietitians of Canada that "appropriately planned vegetarian diets, including total vegetarian or vegan diets, are healthful, nutritionally adequate, and may provide health benefits in the prevention and treatment of certain diseases."

They go on to say, "The results of an evidence-based review showed that a vegetarian diet is associated with a lower risk of death from ischemic heart disease. Vegetarians also appear to have lower low-density lipoprotein cholesterol levels, lower blood pressure, and lower rates of hypertension and type 2 diabetes than non-vegetarians. Furthermore, vegetarians tend to have a lower body mass index and lower overall cancer rates. Features of a vegetarian diet that may reduce risk of chronic disease include lower intakes of saturated fat and cholesterol and higher intakes of fruits, vegetables, whole grains, nuts, soy products, fiber, and phytochemicals."

May this forever dispel the myth that a vegan diet is nutritionally lacking in any way. For anyone concerned about this, please rest assured that vegan foods provide all the protein, calcium, iron, and all other vital nutrients needed for us to thrive.

Preserving the Environment

> *It is increasingly obvious that environmentally sustainable solutions to world hunger can only emerge as people eat more plant foods and fewer animal products. To me, it is deeply moving that the same food choices that give us the best chance to eliminate world hunger are also those that take the least toll on the environment, contribute the most to our long-term health, are the safest, and are also, far and away, the most compassionate towards our fellow creatures.*
>
> —JOHN ROBBINS, AUTHOR OF *NO HAPPY COWS:*
> *DISPATCHES FROM THE FRONTLINES OF THE FOOD REVOLUTION*

It is crystal clear to anyone who takes the time to look at the data that the environmental footprint of a vegan diet is a fraction of that of a meat-based diet. Vegan foods represent the best utilization of the earth's limited resources. It takes 16 pounds of grain and 2,500 gallons of water to produce 1 pound of beef. It's astonishing to realize this, when we see so much in the news about food and water shortages and people going to bed hungry.

We must use the resources of our planet wisely if we are to survive. World scientists agree that global warming poses a serious risk to humanity and life, as we know it. The key to reducing global warming is to reduce activities that produce the greenhouse gases that cause the Earth's temperature to rise. According to a 2006 UN Report "Livestock's Long Shadow," raising livestock for food consumption is responsible for 18 percent of all greenhouse gases emitted.

Here are some additional topics to consider for those wishing to go green:

The livestock population of the United States consumes enough grain and soybeans each year to feed over five times the human population of the country. Animals are fed over 80 percent of the corn and 95 percent of the oats that are grown on our soil.

Less than half of the harvested agricultural acreage goes to feed people.

According to the USDA, 1 acre of land can produce 20,000 pounds of vegetables. This same amount of land can only produce 165 pounds of meat.

It takes 16 pounds of grain to produce 1 pound of meat.

It requires 3 ½ acres of land per person to support a meat-centered diet, 1 ½ acres of land to support a lacto-ovo vegetarian diet, and ⅙ of an acre of land to support a plant-based diet.

If Americans were to reduce meat consumption by just 10 percent, it would free up 12 million tons of grain annually.

Half of the water used in the United States goes to irrigate land growing feed and fodder for livestock. It takes about 2,500 gallons of water to produce a single pound of meat. Similarly, it takes about 4,000 gallons of water to provide a day's worth of food per person for a meat-centered diet, 1,200 gallons for a lacto-ovo vegetarian diet, and 300 gallons for a plant-based diet.

Developing nations use land to raise beef for wealthier nations instead of utilizing that land for sustainable agriculture practices.

Topsoil is the dark, rich soil that supplies the nutrients to the food we grow. It takes five hundred years to produce an inch of topsoil. This topsoil is rapidly vanishing, due to clear cutting of forests and cattle-grazing practices.

For each acre of forestland cleared for human purposes, 7 acres of forest is cleared for grazing livestock or growing livestock feed. This includes federal land that is leased for cattle-grazing purposes. This policy greatly accelerates the destruction of our precious forests. To support cattle grazing, South and Central America are destroying their rain forests. These rain forests contain close to half of all the species on Earth and many medicinal plants. Over a thousand species a year are becoming extinct and most of these are from rain-forest and tropical settings. This practice also causes the displacement of indigenous peoples who have been living in these environments for countless generations.

The factory farm industry is one of the largest polluters of our ground water, due to the chemicals, pesticides, and run-off waste that is inherent in its practices.

Over 60 million people die of starvation every year. This means that we are feeding grain to animals while our fellow humans are dying of starvation in mind-staggering numbers.

For those concerned about our environment, it all boils down to the question of sustainability. What is the most sustainable way for us to feed and support the growing human population? When you look at the disproportionate amount of land, water, and resources it takes to support a meat-based diet, it makes a lot of sense for us to introduce more plant-based foods into our way of life. Whether by going completely vegan or simply including more vegan meals each week, every little bit helps.

Much of this environmental information is provided by John Robbins, a pioneer in the promotion of the health and environmental benefits of a plant-based lifestyle. Robbins founded EarthSave International to educate, inspire, and empower people around the world. He is also the author of the landmark book *Diet for a New America*. His latest book, *No Happy Cows*, gives a current snapshot of the food revolution he helped begin.

Choosing to be Kind

> *There slowly grew up in me an unshakable conviction that we have no right to inflict suffering and death on another living creature, unless there is some unavoidable necessity for it.*
> —ALBERT SCHWEITZER, MD, NOBEL PRIZE recipient

Many people adopt a vegan diet out of a commitment toward nonviolence. For them, we are meant to be stewards and caretakers of the Earth and its inhabitants and do not wish to support practices that inflict suffering on any creature that has the capacity to feel pain.

The small family farm where husbandry practices engendered a certain respect for the animals that were used for food is becoming a thing of the past. Today, most of the world's meat, dairy, and egg production occur on massive factory farms that are owned by agribusiness conglomerates. This has brought about practices that view the raising and transportation of farm animals solely in terms of their ability to generate profits.

Animals are routinely given chemicals and antibiotics to keep them alive in these conditions. To increase the weight of cows, many are fed sawdust, plastic, tallow, grease, and cement dust seasoned with artificial flavors and aromas. Mother pigs on factory farms are kept in crates that are so small they are unable to turn around. Dairy cows are forced to remain pregnant most of their lives and are injected with hormones to increase milk production.

Male calves born from these cows are often raised to become "veal." This practice consists of confining newborn calves to a crate so small that they are unable to turn around. This is to ensure that the flesh remains tender. They are fed diets that are deliberately iron deficient, a practice that induces anemia and allows the flesh to remain white. After four months or so in these conditions, the calf is slaughtered to produce "veal." Simply put, choosing to go vegan or to eat fewer animal products is good for the environment, good for the animals, and good for you. That's the best sort of kindness.

Organically Grown Foods—Our Future Depends upon It

The Organic Trade Association states, "Organic farming is based on practices that maintain soil fertility, while assisting nature's balance through diversity and recycling of energy and nutrients. This method also strives to avoid or reduce the use of synthetic fertilizers and pest controls. Organic foods are processed, packaged, transported, and stored to retain maximum nutritional value, without the use of artificial preservatives, coloring or other additives, irradiation, or synthetic pesticides."

Lately there has been some conflicting information published about the benefits of organically grown food. To me, the bottom line is that many of the chemicals in commercial pesticides and fertilizers have not been tested for their long-term effects on humans. Nonorganic foods substantially increase our exposure to these chemicals, as well as to antibiotic resistant bacteria. Not to mention the tens of thousands agriculture workers on nonorganic farms who are diagnosed with pesticide poisoning each year.

Is it worth it to take that chance with your health and the health of your family? Organically grown foods represent a cycle of sustainability that improves topsoil fertility, enhances nutrition, and ensures food security.

Organic farmers employ farming methods that respect the fragile balance of our ecosystem. This results in a fraction of the groundwater pollution and topsoil depletion that's generated by conventional methods. Many people have also found the taste and nutrient quality of organic products superior to that of conventionally grown food.

Purchasing local, seasonal, and organically grown food is also an extremely effective way to reduce your environmental impact. Buying local saves the huge amount of energy it takes to transport food—sometimes across oceans and continents.

Another reason to support organic farmers has to do with the health of the farmworkers themselves. Farmworkers on conventional farms are exposed to high levels of toxic pesticides on a daily basis. Organic farmworkers don't have to encounter these risks.

Lastly, by supporting organic farmers, we are supporting small, family farms. This once prevalent method of farming is rapidly disappearing. This is due to the small farmer's inability to compete with the heavily subsidized agribusiness farms that use

synthetic soil, pesticides, crop dusters, and heavy machinery on lands that encompass thousands of acres.

For more information on organic farming, visit your local farmers' market and talk to the farmers. You can also check out the websites for the International Federation of Organic Agriculture Movements, the Organic Consumers Association, and the Organic Trade Association, listed in Appendix D.

Not all produce is created equal. The organization called the Environmental Working Group put together a list of those commercially grown foods with the highest level of pesticides, and those with the lowest levels of pesticides.

Those with the highest levels of pesticides are referred to as "The Dirty Dozen," which tested positive for forty-seven to sixty-seven different pesticides. You can identify organic produce by looking at the PLU, which should begin with a "9." Always purchase these organically:

celery	sweet bell peppers
peaches	spinach, kale, and collard greens
strawberries	cherries
apples	potatoes
domestic blueberries	imported grapes
nectarines	lettuce

"The Clean 15" had little to no traces of pesticides:

onions	cabbage
avocados	eggplant
sweet corn	cantaloupe
pineapples	watermelon
mangoes	grapefruit
sweet peas	sweet potatoes
asparagus	sweet onions
kiwifruit	

Say NO to GMO

A GMO (genetically engineered and modified organism) is a plant, animal, or microorganism that has had its genetic code altered—typically by introducing genes from another organism. This process gives the GMO food characteristics that are not present in its original form. Many feel this practice goes against nature and poses a profound threat to people, the environment, and our agricultural heritage.

There are even GMO seeds that are referred to as assassin seeds. The plant that grows from these seeds produces seeds that are infertile. This prevents the replication of the genetic bond. This means that farmers must constantly purchase seeds every year from the companies that manufacture them.

GMO seed manufacturers maintain that this makes the seed more pest resistant, promotes higher yields, or enhances nutrition. The fact is that the long-term effects of these seeds on our health, our genetic pool, the environment, and other life forms that make up the complex web of life we all share, are still unknown. I believe this untested engineering is dangerous to human health in the long term. Is it worth it to take the chance? By definition, eating organic foods eliminates GMO from our food supply.

There is a huge push in the United States to have genetically modified foods labeled as such. This legislation has been fiercely resisted by the companies that manufacture the GMO products and those that profit from their sale. Consider this: over sixty countries around the world, including the entire European Union and even China, insist on labeling. In fact, many communities around the world have succeeded in becoming GMO-free.

Please join us in this critical movement to shift our agriculture away from genetic engineering and toward truly sustainable agriculture. For more information, you may visit the Non-GMO Project at www.nongmoproject.org. You can tell whether your produce has been genetically modified by looking at the PLU label. Numbers beginning with "8" indicate a GMO product.

Composting: The Cycle of Life

Composting is the method of breaking down food waste, grass trimmings, and leaves to create nutrient-rich and fertile soil. It's the next step we can take toward creating a more sustainable method of growing our food. Compost contains nitrogen and micronutrients to keep the soil healthy and can be used as a mulch and soil amendment. When the soil is healthy, plant yields are higher and fertilizers and pesticides aren't as necessary.

Composting completes the cycle of life from seed to table and back to the earth. Many communities sponsor composting programs and can give you all the tools and instructions you need to succeed. Check out www.compostguide.com for a complete guide to composting.

APPENDIX D

Additional Resources

Further Reading

Want to learn more? Explore this section to deepen your knowledge of the information touched upon in *Soup's On!*

Barnard, Neal, MD. *Breaking the Food Seduction: The Hidden Reasons Behind Food Cravings—And 7 Steps to End Them Naturally.* New York, NY: St. Martin's Griffin, 2004.

Brazier, Brendan. *The Thrive Diet: The Whole Food Way to Lose Weight, Reduce Stress, and Stay Healthy for Life.* New York, NY: Da Capo Press, 2007.

Campbell, T. Colin, and Howard Jacobson. *Whole: Rethinking the Science of Nutrition.* Dallas, TX: Benbella Books, 2013.

Campbell, T. Colin, and Thomas M. Campbell II. *The China Study: The Most Comprehensive Study of Nutrition Ever Conducted and the Startling Implications for Diet, Weight Loss, and Long-Term Health.* Dallas, TX: Benbella Books, 2006.

Davis, Brenda, RD, and Vesanto Melina, MS, RD. *The Complete Guide to Adopting a Healthy Plant-Based Diet.* Summertown, TN:. Book Publishing Co., 2000.

Esselstyn, Caldwell. *Prevent and Reverse Heart Disease.* New York, NY: Avery Publishing, 2007.

Fuhrman, Joel. *The End of Diabetes: The Eat to Live Plan to Prevent and Reverse Diabetes.* New York, NY. HarperOne, 2012.

Fuhrman, Joel, MD. Eat to Live: *The Revolutionary Formula for Fast and Sustained Weight Loss.* Boston, MA: Little, Brown, and Company, 2005.

Hever, Julieanna. *The Complete Idiot's Guide to Plant-Based Nutrition.* Indianapolis, IN: Alpha Books, 2011.

Jacobson, Michael, PhD. *Six Arguments for a Greener Diet: How a Plant-Based Diet Could Save Your Health and the Environment.* Washington, DC: Center for Science in the Public Interest, 2006.

Joy, Melanie, *Why We Love Dogs, Eat Pigs, and Wear Cows: An Introduction to Carnism.* Newburyport, MA: Conari Press, 2011.

Klaper, Michael, MD. *Vegan Nutrition: Pure and Simple.* Summertown, TN: Book Publishing Company, 1999.

Krizmaniac, Judy. *A Teen's Guide to Going Vegetarian.* London, UK. Puffin, 1994.

Lyman, Howard. *Mad Cowboy: Plain Truth from the Cattle Rancher Who Won't Eat Meat.* New York, NY: Scribner, 2001.

Marcus, Erik. *Vegan: The New Ethics of Eating.* Ithaca, NY: McBooks Press, 2001.

Norris, Jack, and Virginia Messina. *Vegan for Life: Everything You Need to Know to Be Healthy and Fit on a Plant-Based Diet.* Boston, MA: Da Capo Lifelong, 2011.

Ornish, Dean. *Dr. Dean Ornish's Program for Reversing Heart Disease: The Only System Scientifically Proven to Reverse Heart Disease Without Drugs or Surgery.* New York, NY: Ivy Books, 1995.

Pitchford, P. *Healing with Whole Foods.* Berkeley, CA: North Atlantic Books, 1993.

Reinfeld, Mark. *The 30-Minute Vegan's Taste of Europe.* Boston, MA: DaCapo Lifelong, 2012.

Reinfeld, Mark, and Bo Rinaldi. *Vegan Fusion World Cuisine.* New York, NY: Beaufort Books, 2007.

Reinfeld, Mark, Bo Rinaldi, and Jennifer Murray, *The Complete Idiot's Guide to Eating Raw.* Indianapolis, IN: Alpha Books, 2008.

Reinfeld, Mark, and Jennifer Murray. *The 30-Minute Vegan.* Boston, MA: Da Capo Lifelong, 2009.

———. *The 30-Minute Vegan's Taste of the East.* Boston, MA: DaCapo Lifelong, 2010.

Robbins, John. *Diet for a New America.* Tiburon, CA: H. J. Kramer, 1987.

———. *Healthy at 100.* New York, NY: Random House, 2006.

———. *The New Good Life: Living Better Than Ever in an Age of Less.* New York, NY. Ballantine Books, 2010.

———. *No Happy Cows: Dispatches from the Frontlines of the Food Revolution.* Newburyport, MA. Conari Press, 2012.

Stuart, Tristram. *The Bloodless Revolution: A Cultural History of Vegetarianism from 1600 to Modern Times.* New York, NY: W. W. Norton, 2007.

Tuttle, Will, PhD. *World Peace Diet: Eating for Spiritual Health and Social Harmony.* Brooklyn, NY: Lantern Books, 2005.

Online Resources

Here are some of the more popular websites and blogs promoting a vegan and sustainable way of life. We also list some go-to sites for kitchen equipment and to stock up your veggie pantry.

Vegan & Veg–Friendly Websites

www.earthsave.org

Founded by John Robbins, EarthSave is doing what it can to promote a shift to a plant-based diet. It posts news, information, and resources and publishes a magazine.

www.happycow.net

Happy Cow is a searchable dining guide to vegetarian restaurants, natural health food stores, information on vegetarian nutrition, raw foods, and vegan recipes.

www.veganessentials.com

The ultimate vegan superstore with everything from cosmetics, to clothing, to household products, supplements, and more. When it comes to vegan—you name it, they have it.

www.animalconcerns.org

Animal Concerns Community serves as a clearinghouse for information on the Internet related to animal rights and welfare.

www.farmusa.org

Farm Animal Reform Movement (FARM) is an organization advocating a plant-based diet and humane treatment of farm animals through grassroots programs.

www.vegweb.com

A vegetarian mega site with recipes, photos, articles, online store, and more.

www.vegan.com

The popular site of Erik Markus, geared toward the aspiring and long-term vegan that features articles, interviews, product evaluations, book reviews, and more.

www.vegan.org

Vegan Action is a nonprofit grassroots organization dedicated to educating people about the many benefits of a vegan lifestyle.

www.vrg.org

The Vegetarian Resource Group (VRG) is a nonprofit organization dedicated to educating the public on vegetarianism, including information on health, nutrition, ecology, ethics, and world hunger.

www.vegan.meetup.com

Meet up with other vegans in your town!

www.veganoutreach.com

Amazing resource for aspiring vegans. Vegan outreach is a wonderful organization dedicated to pamphleting and other educational activities.

www.veganfitness.net

Vegan Fitness is a community-driven message board seeking to provide a supportive, educational, and friendly environment for vegans, vegetarians, and those seeking to go vegan.

www.veganpet.com.au

Veganpet provides nutritionally complete and balanced pet food and information on raising vegan pets.

www.vegfamily.com

Comprehensive resource for raising vegan children, including pregnancy, vegan recipes, book reviews, product reviews, message board, and more.

www.veganbodybuilding.com

Vegan Body Building and Fitness is the website of vegan body builder Robert Cheeke and features articles, videos, products, and a forum for the active vegan.

www.vegsource.com

Features over ten thousand vegetarian and vegan recipes, discussion boards, nutritionists, medical doctors, experts, authors, articles, newsletter, and the vegetarian community.

www.pcrm.org

The Physicians Committee for Responsible Medicine (PCRM) is a nonprofit organization that promotes preventive medicine, conducts clinical research, and encourages higher standards for ethics and effectiveness in research.

www.ivu.org

The World Union of Vegetarian/Vegan Societies has been promoting vegetarianism worldwide since 1908.

www.vegetarianteen.com

An online magazine with articles on vegetarian teen lifestyle, activism, nutrition, social issues, and more.

Organic & Gardening Websites

www.ota.com

The Organic Trade Association website will tell you anything you want to know about the term *organic,* from food to textiles to health-care products. The OTA's mission is to encourage global sustainability through promoting and protecting the growth of diverse organic trade.

www.organicconsumers.org

The Organic Consumers Association is an online, grassroots, nonprofit organization dealing with issues of food safety, industrial agriculture, genetic engineering, corporate accountability, and environmental sustainability.

www.avant-gardening.com

A site advocating organic gardening with information on composting, soil building, permaculture principles, botany, companion and intensive planting, and more.

www.gefoodalert.org

GE Food Alert Campaign Center is a coalition of seven organizations committed to testing and labeling genetically engineered food.

www.biodynamics.com

The Biodynamic Farming and Gardening Association supports and promotes biodynamic farming, the oldest nonchemical agricultural movement.

www.kidbean.com

Organic, earth-friendly, and vegan products for families.

www.veganorganic.net

Organic growing, green, clean, cruelty-free articles and information.

Environmental & Sustainability Websites

www.conservation.org

Conservation International is involved in many conservation projects worldwide. On their site you can calculate your carbon footprint based on your living situation, car, travel habits, and diet.

www.nrdcwildplaces.org

Natural Resources Defense Council (NRDC) is an environmental action group with over 1 million members working to safeguard the American continents' natural systems.

www.dinegreen.com

The Green Restaurant Association (GRA) is a national nonprofit organization that provides a convenient way for all sectors of the restaurant industry, which represents 10 percent of the US economy, to become more environmentally sustainable.

www.ran.org

Rainforest Action Network is working to protect tropical rainforests around the world and the human rights of those living in and around those forests.

www.childrenoftheearth.org

Children of the Earth United is a children's environmental education website that educates the public on ecological concepts and aims to provide a forum for people to share knowledge and ideas.

Specialty Foods and Products

www.goldminenaturalfood.com

An online source for a vast selection of organic foods, raw foods, macrobiotic, vegan, gluten-free, Asian, gourmet, and specialty foods as well as natural cookware and home products.

www.amazon.com

Amazon.com is perhaps the world's largest superstore. Check it out to order any kitchen equipment or specialty food items, including immersion blenders, gnocchi boards, Microplane zesters, spiralizers, and more.

Eco-Friendly Products & Services

www.foodfightgrocery.com

Food Fight! Grocery is an all-vegan convenience store located in Portland, Oregon, with an online market that emphasizes junk foods, imports, and fun stuff.

www.vitamix.com

Find the latest Vitamix blenders here on the official site, including factory-reconditioned models that still come with a seven-year warranty. For free shipping in the continental United States, enter code 06-002510.

www.877juicer.com

This website carries way more than juicers, including everything kitchen related, plus air purifiers, books, and articles.

www.greenpeople.org

Green People provides a directory of eco-friendly products and services.

Raw Food Lifestyle Websites

www.livesuperfoods.com

The go-to site for all of your raw food needs, from food and supplements to appliances, such as juicers, blenders, dehydrators, and spiralizers.

www.goneraw.com

Gone Raw is a website created to help people share and discuss raw, vegan food recipes from around the world.

www.rawfoods.com

Living and Raw Foods is the largest raw online community with appliances for the raw foodist, chat rooms, blogs, articles, classified ads, and recipes.

www.gliving.tv

The G Living Network is a hip and modern green lifestyle network with videos and articles on living in an earth-friendly way, including raw recipes, sustainable fashion, technology, and household design.

Contributor Bios

AMY GREEN, *Food Photographer*
Amy was the award-winning photographer for *Vegan Fusion World Cuisine* who makes her home on the beautiful island of Kauai. Her love for the creative expression of food is evident in all of her works. She can be contacted at green leafkauai@gmail.com.

ROLAND BARKER, *Recipe Tester*
Roland is inspired by nature's abundance and ability to nourish and heal us, and as a cook, he tries to add to that his intention for healing and joy in the preparation of natural, whole foods. Xnau Web design: www.xnau.com

SUZANNE RUDOLF, *Recipe Tester*
Suzanne is an avid world traveler with a lifelong passion for food. Her palate has been strongly influenced by the cuisines she has eaten while on trips to over thirty countries. Suzanne divides her time with catering and teaching classes for home cooks at the Auguste Escoffier School of Culinary Arts in Boulder, Colorado. www.rudymademeals.com and www.examiner.com/user-suzannerudolph

LISA PARKER, *Recipe Tester*
An alchemist at heart, Lisa loves plants, colors, flavors, textures, and smells. She loves measuring and stirring and filling the kitchen with delectable fragrances. These days she cooks a lot for friends and family, has a botanical body product business, and works with her husband to create a tropical food forest and sanctuary at their home on Kauai. www.greensongbotanicals.com

GERIT WILLIAMS, *Recipe Tester*
Gerit Williams is a professional guitarist and skilled chef whose creative genius is uniquely expressed both on the stage and in the kitchen. Guided by pure intuition and years of training, Gerit offers music and food that cater to the soul. www.gerit williams.com

Acknowledgments

It is amazing to me that I am completing my sixth cookbook. I always dreamed of being a travel writer and never imagined that my writings would be about my culinary travels. I am in deep and continuous gratefulness for the support of my family and friends. I feel special gratitude for the loving presence of Ashley Boudet, who has been a guiding light in the process of writing this book.

Thanks go to my family: my mother, Roberta Reinfeld, and sisters Jennifer and Dawn Reinfeld. Also to Roger Vossler, Richard Slade, Bill Townsend, Cody Martin Townsend, and Sierra Molly Townsend.

Big thanks to my outstanding team of recipe testers: Roland Barker, Lisa Parker, Suzanne Rudolph, and Gerit Williams. I am honored to feature the incredible food photography of Amy Green, who was the food photographer for our first cookbook, the multiple award–winning *Vegan Fusion World Cuisine*. She was assisted in the shoots by Carly Boardman. Props were donated by Pottery and Ceramic Art Shop on Kauai, Hawaii, www.lightwavepottery.com.

Thanks to all the recipe tasters and feedback givers—Chef Susan Teton (www.susan tetoncampbell.com), Gerit Williams (www.geritwilliams.com), Ashley Boudet, Jayson Weisz, Brook and Dana Theodros, Jennifer Jenson, Manaka, Troy Gagliano, Ganesha Michael Shapiro, Suzie Shwartz, Cristalle Caceres, and Nicole Davis. Thanks to Cyndi Slick for her assistance with the seasonal growing charts.

Special thanks to my partners in Vegan Fusion, Bo and Star Rinaldi, for being such an integral part of this vegan journey of transformation.

Thanks also go to Jennifer Murray for her contributions to other books in the 30-Minute Vegan series, *The 30-Minute Vegan* and *The 30-Minute Vegan's Taste of the East*, as well as *The Complete Idiot's Guide to Eating Raw*.

As always, thanks go to my incredible literary agent Marilyn Allen, and to my friend Daniel Rhoda who introduced me to her. Special thanks to my editor at Da Capo, Renée Sedliar, for her impeccable edits and contributions. It is a true pleasure to work with you.

About the Author

The winner of Vegan.com's Recipe of the Year Award for 2011, Mark Reinfeld has over twenty years of experience preparing creative vegan and raw food cuisine. Mark was the executive chef for the North American Vegetarian Society's 2012 and 2013 Summerfest, one of the largest vegetarian conferences in the world. He is described by VegCooking.com as being "poised on the leading edge of contemporary vegan cooking." He is the founding chef of the Blossoming Lotus Restaurant, winner of *Honolulu Advertiser*'s Ilima Award for Best Restaurant on Kaua'i. Mark is also the recipient of a Platinum Carrot Award for living foods—a national award given by the Aspen Center of Integral Health to America's top "innovative and trailblazing healthy chefs."

Mark received his initial culinary training from his grandfather Ben Bimstein, a renowned chef and ice carver in New York City. He developed his love for world culture and cuisine during travel journeys through Europe, Asia, and the Middle East. In 1997, Mark formed the Blossoming Lotus Personal Chef Service in Malibu, California. To further his knowledge of the healing properties of food, he received a master's degree in holistic nutrition.

His first cookbook, *Vegan World Fusion Cuisine*, coauthored with Bo Rinaldi and with a foreword by Dr. Jane Goodall, has won several national awards, including Cookbook of the Year, Best New Cookbook, Best Book by a Small Press, and a Gourmand Award for Best Vegetarian Cookbook in the USA. In addition Mark coauthored *The Complete Idiot's Guide to Eating Raw*.

Mark's last book, *The 30-Minute Vegan's Taste of Europe*, was selected as one of the top five books by *Vegetarian Times* and one of the top ten cookbooks of 2012 by *VegNews* magazine.

Mark specializes in vegan recipe development and offers chef training and consulting services internationally. He conducts online vegan culinary lessons at veganfusion.com as well as vegan and raw food workshops, immersions, and retreats worldwide.

The 10-Day Vegan
Fusion Culinary Immersion

Want to learn more? Consider attending an immersion or workshop with Mark Reinfeld. Courses are offered internationally and online at www.veganfusion.com.

Prepare to transform your life as you immerse yourself in the world of vegan and raw food cuisine!

Whether you are a trained chef, foodie, novice, or homemaker, we guarantee that you will learn the skills to create a lifetime of health:

- Experience greater confidence in the kitchen.
- Save money by learning how to prepare more delicious and healthy cuisine on your own.
- Learn new tips and tricks that will greatly enhance your culinary abilities.
- Connect with others who share a similar interest in vegan and raw foods.
- Deepen your knowledge of the healing qualities of vegan foods.
- Discover new ideas for presentation that will transform an ordinary meal into a gourmet experience.

Topics include Vegan Soups; Salads & Dressings; the World of Grains and Beans; Tofu, Tempeh & Seitan Dishes; Casseroles and Sauces; Wraps, Spreads, Sandwiches and Rolls; Vegan Desserts; Raw Cuisine 1-Smoothies, Pâtés, Pasta and Pudding; Raw Cuisine 2-Elixirs, Soups, Plant Cheeses, Ravioli, Lasagna, Parfaits, and Ice Cream; Raw Cuisine 3-Nut and Seed Milks, Granola, Pizza, Tacos, and Live Pies.

The 10-day Immersion includes daily gourmet vegan feasts and the Vegan Fusion Cuisine Chef Training manual.

Index

Adzuki Bean Soup with Enoki
    Mushrooms, 116
African Peanut Soup, 65
Amaranth
    about, 7
    Ethiopian Stew, 92
Andean Incan Stew with
    Quinoa, 70
Apricots
    Danish Fruit Soup, 170
    Pineapple Ginger Soup with
        Apricot Puree, 162–163
Arame
    about, 9
    Dashi, 28
Artichokes
    Creamy White Bean Soup
        with Broiled Artichoke
        Hearts, 148–149
    Crispy Sunchokes, 202
    Spanish Rice and Artichoke
        Heart Stew, 107
Asparagus
    Bavarian Asparagus Soup
        with Hazelnuts, 139
    Grilled Asparagus, 36
    Ragout of Spring/Summer
        Vegetables, 45
    Truffled Wild Mushroom
        Consommé with Grilled
        Baby Asparagus, 36–37
Avocados
    Chilled Avocado Soup with
        Cherry Tomato Salsa
        Fresca, 183
    Guacamole, 204

Balsamic Reduction, 189
Bamboo shoots
    Szechuan Hot and Sour
        Vegetable Soup, 47
Barley
    Mushroom Barley Soup, 119
Basic Nut or Seed Milk, 222
Basic Tamari Stock, 29
Basil
    Basil Oil, 188
    Italian Pesto Soup with
        Gnocchi, 146–147
    Pesto Magnifico, 206
Bavarian Asparagus Soup with
    Hazelnuts, 139
BBQ Tempeh and Roasted Corn
    Stew, 99–100
Beans
    Adzuki Bean Soup with
        Enoki Mushrooms, 116
    anasazi, about, 7
    Black Bean Tomato Soup
        with Polenta Dumplings,
        109–111
    Brazilian Black Bean Soup
        with Baked Plantain, 114–
        115
    Caribbean Red Bean and
        Rice Soup, 86–87
    Cha-Cha Chili with Tempeh,
        120
    Creamy White Bean Soup
        with Broiled Artichoke
        Hearts, 148–149
    Greek Fasolada Soup with
        Cannellini Beans, 102

Green Bean Amandine Soup,
    151
    Orzo Minestrone with
        Broiled Fennel, 88–89
    Persian Lima Bean and Dill
        Soup, 90
    Three Sisters Soup, 91
Beer
    Irish Cabbage and Potato
        Stew, 55
Beets
    Roasted Beet Borscht, 64
    Vegetable Chips, 201
Berbere spice mix, 7, 93
Beyond Meat
    about, 7
    Un-chicken Noodle Soup, 79
    Veggie Coq au Vin, 112
Bisque, defined, 20
Black Bean Tomato Soup with
    Polenta Dumplings, 109–
    111
Black-eyed peas
    Black-eyed Peas and
        Collards Stew, 85
Blending soups, 124
Blueberries
    Cantaloupe Rose Soup with
        Blueberry Cream, 165
Bok choy
    Hot Pot with Soba Noodles,
        Seared Shiitake
        Mushrooms, and Baby
        Bok Choy, 80–81
Bouillon, defined, 20
Bouquet garni, making, 78

INDEX

Brazilian Black Bean Soup with
  Baked Plantain, 114–115
Bread
  Cosmic Corn Bread, 211
  Crostini, 198
  Croutons (in French Onion
    Soup), 40
  Herbed Bread Sticks, 209–
    210
  Herbed Croutons, 200
  Pita Chips, 199
Broccoli
  Creamy Broccoli Soup with
    Shiitake Mushrooms,
    137–138
  Szechuan Hot and Sour
    Vegetable Soup, 47
Broccoli rabe
  Ratatouille Stew with Grilled
    Broccoli Rabe, 61–62
Broiled Zucchini Soup with
  Saffron, 42
Brussels sprouts
  Roasted Brussels Sprouts
    and Red Cabbage Soup, 49
Burdock root
  about, 7
  Adzuki Bean Soup with
    Enoki Mushrooms, 116
  Cleansing Burdock Soup
    with Ginger and
    Dandelion Greens, 35
Butter, vegan, about, 10

Cabbage
  Ethiopian Stew, 92
  Irish Cabbage and Potato
    Stew, 55
  Ragout of Fall Vegetables, 60
  Roasted Beet Borscht, 64
  Roasted Brussels Sprouts
    and Red Cabbage Soup, 49
  Tibetan Noodle Soup
    (Thenthuk), 98
  Vietnamese Pho Real Bowl,
    74
  Wonton Soup, 72–73
Cantaloupe Rose Soup with
  Blueberry Cream, 165
Capers, about, 7
Caramelized Onions, 205

Caribbean Red Bean and Rice
  Soup, 86–87
Carrots
  Coconut Carrot Soup with
    Ginger and Dill, 128
Cauliflower
  Cheesy Cauliflower Soup,
    144
Cha-Cha Chili with Tempeh,
  120
Cheese, vegan
  about, 10
  Cheesy Cauliflower Soup,
    144
  French Onion Soup, 40–41
  Fried Green Tomato Soup
    au Gratin, 46
Cherries
  Creamy Brazil Nut Fig Soup
    with Kiwi Compote, 168
Chickpeas
  Himalayan Dal with Curried
    Chickpeas, 103–104
  Mideast Chickpea Soup, 135
Chilled Avocado Soup with
    Cherry Tomato Salsa
    Fresca, 183
Chinese cuisine spices, about, 7
Chipotle chile powder, about, 7
Chocolate
  Holy Mole Soup with
    Veggies, 145
  Raw Chocolate Mint Soup
    with Raspberries (or
    Strawberries), 167
Chowder, defined, 20
Cleansing Burdock Soup with
    Ginger and Dandelion
    Greens, 35
Coconut milk
  about, 8
  African Peanut Soup, 65
  Caribbean Red Bean and
    Rice Soup, 86–87
  Coconut Carrot Soup with
    Ginger and Dill, 128
  Coconut Curry Veggie Soup
    with Tofu, 97
  Coconut Greens Soup with
    Polenta, 96
  Indian Mulligatawny, 101

Jamaican Jerk Plantain Soup,
  56–57
Roasted Squash with
  Coconut Soup, 136
Thai Coconut Soup with
  Lemongrass, 43–44
Tropical Coconut Yam
  Soup, 58–59
Coconut oil, about, 8
Coconut(s)
  opening, 182
  Raw Thai Coconut Soup,
    181
  Toasted, 190
Collard greens
  Black-eyed Peas and
    Collards Stew, 85
Composting, 242
Consommé, defined, 20
Corn
  BBQ Tempeh and Roasted
    Corn Stew, 99–100
  Corn Chowder, 129
  Mayan Tomato and Corn
    Soup, 38
  New Orleans Corn and Bell
    Pepper Soup (Maque
    Choux), 50
  Raw Corn Chowder, 179
  Three Sisters Soup, 91
Cornmeal
  BBQ Tempeh and Roasted
    Corn Stew, 99–100
  Black Bean Tomato Soup
    with Polenta Dumplings,
    109–111
  Coconut Greens Soup with
    Polenta, 96
  Cosmic Corn Bread, 211
  Herbed Bread Sticks, 209–
    210
  Polenta Dumplings, 109–110
Couscous
  Israeli Couscous Soup with
    Sun-dried Tomatoes, 83–
    84
  pearled, about, 8
Cream of Mushroom Soup, 127
Creamer, soy. See Soy creamer
Creamy Brazil Nut Fig Soup
    with Kiwi Compote, 168

Creamy Broccoli Soup with Shiitake Mushrooms, 137–138
Creamy Fire-Roasted Tomato Soup with Dill, 125
Creamy Grilled Vegetable Soup with Cilantro Cream, 140–141
Creamy Parsnip Soup with Smoked Cherry Tomatoes, 131–132
Creamy White Bean Soup with Broiled Artichoke Hearts, 148–149
Crispy Sunchokes, 202
Crostini, 198
Croutons (in French Onion Soup), 40
Cucumbers
    Golden Gazpacho with Saffron, 171
    Raw Cucumber Mint Soup, 172
Curry powder
    Coconut Curry Veggie Soup with Tofu, 97
    Curried Pumpkin Soup, 150
    Himalayan Dal with Curried Chickpeas, 103–104

Dandelion greens
    Cleansing Burdock with Ginger and Dandelion Greens, 35
Danish Fruit Soup, 170
Dashi, 28
Date Syrup, 229
Deglazing, 205
Dried herbs, substituting for fresh, 87
Dumplings, Polenta, 109–110

Egg replacers, about, 76
Eggplant
    Grilled Eggplant Soup with Pine Nuts, 142–143
    Ratatouille Stew with Grilled Broccoli Rabe, 61–62
Ethiopian cuisine, about, 93
Ethiopian Stew, 92

Fennel
    Orzo Minestrone with Broiled Fennel, 88–89
    Raw Chopped Vegetable Soup with Shaved Fennel, 174
    shaving, 175
Figs
    Creamy Brazil Nut Fig Soup with Kiwi Compote, 168
Fire-Roasted Tomato and Rice Soup with Spinach, 69
Flaxseeds, as egg replacer, 76
Flour
    Gluten-Free Flour Mix, 11, 223
    spelt, white, about, 11, 15
Food preparation, guidelines for, 11–13
Four Mushroom and Baby Spinach Soup, 48
French Bouillabaisse, 77–78
French Onion Soup, 40–41
Fried Green Tomato Soup au Gratin, 46

Garam masala, making, 104
Garlic
    Garlic Lovers' Roasted Garlic Soup, 133–134
    Roasted Garlic Spread, 194
Gluten, about, 11
Gluten-Free Flour Mix, 11, 223
GMO (genetically engineered and modified organism), 241–242
Gnocchi, making, 147
Gnocchi (in Italian Pesto Soup), 146
Golden Gazpacho with Saffron, 171
Grains, cooking, 217–219
Greek Fasolada Soup with Cannellini Beans, 102
Greek Lentil Soup with Grilled Bell Pepper, 94–95
Green Bean Amandine Soup, 151
Grilled Asparagus, 36
Grilled Eggplant Soup with Pine Nuts, 142–143

Grilling, 216–217
Guacomole, 204

Heart of palm
    about, 39
    Mayan Tomato and Corn Soup, 38
Herbed Bread Sticks, 209–210
Herbed Croutons, 200
Herbes de Provence, about, 36
Himalayan Dal with Curried Chickpeas, 103–104
Holy Mole Soup with Veggies, 145
Hot peppers, about, 57
Hot Pot with Soba Noodles, Seared Shiitake Mushrooms, and Baby Bok Choy, 80–81

Ice Cubes, Flavored, 186
Indian Chutney Stew with Tamarind, 52–53
Indian Mulligatawny, 101
Irish Cabbage and Potato Stew, 55
Israeli Couscous Soup with Sun-dried Tomatoes, 83–84
Italian Pesto Soup with Gnocchi, 146–147
Italian Wedding Stew with Vegan Sausage, 108

Jamaican Jerk Plantain Soup, 56–57
Jicama
    Savory Brazil Nut Soup with Jicama, 178

Kale
    Krispy Kale, 203
    Portuguese Kale and Potato Soup (Caldo Verde), 54
    Spicy Kale Soup with Pepitas, 177
Kitchen gear, 13
Kiwi
    Creamy Brazil Nut Fig Soup with Kiwi Compote, 168
Kombu
    about, 9

Kombu (*continued*)
Dashi, 28
Krispy Kale, 203

Lavender flowers
about, 160
Lavender-Infused
Watermelon Soup, 159
Leeks
Mushroom Stock, 26
Ragout of SpringSummer
Vegetables, 45
Roasted Vegetable Stock, 27
Rosemary Potato Soup with
Roasted Leek and Garlic,
152–153
Legumes, cooking, 220–221
Lemon Dijon Marinade, 225
Lemongrass
Thai Coconut Soup with
Lemongrass, 43–44
working with, 44
Lentils
Ethiopian Stew, 92
Greek Lentil Soup with
Grilled Bell Pepper, 94–95
Himalayan Dal with Curried
Chickpeas, 103–104
Indian Mulligatawny, 101

Mandolines, working with, 201
Maple Balsamic Marinade, 225
Marinades
about, 224–225
Lemon Dijon Marinade, 225
Maple Balsamic Marinade,
225
Matzo meal
Matzo Ball Soup, 75–76
Mayan Tomato and Corn Soup,
38
Mayonnaise, vegan
about, 10
Creamy Grilled Vegetable
Soup with Cilantro
Cream, 140–141
Vegan Crème Fraîche, 195
Vegan Mayonnaise, 226
Melon Balls, Frozen, 186
Metric conversion charts, 212
Mideast Chickpea Soup, 135

Milk, nondairy
about, 8
Bavarian Asparagus Soup
with Hazelnuts, 139
Cream of Mushroom Soup,
127
Creamy Fire-Roasted
Tomato Soup with Dill,
125
Creamy Parsnip Soup with
Smoked Cherry
Tomatoes, 131–132
Curried Pumpkin Soup, 150
New England Chowder, 154
New Orleans Corn and Bell
Pepper Soup (Maque
Choux), 50
Rosemary Potato Soup with
Roasted Leek and Garlic,
152–153
See also Soy creamer
Millet
Cosmic Corn Bread, 211
Mirin, about, 8
Miso paste
about, 8, 34
Cleansing Burdock Soup
with Ginger and
Dandelion Greens, 35
Raw Creamy Greens Soup,
180
Tofu Feta, 207
Versatile Miso Soup with
Pickled Ginger, 34
Mushrooms
Adzuki Bean Soup with
Enoki Mushrooms, 116
Cream of Mushroom Soup,
127
Creamy Broccoli Soup with
Shiitake Mushrooms,
137–138
Four Mushroom and Baby
Spinach Soup, 48
Hot Pot with Soba Noodles,
Seared Shiitake
Mushrooms, and Baby
Bok Choy, 80–81
Mushroom Barley Soup, 119
Mushroom Stock, 26
Roasted Vegetable Stock, 27

Truffled Wild Mushroom
Consommé with Grilled
Baby Asparagus, 36–37

Nectarines
Slushy Summer Fruit Soup,
169
New England Chowder, 154
New Orleans Corn and Bell
Pepper Soup (Maque
Choux), 50
Nori
about, 9
Sweet and Spicy Toasted
Nori Sheets, 191
North African Tagine with
Broiled Tofu, 117–118
Nutritional yeast, about, 8
Nuts
African Peanut Soup, 65
Basic Nut or Seed Milk, 222
Bavarian Asparagus Soup
with Hazelnuts, 139
Cantaloupe Rose Soup with
Blueberry Cream, 165
Cheesy Cauliflower Soup,
144
Corn Chowder, 129
Creamy Brazil Nut Fig Soup
with Kiwi Compote, 168
Creamy Broccoli Soup with
Shiitake Mushrooms,
137–138
Creamy Grilled Vegetable
Soup with Cilantro
Cream, 140–141
Green Bean Amandine
Soup, 151
Grilled Eggplant Soup with
Pine Nuts, 142–143
Italian Pesto Soup with
Gnocchi, 146–147
Pesto Magnifico, 206
Raw Chocolate Mint Soup
with Raspberries (or
Strawberries), 167
Raw Corn Chowder, 179
Raw Cream of Tomato Soup,
173
Raw Creamy Greens Soup,
180

Raw Crème Fraîche, 196
Raw Papaya Soup with Red
  Pepper Cream, 164
Raw Peaches and Cream
  Soup, 166
Savory Brazil Nut Soup with
  Jicama, 178
Sweet Cashew Cream, 166
Nuts, soaking chart, 222

Oils, about, 8, 10, 14
Okra
  Veggie Gumbo, 82
Olives
  Tapenade, 193
Onions
  Caramelized Onions, 205
  French Onion Soup, 40–41
  Raw Mediterranean Onion
    Soup, 176
Oranges
  Brazilian Black Bean Soup
    with Baked Plantain, 114–
    115
  North African Tagine with
    Broiled Tofu, 117–118
  Pineapple Ginger Soup with
    Apricot Puree, 162–163
  Spicy Strawberry Soup, 161
Organic farming, 240–241
Organic food, defined, 2
Orzo, about, 8
Orzo Minestrone with Broiled
  Fennel, 88–89

Papayas
  Raw Papaya Soup with Red
    Pepper Cream, 164
Paprika, smoked, about, 10
Parsnips
  Creamy Parsnip Soup with
    Smoked Cherry
    Tomatoes, 131–132
  Ragout of Fall Vegetables, 60
Pasta
  brown rice pasta, 7
  Hot Pot with Soba Noodles,
    Seared Shiitake
    Mushrooms, and Baby
    Bok Choy, 80–81
  Orzo Minestrone with
    Broiled Fennel, 88–89

Tibetan Noodle Soup
  (Thenthuk), 98
Un-chicken Noodle Soup, 79
Vietnamese Pho Real Bowl,
  74
Peaches
  Raw Peaches and Cream
    Soup, 166
Peanut butter
  African Peanut Soup, 65
Peas
  Ragout of Spring/Summer
    Vegetables, 45
  Split Pea Soup, 113
  See also Snow peas
Peasant Vegetable and Toasted
  Spice Soup, 51
Pepitas. See Pumpkin seeds
Peppers, bell
  Greek Lentil Soup with
    Grilled Bell Pepper,
    94–95
  New Orleans Corn and Bell
    Pepper Soup (Maque
    Choux), 50
  Raw Papaya Soup with Red
    Pepper Cream, 164
  Red Pepper Coulis, 197
  Roasted Red Pepper Soup,
    126
Persian Lima Bean and Dill
  Soup, 90
Pesticides, in food, 241
Pesto Magnifico, 206
Pineapple
  Pineapple Ginger Soup with
    Apricot Puree, 162–163
Pita Chips, 199
Plantains
  Brazilian Black Bean Soup
    with Baked Plantain, 114–
    115
  Jamaican Jerk Plantain Soup,
    56–57
  working with, 57
Polenta
  about, 8
  See also Cornmeal
Polish Vegan Sausage and
  Sauerkraut Stew, 105
Portuguese Kale and Potato
  Soup (Caldo Verde), 54

Potatoes
  Basic Vegetable Stock, 25
  Irish Cabbage and Potato
    Stew, 55
  Italian Pesto Soup with
    Gnocchi, 146–147
  New England Chowder, 154
  Peasant Vegetable and
    Toasted Spice Soup, 51
  Portuguese Kale and Potato
    Soup (Caldo Verde), 54
  Ragout of Fall Vegetables, 60
  Ragout of Spring/Summer
    Vegetables, 45
  Rosemary Potato Soup with
    Roasted Leek and Garlic,
    152–153
  Vegetable Chips, 201
  Vegetable Stock, Basic, 25
Prunes
  Danish Fruit Soup, 170
Pumpkin/pumpkin seeds
  Candied Pepitas, 192
  Curried Pumpkin Soup, 150
  Spicy Kale Soup with
    Pepitas, 177
Puree, defined, 20

Quinoa
  about, 9
  flour, making, 76
  rinsing, 71
Quinoa, recipes for
  Andean Incan Stew with
    Quinoa, 70
  Ethiopian Stew, 92
  Matzo Ball Soup, 75–76

Ragout of Fall Vegetables, 60
Ragout of Spring/Summer
  Vegetables, 45
Raspberries
  Raw Chocolate Mint Soup
    with Raspberries (or
    Strawberries), 167
Ratatouille Stew with Grilled
  Broccoli Rabe, 61–62
Raw Chocolate Mint Soup with
  Raspberries (or
  Strawberries), 167
Raw Chopped Vegetable Soup
  with Shaved Fennel, 174

Raw Corn Chowder, 179
Raw Cream of Tomato Soup,
    173
Raw Creamy Greens Soup, 180
Raw Crème Fraîche, 196
Raw Cucumber Mint Soup, 172
Raw foods, about, 15–16
Raw Mediterranean Onion
    Soup, 176
Raw Papaya Soup with Red
    Pepper Cream, 164
Raw Peaches and Cream Soup,
    166
Raw soups, garnishes for, 158
Raw Thai Coconut Soup, 181
Red Oil, 187
Red Pepper Coulis, 197
Rice
    Caribbean Red Bean and
        Rice Soup, 86–87
    Fire-Roasted Tomato and
        Rice Soup with Spinach,
        69
    Indian Mulligatawny, 101
    Spanish Rice and Artichoke
        Heart Stew, 107
    Tofurky and Rice Soup, 106
Roasted Beet Borscht, 64
Roasted Brussels Sprouts and
    Red Cabbage Soup, 49
Roasted Garlic Spread, 194
Roasted Red Pepper Soup, 126
Roasted Root Vegetable Soup,
    63
Roasted Squash with Coconut
    Soup, 136
Roasted Vegetable Stock, 27
Rose water
    about, 160
    Cantaloupe Rose Soup with
        Blueberry Cream, 165
Rosemary Potato Soup with
    Roasted Leek and Garlic,
    152–153

Saffron
    Broiled Zucchini Soup with
        Saffron, 42
    French Bouillabaisse, 77–78
    Golden Gazpacho with
        Saffron, 171

North African Tagine with
    Broiled Tofu, 117–118
Spanish Rice and Artichoke
    Heart Stew, 107
Salsa Fresca, Cherry Tomato,
    183
Salts, types of, 9
Sauerkraut
    Polish Vegan Sausage and
        Sauerkraut Stew, 105
Sausage, vegan
    about, 10
    Italian Wedding Stew with
        Vegan Sausage, 108
    Polish Vegan Sausage and
        Sauerkraut Stew, 105
Savory Brazil Nut Soup with
    Jicama, 178
Scoville units, 57
Sea vegetables, about, 9
Seasonal growing charts, 231–
    234
Seeds
    Basic Nut or Seed Milk, 222
    soaking chart, 222
Seitan
    Un-chicken Noodle Soup, 79
    Veggie Coq au Vin, 112
    Vietnamese Pho Real Bowl,
        74
    working with, 216
Serving sizes, 17
Slushy Summer Fruit Soup, 169
Smoke, liquid, about, 8
Snow peas
    Raw Thai Coconut Soup,
        181
    Szechuan Hot and Sour
        Vegetable Soup, 47
    Thai Coconut Soup with
        Lemongrass, 43–44
Sodium, 15, 23
Soy, substitutes for, 15
Soy creamer
    Bavarian Asparagus Soup
        with Hazelnuts, 139
    Cream of Mushroom Soup,
        127
    Creamy Fire-Roasted
        Tomato Soup with Dill,
        125

Curried Pumpkin Soup, 150
Indian Mulligatawny, 101
New England Chowder, 154
Rosemary Potato Soup with
    Roasted Leek and Garlic,
    152–153
Spanish Rice and Artichoke
    Heart Stew, 107
Spice Mixes
    Berbere, 93
    Indian, 104, 223
    Italian, 223
    Mexican, 224
    Moroccan, 224
Spicy Kale Soup with Pepitas,
    177
Spicy Strawberry Soup, 161
Spinach
    Coconut Greens Soup with
        Polenta, 96
    Fire-Roasted Tomato and
        Rice Soup with Spinach,
        69
    Four Mushroom and Baby
        Spinach Soup, 48
    Raw Creamy Greens Soup,
        180
    Spinach Soup with Vegan
        Yogurt and Toasted
        Sesame Seeds, 130
Split Pea Soup, 113
Squash
    Roasted Squash with
        Coconut Soup, 136
    Three Sisters Soup, 91
Steam/water sautéing, 217
Stocks
    about, 22–23
    Basic Tamari, 29
    Basic Vegetable, 25
    Dashi, 28
    Mushroom, 26
    Roasted Vegetable, 27
Strawberries
    Raw Chocolate Mint Soup
        with Raspberries (or
        Strawberries), 167
    Spicy Strawberry Soup, 161
Sugar, white, alternatives to, 15
Sweet and Spicy Toasted Nori
    Sheets, 191

Sweet Cashew Cream, 166
Sweet potatoes
    African Peanut Soup, 65
    Ethiopian Stew, 92
Sweeteners, natural, 226–228
Szechuan Hot and Sour
        Vegetable Soup, 47

Tamari
    stock, 29
    wheat-free, about, 10
Tamarind paste
    about, 10
    Indian Chutney Stew with
        Tamarind, 52–53
Tapenade, 193
Teff
    about, 10
    Ethiopian Stew, 92
Tempeh
    about, 10
    BBQ Tempeh and Roasted
        Corn Stew, 99–100
    Cha-Cha Chili with Tempeh,
        120
    roasting, 215
    Split Pea Soup, 113
    Tempeh Bacon, 208
    working with, 215
Template recipes, 20–21
Thai Coconut Soup with
        Lemongrass, 43–44
Thai food essentials, 10
Three Sisters Soup, 91
Tibetan Noodle Soup
        (Thenthuk), 98
Toaster oven, using, 216
Toasting spices, nuts, and seeds,
        213
Tofu
    Coconut Curry Veggie Soup
        with Tofu, 97
    Cosmic Corn Bread, 211
    French Bouillabaisse,
        77–78
    Hot Pot with Soba Noodles,
        Seared Shiitake
        Mushrooms, and Baby
        Bok Choy, 80–81
    North African Tagine with
        Broiled Tofu, 117–118

Roasted Red Pepper Soup, 126
    roasting, 215
    Tofu Feta, 207
    Versatile Miso Soup with
        Pickled Ginger, 34
    Wonton Soup, 72–73
    working with, 214
Tofurky and Rice Soup, 106
Tomatoes
    Black Bean Tomato Soup
        with Polenta Dumplings,
        109–111
    Cha-Cha Chili with Tempeh,
        120
    Chilled Avocado Soup with
        Cherry Tomato Salsa
        Fresca, 183
    Creamy Fire-Roasted
        Tomato Soup with Dill,
        125
    Creamy Parsnip Soup with
        Smoked Cherry
        Tomatoes, 131–132
    Fire-Roasted Tomato and
        Rice Soup with Spinach, 69
    Fried Green Tomato Soup
        au Gratin, 46
    Golden Gazpacho with
        Saffron, 171
    Greek Fasolada Soup with
        Cannellini Beans, 102
    Israeli Couscous Soup with
        Sun-dried Tomatoes,
        83–84
    Mayan Tomato and Corn
        Soup, 38
    Ragout of Spring/Summer
        Vegetables, 45
    Ratatouille Stew with Grilled
        Broccoli Rabe, 61–62
    Raw Cream of Tomato Soup,
        173
    Roasted Vegetable Stock, 27
Tomatoes, seeding, 39
Tropical Coconut Yam Soup,
        58–59
Truffle oil
    about, 10, 37
    Truffled Wild Mushroom
        Consommé with Grilled
        Baby Asparagus, 36–37

Turnips
    Ragout of Fall Vegetables,
        60

Un-chicken Noodle Soup, 79

Vegan Crème Fraîche, 195
Vegan diet
    environment and, 237–239
    health and, 236–237
    nonviolence and, 239–240
    reasons for, 235–236
Vegan fusion, defined, 1
Vegan Fusion, website, 3
Vegan lifestyle, defined, 235
Vegan Mayonnaise, 226
Vegetable Chips, 201
Vegetable Stock
    about, 41
    Basic, 25
    Roasted, 27
Veggie Coq au Vin, 112
Veggie Gumbo, 82
Versatile Miso Soup with
        Pickled Ginger, 34
Vietnamese Pho Real Bowl,
        74

Wakame, about, 9
Water chestnuts
    Szechuan Hot and Sour
        Vegetable Soup, 47
Watermelon
    Lavender-Infused
        Watermelon Soup, 159
Wild greens, about, 35
Wonton Soup, 72–73
Yams
    Ethiopian Stew, 92
    Tropical Coconut Yam
        Soup, 58–59
    yam-sweet potato debate, 59
Yogurt
    Spinach Soup with Vegan
        Yogurt and Toasted
        Sesame Seeds, 130
Zucchini
    Basic Vegetable Stock, 25
    Broiled Zucchini Soup with
        Saffron, 42
    Roasted Vegetable Stock, 27

263

the
30-MINUTE VEGAN SERIES

If you have enjoyed *Soup's On!* please check out the other books in the 30-Minute Vegan series:

The 30-Minute Vegan
by Mark Reinfeld
& Jennifer Murray

Paperback: 978–0-7382–1327–9
Ebook: 978–0-7867–4814–3

The book that started it all! Do you want to cook fresh and healthy vegan cuisine, but don't have a lot of time? With over 175 simple and delectable whole foods recipes, *The 30-Minute Vegan* demystifies the art of vegan food preparation for both experienced cooks and novices alike, with chapters devoted to smoothies and satiating beverages, snacks, wraps, rolls, wholesome suppers, guilt-free comfort food, and, of course, divine desserts. With at-a-glance cooking charts, delicious raw foods recipes, kid-friendly dishes, and exciting menu suggestions for every occasion, *The 30-Minute Vegan* is an essential everyday cookbook.

The 30-Minute Vegan's Taste of Europe
by Mark Reinfeld

Paperback: 978–0–7382–1433–7
Ebook: 978–0–7382–1616–4

Do you long for the robust flavors of Italy, France, Spain, or Greece but haven't found tasty animal-free recipes? Look no further: with inspired plant-based versions of everything from manicotti to French onion soup, moussaka to "notwurst," as well as raw and gluten-free options, and suggestions for wine and beer pairings, *The 30-Minute Vegan* is where the joie de vivre meets la dolce vita!

*One of the top five cookbooks of 2012—*Vegetarian Times*
*One of the top ten cookbooks of 2012—*VegNews*

The 30-Minute Vegan's Taste of the East
by Mark Reinfeld & Jennifer Murray

Paperback: 978–0–7382–1382–8
Ebook: 978–0–7382–1416–0

This definitive guide to Asian vegan cuisine offers more than 150 irresistible dishes from India, Thailand, China, Japan, as well as a wide selection of fusion dishes from Korea, Vietnam, Nepal, the Philippines, Tibet, Indonesia, Afghanistan, Iran, Uzbekistan, and Turkmenistan.

Complete with at-a-glance cooking charts, key Asian pantry ingredients, and unique cooking tips, *The Taste of the East* will greatly expand your culinary repertoire.